Solon the Singer

Greek Studies: Interdisciplinary Approaches

General Editor: Gregory Nagy, Harvard University

On the front cover: A calendar frieze representing the Athenian months, reused in the Byzantine Church of the Little Metropolis in Athens. The cross is superimposed, obliterating Taurus of the Zodiac. The choice of this frieze for books in *Greek Studies: Interdisciplinary Approaches* reflects this series' emphasis on the blending of the diverse heritages—Near Eastern, Classical, and Christian—in the Greek tradition. Drawing by Laurie Kain Hart, based on a photograph.

Solon the Singer

Politics and Poetics

Emily Katz Anhalt

Rowman & Littlefield Publishers, Inc.

ROWMAN & LITTLEFIELD PUBLISHERS, INC.

Published in the United States of America
by Rowman & Littlefield Publishers, Inc.
4720 Boston Way, Lanham, Maryland 20706

British Cataloging in Publication Information Available

Library of Congress Cataloging-in-Publication Data

Anhalt, Emily Katz.
Solon the singer : politics and poetics / Emily Katz Anhalt.
p.   cm. — (Greek studies)
Includes bibliographical references and index.
1. Solon, ca. 630 B.C.–ca. 560 B.C.—Poetic works.   2. Politics and
literature—Greece—History.   3. Athens (Greece)—Politics and
government.   4. Greek language—Metrics and rhythmics.   I. Title.
II. Series.
PA4412.S8Z54   1993
881'.01—dc20   92–38035 CIP

ISBN 0–8476–7782–6 (cloth : alk. paper)
ISBN 0–8476–7783–4 (paper : alk. paper)

PA
4412
S8
254
1993

Printed in the United States of America

For my father,
Maurice B. Katz,
whose *aretê* 'excellence'
is remembered.

ἄστρα τε καὶ ποταμοὶ καὶ κύματα πόντου
τὴν ἀωρίαν τὴν σὴν ἀνακαλεῖ
(Pindar fr. 136)

The stars and the rivers and the waves
of the sea call you back from your untimely death.

Contents

Greek Studies: Interdisciplinary Approaches

Foreword

by Gregory Nagy, General Editor

Building on the foundations of scholarship within the disciplines of
philology, philosophy, history, and archaeology, this series spans the
continuum of Greek traditions extending from the second millennium
B.C. to the present, not just the Archaic and Classical periods. The aim
is to enhance perspectives by applying various different disciplines to
problems that have in the past been treated as the exclusive concern of
a single given discipline. Besides the crossing-over of the older
disciplines, as in the application of history to literature, the series
encourages the application of such newer disciplines as linguistics,
sociology, anthropology, and comparative literature. It also encourages
encounters with current trends in methodology, especially in the realm
of literary theory.

   Solon the Singer: Politics and Poetics, by Emily Katz Anhalt, examines
objectively the poetic heritage of the great Athenian lawgiver, treating
the poetry attributed to Solon as a medium that not only expresses the
political and ethical teachings of a revered statesman but also
perpetuates the traditions associated with wisdom poetry and even with
sympotic songmaking. The author's thorough understanding of Solon's
poetics sheds new light on the historical circumstances in which this
poetry was created. This book shows clearly that the poetry of Solon is
not just a source for studying the history of the world's first democracy:
it is also an integral part of that history.

Note on Sources and Translations

Sources are cited in full at first appearance in each chapter; subsequent citations are shortened.

Translations of the *Iliad* and the *Odyssey* are from Richmond Lattimore's versions (*The Iliad of Homer* [Chicago, 1951]; *The Odyssey of Homer* [New York, 1965]); of Hesiod by R. M. Frazer, *The Poems of Hesiod* (Norman, Okla., 1983, reprint, 1985); and of Pindar by Frank J. Nisetich, *Pindar's Victory Songs* (Baltimore and London, 1980).

For all of the other poets, including Solon himself, I have provided my own translations, and in these I have tried to preserve, as much as possible, the literal intention of the Greek. As will be obvious, my translations make no claim to poetic merit.

For the editions of poets cited in this book, see the list on p. 149. For the text and numbering of poems by Solon, Tyrtaeus, Archilochus, Theognis, Simonides, Semonides, and Mimnermus, I have used the edition of M. L. West, *Iambi et elegi Graeci* (Oxford, 1971—1972). For Sappho and Alcaeus, see the edition of E. Lobel and D. L. Page, *Poetarum Lesbiorum fragmenta* (Oxford, 1955). For Alcman, Anacreon, Ibycus, and Simonides, see the edition of D. L. Page, *Poetae melici Graeci* (Oxford, 1962).

Acknowledgements

I wish to thank Donald Kagan and Victor Bers for their wise counsel and encouragement. I am especially grateful to A. Thomas Cole and Richard Garner, whose perceptive analyses and constructive criticisms were both indispensable and inspiring. I would also like to thank Gregory Nagy for his invaluable guidance, criticism, and kindness. Most of all, I am grateful to my husband, Eduardo, my daughters, Erica and Ariela, and my mother, Marilyn Katz, for their unfailing patience and enthusiasm.

Introduction

As an Athenian statesman in the sixth century B.C., Solon enacted legislative reforms which ended the exclusive political control of the aristoc-
racy in Athens. His legislation began a process which culminated in the
Athenian democracy of the fifth century. As a poet, Solon is the first
Athenian (and the *only* Athenian until Aeschylus) whose compositions
have survived from antiquity. His poetry marks a starting point on both
a political and a literary level, and, at the same time, a starting point
that must be understood in the context of the intense poetic activity
elsewhere in Greece which both preceded and coincided with his own
efforts. There is a need, therefore—although Solon's verses have certainly not suffered from scholarly neglect—for a re-examination of his
poetry in the context of archaic ethical and political thought. Neither
his position nor his contribution has been sufficiently determined.

Solon was appointed Chief Archon at Athens for the year 594/593
B.C. during a period of acute conflict between the noble ruling families
and the impoverished peasants, many of whom had already been
reduced to debt slavery. Fearing the possibility of a general uprising
and the installation of a popular tyrant, the nobles appear to have been
willing to make certain concessions. Although Solon was born into a
noble family, he was not himself wealthy. He was perceived as a
moderate, and yet, remarkably, each faction apparently expected him
to protect its interests.

Solon was not a revolutionary. He did not redistribute the land, as
many of the populace undoubtedly wished, nor did he make himself
tyrant, as might have been expected. Instead, he instituted an
unprecedented set of economic and political reforms. The former,
called the *Seisachtheia* 'shaking off of burdens', cancelled existing debts
(either all debts, or only those secured by the person of the borrower),
abolished the use of personal security for debts, and freed those already

1

enslaved under such contracts. The *Seisachtheia* further abolished the terms of serfdom under which peasants were obligated to pay landowners one sixth (or, possibly, five sixths) of their annual produce. Solon combined these reforms with others intended to ease Athens' economic troubles by promoting trade and industry.

His constitutional reforms were even more innovative. He divided the citizenry into four classes based on yearly income and ascribed political responsibilities accordingly, with the two highest classes entitled to hold the highest political offices. The lowest class gained voting power in the general assembly (*Ekklêsia*), whose activities Solon was probably the first to delineate. It is also likely that Solon established a Council of Four Hundred with probouleutic functions. By substituting wealth for birth as the criterion for political office, Solon ended the nobles' exclusive control of political power. In addition, he granted to all citizens the right of appeal to popular courts (*Hêliaia*), thus freeing them from the arbitrary decisions of noble magistrates. He also created a new, more humane law code to replace the severe code of Draco except in cases of homicide.

Although democracy was as yet unimagined, Solon's reforms must be seen as the first pre-requisites for it. How did he come to these ideas? On what understanding of human nature and of the problems of communal existence must he have based his decisions? Our knowledge of the details of Solon's life and work is sketchy and open to various interpretations. The earliest biographical accounts were probably not written until the fourth century B.C. Later ancient accounts, based upon these, are riddled with puzzling inconsistencies and frustrating omissions.[1] Thus, our best source of information about Solon's thought remains Solon's own poetry. Only his own verses can reveal the way in which he took traditional forms and ideas and transformed them into the novel bases for radically new political structures, thus setting the stage for democracy.

---

1. The earliest accounts were based upon Solon's poems, surviving fragments of his law code, and on oral tradition. Surviving are extended (often conflicting) accounts drawn from these earliest sources. These were written by Aristotle, Diodorus Siculus, Plutarch, and Diogenes Laertius. Solon is also mentioned by Herodotus, Plato, Demosthenes, Aristides, and others.

For detailed modern studies of Solon's life and work, see: K. Freeman, *The Life and Work of Solon* (London, 1926); I. Linforth, *Solon the Athenian* (Berkeley, 1919); W. J. Woodhouse, *Solon the Liberator* (London, 1938).

The problems which confront the literary and intellectual historian exist on three levels. They derive, first, from Solon's general uninformativeness about his political program, second, from the continued uncertainty as to where to place him in an assessment of the Greek moral consciousness, and, third, from the difficulty of adequately evaluating his poetic achievement. The persistence of scholarly disagreement in spite of extensive examination testifies to the difficulty of finding a practicable approach to Solon's poetry. A more unified, thematic approach is needed, one that resists creating artificial distinctions between poems and seeks not simply to understand Solon as a moralist but to examine his general position as an Athenian politician and poet.

As political history or as treatises of political theory, Solon's poems are decidedly cryptic and uninformative, at least to the modern reader. But since, as a statesman, Solon is a figure of considerable historical importance, scholars have, understandably, sought to find in his poetry descriptions, explanations, and clarifications of his political actions and views. The results of such inquiries have been dissatisfying. Solon's statements seem straightforward on the surface but perplexing when examined more closely. One critic comments that Solon's verses "speak to us in terms that seem to bear their meaning on their face, but prove on closer scrutiny to carry no really intelligible, certainly no indubitable, significance."[2] If, as seems probable, the lack of specificity is due neither to accident nor to deliberate selection by later authors, one might well conclude that Solon employed generalities because his verses were designed for his contemporaries.[3] Yet, granted that the details of Solon's legislative achievements are likely to remain forever disputable, one may still ask why Solon would choose to address his contemporaries in generalities, and whether the modern reader should be so reluctant to suspect that Solon had a desire to address posterity as well.

If Solon's poems are frustrating to the historian, they are not less so to the literary critic. Little of his poetic achievement survives, and the surviving sample is sadly fragmentary. One consequence of this is that in comparison with the work of other poets whose work has been better preserved, Solon's poetic efforts tend to be overshadowed. Often, in studies of archaic thought, his verses come to provide a context for

---

2. Woodhouse, *Solon the Liberator*, pp. 9–10.

3. Woodhouse, *Solon the Liberator*, pp. 12–13.

examination of other poets, rather than a focus for examination in their own right. Not surprisingly, there is as little consensus of opinion about the significance of his poetic activity as there is about the interpretation of his ethical and political theories.

The lack of agreement as to the substance of Solon's ethical and political contribution makes it difficult to assess his position in the Greek moral consciousness. Scholars debate heatedly Solon's position in the development of archaic thought. The question of development is itself controversial. Some literary critics reject the view that the ethical conceptions manifest in Homer or Hesiod are significantly different from a modern, post-Kantian understanding of morality. But neither they nor those who argue in favor of a developmental process agree as to Solon's contribution. Some ascribe to him a virtually modern ethical viewpoint, seeing in his verses reference to concepts of moral responsibility,[4] universal truths, immanent laws binding communities,[5] and moral self-consciousness.[6] In contrast, other scholars do not consider Solon's ethical conceptions to be significantly different from those of Homer or Hesiod. They see little difference between his conception of *Dikê* 'Justice' and Hesiod's,[7] and reject the view that his imagery depicts universal ethical truths or adds significantly to the ethical contributions of Homer and Hesiod.[8] According to this view,

---

4. Thus W. Jaeger describes his "dynamic didactic ethos which lays hold of men as responsible agents" ("Solons Eunomie," in *Five Essays,* translated by A. M. Fiske [Montreal, 1966], p. 88).

5. In Jaeger's view, the "recognition of the universal truth that every community is bound by immanent laws implies that every man is a responsible moral agent with a duty to be done" (*Paideia,* translated by G. Highet, vol. I [New York, 1939], p. 143).

6. According to F. Will, Solon's "self-consciousness is distinctively moral and radiates an appeal to moral self-consciousness in other men" ("Solon's Consciousness of Himself," *Transactions of the American Philological Association* 89 [1958], p. 311).

7. A. W. H. Adkins comments that "Hesiod's *Dikê* 'Justice' complains to Zeus, whereas Solon's silently punishes on her own account; but we are in the same world of thought" (*Poetic Craft in the Early Greek Elegists* [Chicago and London, 1985], p. 117).

8. In the opinion of E. A. Havelock, Solon's imagery contains no "conceptual grasp of a profound moral and cosmic principle" and "his elegies make no conceptual contribution which carries one beyond Hesiod" (*The Greek Concept of Justice From Its Shadow in Homer to Its Substance in Plato* [Cambridge, Mass., 1978], p. 262).

Solon's poems reveal that inherited traditional concepts could easily be applied to situations occuring in the new *polis* 'city-state' of his time.[9]

Some literary critics reject both the opinion that Solon's ethical views are essentially modern and the conclusion that his doctrines come directly from Hesiod and from Homer. These scholars adopt an intermediate position, recognizing that Solon opposes greed for wealth and power not with a conscience which reminds one of one's duty— since the conscience as such did not exist yet—but rather with concern for reputation, that is, respect for public opinion.[10] Perhaps because the text is so fragmentary, it can be (and has been) interpreted to support such widely differing conclusions. The range of opinion indicates the need for a re-examination of Solon's poetry in the appropriate context.

That context will, inevitably, include not only archaic thought, but poetry in its formal, stylistic, and occasional aspects. The tendency to neglect Solon's achievement in that area may, in part, be a further consequence of the loss of most of his work. Much critical debate reveals an interpretive bias in favor of viewing him as primarily a statesman and political thinker rather than as a poet.[11] It has been argued that, in fact, Solon is neither a true philosopher, in that he does not construct a closed system, nor a true poet, in that he does not create a new world of thought and form.[12] Be that as it may, Solon, at least, seems to have considered *himself* a true poet, inasmuch as he sought to make a permanent contribution to political and ethical discourse in Athens, a contribution over and above the immediate political value of his efforts. This point is essential to a re-examination

---

9. Although he is far from sharing Adkins' position, H. Lloyd-Jones makes this argument and insists: "Jaeger's attempt to mark him off from his predecessors by drawing delicate distinctions seems to me to be a failure" (*The Justice of Zeus* [Berkeley, 1971], p. 169). He concludes that "it is no disparagement of the achievement of the great statesman and political thinker to point out that the doctrines he puts forward come to him from Hesiod and from Homer" (*The Justice of Zeus*, p. 45).

10. H. Fränkel makes this argument (*Dichtung und Philosophie des frühen Griechentums* [New York, 1951] p. 297). E. R. Dodds explains that a shame culture acquires elements of guilt culture only through the internalization of conscience, which does not occur until late in the Hellenic world (*The Greeks and the Irrational* [Berkeley, 1951], pp. 36–37).

11. Lloyd-Jones' comment (note 9 above) is a good example.

12. Fränkel, *Dichtung und Philosophie des frühen Griechentums*, p. 313.

of his ethical, political, and social vocabulary, as well as the similes and metaphors he employs. Comparison of his usage with that of Homer, Hesiod, and other poets of the period down to, but not including, Aeschylus reveals not only Solon's sensitivity to the relationship between the individual and the community, but also his acute awareness of his own poetic activity, of the relationship between poet and audience, and of the social purposes of his poetry. Examination of his understanding of these issues facilitates appreciation of the extent of his contribution to the problems posed by the concept of community.

In seeking to appreciate Solon's contribution, rigid distinctions between periods and types are likely to be as unhelpful as distinctions between 'Solon the statesman' and 'Solon the poet'. It is, for example, limiting to divide Solon's poetry into categories such as "early" vs. "late"; "political" vs. "not political"; or "general (or religio-ethical or political) theory" vs. "self-explanation." Such categories limit interpretation because they limit the possibilities for comparing Solon's poems with one another and with other poems of the archaic period. So much of archaic poetry failed to survive; it seems a shame not to make full use of what little is available to us. To the modern reader, Solon's poetry often appears vague and puzzling. The only hope for understanding both its emotional impact and its political import lies in examining it in its archaic context, free from artificially and anachronistically imposed distinctions.

Even obvious categories based on metrical distinctions have their pitfalls. The difference between epic and lyric poetry, vast as it is, need not obscure the fact that all poets drew on Homeric poetry, that epic poetry informs lyric. In regard to modes of poetic compositon, there is significant continuity between epic and lyric poetry, and oral compositional techniques were, arguably, used in lyric poetry as well as in epic.[13] In any case, whether Solon composed orally or in writing, it is impossible to imagine his composing without assimilating and responding to other poetry of his period and earlier, without drawing

---

13. B. Gentili, *Poetry and its Public in Ancient Greece*, translated by A. T. Cole, (Baltimore, 1988), pp. 19–21. G. Nagy provides ample support for this view, arguing persuasively against the assumption that archaic Greek poetry required the medium of writing for its performance and composition. Nagy differentiates oral *poetry* (dactylic hexameter, elegaic distich, iambic trimeter) from *song* (optionally accompanied by *aulos* 'reed' or *kithara* 'lyre') and argues that the former actually derives from the latter (*Pindar's Homer: The Lyric Possession of an Epic Past* [Baltimore, 1990], especially c. 1).

upon familiar themes and associations and manipulating their emotional resonances and social purposes.

In the case of elegy and iambus, it is important to remember that meter never fully determined subject matter. Elegiac meter was undoubtedly employed for diverse themes and functions, and what was considered "iambic" subject matter, the poetry of blame as against the poetry of praise, could also be treated in a variety of meters, including elegy and hexameter.[14] The antithesis between praise and blame, which has been shown to be powerfully pervasive in archaic thought,[15] found expression in diverse meters. More important than such traditional associations was the occasional or non-occasional character of the poetry. Epic poetry contains praise (or blame) of people and events from the past; occasional poetry accords praise or blame to people of the moment. One consequence of this difference is that, unlike narrative poetry, occasional poetry at times requires a certain tact or veiling of language depending upon the composition of the audience. Solon manipulates many of the poetic traditions associated with praise and blame in reassessing the relationship between poet and audience. Although his attitudes about the social function of poetry and of the poet derive from traditional archaic views, he must adapt them to fit a new political situation. Traditional poetry is designed, by and large, to serve the needs of small, cohesive (and exclusive) groups of *philoi* 'friends'; Solon seeks to create poetry that will serve the needs of the *polis* as a whole.

Each of the three chapters which follow examines one of the three largest surviving fragments of Solon's poetry (Poems 13, 4, and 36 respectively).[16] All three poems share important themes and preoccupations. All three emphasize Solon's consciousness of his role as a poet, his understanding of the causal connections between actions and their consequences, and his assessment of human nature and the problems of communal existence.

---

14. Gentili, *Poetry and its Public in Ancient Greece*, pp. 33–34, and 109. And see M. L. West's discussion in *Studies in Greek Elegy and Iambus* [Berlin and New York, 1974], especially pp. 4, 7, and 22–24.

15. M. Detienne, *Les maîtres de vérité dans la Grèce archaïque* (Paris, 1981), pp. 18–25.

16. All references to and quotations of Solon's poetry will be from M. L. West's edition, *Iambi et elegi Graeci*, vol. II (Oxford, 1972).

Chapter 1 discusses Poem 13, probably the most difficult of Solon's extant poems. Is this a single, unified work? Does the invocation to the Muses relate to the rest of the poem and, if so, in what way? The question is more than merely academic since upon it must rest full appreciation of the content of Solon's message. Pursuit of this question will reveal Solon's innovative interpretation of crucial terms in the invocation, namely *Mnêmosunê* 'Memory', *olbos* 'prosperity', and *doxa* 'expectation' or 'reputation'. The novel emphases that Solon gives to these traditional terms clarify later transitions in the poem. Exploring the relationship between human actions and human fortunes, Solon finds in human nature the key to the form that human fortunes take. In so doing, he challenges, in subtle and unexpected ways, unexamined acceptance of conventional goals of human achievement in general and of poetic *sophiê* 'skill' or 'wisdom' in particular.

Chapter 2 examines Solon's Poem 4. In contrast to poem 13, which scholars tend to classify as "ethical," Poem 4 is generally considered "political" and, as a result, examined under a different microscope. Nevertheless, thematic similarities between the two poems are marked. Both stress the value of intellectual understanding, human responsibility for human fortunes, and optimism and insatiability as elements of human nature. Although Poem 4 identifies the interrelationship between individuals in the *polis*, the responsibility of individuals for the consequences of their own actions, and the interdependence between individual fortunes and the fortunes of the *polis* as a whole, the poem is vague and unenlightening when read simply as "political theory." What is Solon actually advocating? How is the modern reader to interpret *Eunomiê* 'good order'? Examined as to its language, imagery and emotional impact, however, the poem becomes far more informative. In this chapter it will be seen that Solon shares with other poets the recognition that the relationship between individual satisfaction and communal harmony is problematic, but questions the language and imagery traditionally employed to address the problem. His use of words such as *episkopos* 'guardian', *koros* 'satiety', and *euphrosunê* 'festivity' simultaneously recalls and re-evaluates conventional ideals of communal organization and of the role of poetry in the furthering of communal harmony. Poem 4 thus reveals, as does Poem 13, both Solon's awareness of the traditional attitudes and functions of poetic composition and the novelty of his own vision.

In Chapter 3 it will be seen that Poem 36 explores many of the same themes as Poem 4 and presents a similar problem. As in Poem 4, here, too, Solon acknowledges the dire threat of enslavement, the direct responsibility of human beings for the consequences of their actions, and the sensitive relationship between the individual and the community. While Poem 4 considers the possibilities for conflict and resolution in the relationship between citizens of the *polis,* Poem 36 reveals Solon's view of himself and his own relationship to his fellow citizens and to his city. But, just as Poem 4 seems vague as political theory, Poem 36 seems unaccountably abstract if it is read merely as a defense of Solon's political actions. The poem contains frustratingly little reference to the specifics of his legislative reforms. It concludes, moreover, with a surprising simile, explicable only by reference to other similes and metaphors in Solon's poetry as well as to the connotations of its terms in epic poetry and the poetry of praise and blame. In voicing his understanding of his own relationship to his fellow citizens, Solon expresses the interconnection between his political and his poetic activity. Far more than simply a defense of his political program, the poem invites scrutiny of the act of poetic composition itself and of the way in which that act may, in fact, be Solon's most successful *political* achievement.

The modern reader needs to overcome the perhaps natural temptation to view Solon as a statesman who happened to compose poetry as a convenient means of disseminating his views. Rather, one may recognize that in composing his verses, Solon considered himself a *poet,*[17] who happened, perhaps, also to be a statesman. That is, he considered that his primary function in demonstrating his *sophiê* 'skill' or 'wisdom' was to transmit and improve upon traditional wisdom, whatever the subject of his discourse.

---

17. In justification of my title, *Solon the Singer,* I cite Plato *Timaeus* 21b. In this passage, Critias describes contests in which boys recited the poems of well-known poets and many boys *sang* (*aeidô* 'sing') the poems of Solon.

Chapter One

Poem 13: Memory and Destiny

Solon's Elegy to the Muses (Poem 13) has excited more scholarly comment than any other of his extant poems or fragments.[1] It is a difficult poem, complex and puzzling in both its content and its structure. Is this a single, unified work, and, if so, in what way? How does it relate to the rest of Solon's poetry? Is this religious theory? ethical theory? political theory? And—ultimately the most compelling question of all, but inextricably connected to all of the others—what exactly is the content of Solon's message? These interrelated "problems" may appear to be insoluble, if for no other reason than that they have received a plethora of "solutions," each the less definitive by virtue of the sheer number of all the others. Additional investigation is not, then, unjustified. And, indeed, the problems appear less insoluble if the poem—and particularly its central passage (lines 33–43)—is further examined in the context of other poetry of the period and earlier. Such examination reveals Solon's consciousness of his own poetic activity, his understanding of the purposes of poetic *sophiê* 'skill' or 'wisdom', and the subtle and unexpected emphases with which he communicates that understanding.

The opening address to the Muses seems, to many critics, unrelated to the rest of the poem. The bulk of the poem sets forth arguments on the inevitability of punishment for wrongdoing and on the uncertainty

---

1. As previously noted (Introduction, note 16), all references to and quotations of Solon's poetry will be from M. L. West's edition in vol. II of *Iambi et elegi Graeci* (Oxford, 1972). I have also used West's edition for Archilochus, Tyrtaeus, Theognis, Simonides, Semonides, and Mimnermus. For Sappho and Alcaeus, see the edition of E. Lobel and D. L. Page, *Poetarum Lesbiorum fragmenta* (Oxford, 1955). For Alcman, Anacreaon, Simonides, and Ibycus, see the edition of D. L. Page, *Poetae melici Graeci* (Oxford, 1962). For Homer, Hesiod, Pindar, Herodotus, Bacchylides, Aeschylus, and Sophocles, see the editions listed on p. 149 below.

11

of human affairs. What is the relationship between these two ideas? Are they simply incompatible views oddly juxtaposed? Can the future be simultaneously knowable (if all wrongdoing is inevitably punished) and not (if uncertainty is inherent in all human affairs)? One solution is to view Poem 13 as neither a single, unified poem, nor addressed to the Muses throughout.[2] But there is a connection between the invocation and the remainder of the poem. It derives from the Muses' association with Memory and from the relevance of Memory to the admonitory character of the poem.

Indeed Solon's opening address to the Muses is puzzling. Why does he address his prayer to these divinities? Is it because they have the power to grant his request? And for what, precisely, is he asking them? Seen in its archaic context, however, the request appears both lucid and elucidating. The explanation lies not only in what it contains but also in what it excludes. Solon begins by saying:

Μνημοσύνης καὶ Ζηνὸς Ὀλυμπίου ἀγλαὰ τέκνα,
    Μοῦσαι Πιερίδες, κλῦτέ μοι εὐχομένωι·
ὄλβόν μοι πρὸς θεῶν μακάρων δότε, καὶ πρὸς ἁπάντων
    ἀνθρώπων αἰεὶ δόξαν ἔχειν ἀγαθήν·
εἶναι δὲ γλυκὺν ὧδε φίλοις, ἐχθροῖσι δὲ πικρόν,
    τοῖσι μὲν αἰδοῖον, τοῖσι δὲ δεινὸν ἰδεῖν.

                                                (Solon 13.1–6)

Shining children of Memory [*Mnêmosunê*] and of Olympian Zeus,
    Pierian Muses, hear me as I pray.
Grant me prosperity [*olbos*] at the hands of the blessed gods,
    and always a good reputation [*agathê doxa*] at the hands of men;
and so to be sweet [*glukus*] to friends and bitter [*pikros*] to enemies,
    an object of reverence to the former, but to the latter terrible to
    look upon.

The problem is that Solon is asking for things generally thought to be bestowed not by the Muses but by Zeus or other gods. Experts have expressed surprise that Solon would choose to call upon the Muses for such general assistance.[3] This assessment reflects the reluctance of

2. H. Fränkel reaches this conclusion (*Dichtung und Philosophie des frühen Griechentums* [New York, 1951], p. 310).

3. I. Linforth comments that Solon "must have believed that he enjoyed an unusually intimate relation with these divinities if he was moved to turn to them for aid in the general conduct of his life" (*Solon the Athenian* [Berkeley, 1919], p. 106).

many critics to suspect that Solon may have considered himself a poet no less than a lawgiver. This issue receives expanded attention in Chapter 3, but for now the point remains that if Solon regarded himself in this way, it would not be at all unusual for him to begin an important work with an address to the Muses.

Although the address to the Muses has been recognized as a traditional theme in archaic poetry and one which reflects the social importance of the Muses as the guardians of traditional lore,[4] Solon's lines have not been fully interpreted in this light. Solon calls upon the Muses in their traditional capacity as the daughters of Memory (see Hesiod *Theogony* 54ff.). He even highlights this fact of their lineage in a particularly direct, unsubtle way, by making *Mnêmosunê* 'Memory' the first word in his poem, and then he proceeds to ask these daughters of Memory for something that seems to have little to do with Memory. If it is to be comprehensible to the modern reader, Solon's request must, therefore, be examined in connection with traditional archaic themes involving, in different ways, the relationship between the poet, the Muses, and poetic Memory. But one must also consider an additional conception of Memory, distinct from but related to the others, to which Solon gives increasing emphasis throughout Poem 13 and indeed throughout much of his extant poetry.

The importance of Memory in Greek poetic thought is multifaceted. The Muse, as rhythmical song, is inseparable from Memory.[5] In epic poetry Memory is not only the psychological function underlying the formulaic technique of oral composition, it is also and especially the religious power which confers magico-religious status on the poetic utterance. This gives the poet the ability both to celebrate human exploits (*klea andrôn*, as, for example, at *Iliad* 9.189 and 520), and to retell stories of the gods.[6] The traditional position of the epic poet is that he presents to his audience things that he has heard directly from

---

4. See, for example, M. Detienne, *Les maîtres de vérité dans la Grèce archaïque* (Paris, 1981), pp. 9ff.; G. Nagy, *The Best of the Achaeans: Concepts of the Hero in Archaic Greek Poetry* (Baltimore, 1979), pp. 271–272; B. Gentili, *Poetry and its Public in Ancient Greece*, translated by A. T. Cole (Baltimore, 1988), p. 159.

5. Detienne, *Les maîtres de vérité dans la Grèce archaïque*, pp. 10–15.

6. Detienne, pp. 15–16.

the Muses. In this way the Muses grant him access to events of which he can have had no firsthand knowledge.[7] This traditional position is not the exclusive province of the epic poet. Other poets, too, claim to receive their subject matter directly from the Muses. Theognis, for example, allies himself with epic tradition by repeating an *epos* 'song' or 'utterance' of the Muses:

Μοῦσαι καὶ Χάριτες, κοῦραι Διός, αἵ ποτε Κάδμου
ἐς γάμον ἐλθοῦσαι καλὸν ἀείσατ' ἔπος,
"ὅττι καλὸν φίλον ἐστί, τὸ δ' οὐ καλὸν οὐ φίλον ἐστί"
τοῦτ' ἔπος ἀθανάτων ἦλθε διὰ στομάτων.

(Theognis 15–18)

Muses and Graces, daughters of Zeus, who once
came to the wedding of Cadmus, you sang this beautiful song:
"That which is beautiful is near and dear, that which is not beautiful
is not."
This song came through your immortal lips.[8]

Similarly, for Bacchylides, inspiration from the Muses comes in the form of a dictated announcement (13.228–231). By contrast, Solon does not ask the Muses to give him his subject matter. His opening lines thus indicate a departure from tradition and emphasize the personal immediacy of the verses which follow. Solon does not intend to describe *klea andrôn* 'glorious deeds' of past generations. Rather, he will describe present conditions and speak directly from his own personal experience. To this extent the request must be understood in the context of Hesiod's *prooimion* to the *Theogony*.[9] But while it may be clear

7. Nagy, *The Best of the Achaeans*, pp. 271–272 regarding *Iliad* 1.1; 2.485–486; 20.203–205; *Odyssey* 1.1; and p. 271, n. 4 regarding Hesiod *Theogony* 27–28. Nagy terms this the "inherited conceit" of the epic poet. See also Detienne, *Les maîtres de vérité dans la Grèce archaïque*, pp. 9ff.

8. See L. Edmunds, "The Genre of Theognidean Poetry," in *Theognis of Megara*, edited by T. J. Figueira, and G. Nagy (Baltimore and London, 1985), pp. 96–97 regarding the desacralization of memory in elegy, wherein "the poet on his own authority can determine the application of Memory." See also Edmunds, pp. 101–102 and V. Cobb-Stevens, "Opposites, Reversals, and Ambiguities: The Unsettled World of Theognis," in *Theognis of Megara*, p. 173 regarding Theognis' understanding of the Muses' function.

9. H. Eisenberger argues that while the Muses do not have the power to give wealth themselves or to influence men directly, they can mediate on Solon's behalf, if they think him worthy. Solon's request to the Muses is unexpected and should cause some discomfort, according to Eisenberger, because the poet is striving for a strong surprise

what Solon is *not* asking of the Muses, it remains to be seen precisely what it is that he *is* asking from them.

One must therefore consider what else the Muses are traditionally empowered to grant as well as the actual content of Solon's request. Both questions reveal additional aspects of the concept of poetic Memory and its relation to the Muses. In Hesiod's *Theogony*, the Muses claim:

ἴδμεν ψεύδεα πολλὰ λέγειν ἐτύμοισιν ὁμοῖα,
ἴδμεν δ᾽, εὖτ᾽ ἐθέλωμεν, ἀληθέα γηρύσασθαι.

(*Theogony* 27–28)

We know how to tell numerous lies which seem to be truthful,
but whenever we wish we know how to utter the full truth.

The poet asserts that after giving him a staff of blooming laurel, the Muses provided the necessary poetic inspiration:

ἐνέπνευσαν δέ μοι αὐδὴν
θέσπιν, ἵνα κλείοιμι τά τ᾽ ἐσσόμενα πρό τ᾽ ἐόντα

(*Theogony* 31–32)

they breathed a divine voice
into me to sing of what will be and what was before.

It is the Muses who delight Zeus in Olympos εἰρεῦσαι τά τ᾽ ἐόντα τά τ᾽ ἐσσόμενα πρό τ᾽ ἐόντα 'as they reveal what is and what will be and what was before' (*Theogony* 38). The Muses, it seems, have the power of knowledge of truth and the ability to inspire others with this power if they care to. It is this ability to tell "what is, what will be and what was" (*Theogony* 32 and 38) which signifies the connection between Truth and Memory.[10]

---

effect intended to secure the intense attention of his hearers. Eisenberger concludes that the gesture of prayer signifies Solon's reverential attitude toward the gods, while the contents of the request indicate to listeners that the elegy will not contain a narrative, but rather will discuss issues connected to human striving toward happiness ("Gedanken zu Solons Musenelegie," *Philologus* 128 [1984], p. 11).

10. Detienne, *Les maîtres de vérité dans la Grèce archaïque*, p. 18. For the relationship between *mnêmosunê* 'memory', *lêthê* 'forgetting', and *alêtheia* 'truth', see G. Nagy, *Pindar's Homer: The Lyric Possession of an Epic Past* (Baltimore, 1990), pp. 58–60, and n. 39. Nagy cites A. T. Cole's formulation that the reference of *alêtheia* is "not simply to non-omission of pieces of information...but also to not forgetting from one minute to the next what was said a few minutes before, and not letting anything, said or unsaid, slip by without being mindful of its implications" (A. T. Cole, "Archaic Truth," *Quaderni Urbinati di Cultura Classica* 13 [1983], p. 12).

In this connection, Truth can also mean "consecration by Memory."[11] This sense of Memory is essential to the antithesis between praise and blame which is a fundamental principle in archaic thought. The Muses are important in their ability to memorialize exploits in song. The poet thus becomes the supreme arbiter of values by choosing to accord or refuse poetic remembrance,[12] whether in the poetry of invective or its formal opposite, the poetry of praise.[13] Although Solon is not composing praise or invective poetry *per se*, his address to the Muses and his emphasis on *Mnêmosunê* (but not—as in epic poetry—of the exploits of past generations) invites comparison with this genre. Such comparison proves useful not only for understanding Poem 13 but, in fact, for interpreting much of Solon's poetry. Given this context, Solon's address to the Muses as daughters of Memory seems neither unique nor inexplicable. The didactic element in his verses participates unmistakably in the traditional sense of the poet's social function as an arbiter of values. But whereas epic and occasional poetry draw primarily upon the Muses' knowledge of the past and the present, leaving their knowledge of the future as merely the potential source of subjects for poetic remembrance, Solon in this poem is concerned with knowledge of the future or lack of it. Recognizing this as a crucial ingredient in human affairs, he draws upon a particular sense of the Muses' knowledge of the future, in attempting to understand the relationship between human nature and human fortunes.

But in what sense can memory be said to concern the future? To be sure, a traditional parallelism exists between the *aoidos* 'singer' and the *mantis* 'seer'.[14] As the servant and companion of the Muses, the poet is

---

11. A. P. Burnett, *The Art of Bacchylides* (Cambridge, Mass., 1985), p. 44.

12. Detienne, *Les maîtres de vérité dans la Grèce archaïque,* pp. 18–27. This subject has received a great deal of attention. See for example: Edmunds, "The Genre of Theognidean Poetry," pp. 98ff., citing Theognis 797–798, 237–250, and Semonides 7.112–113; G. Nagy "Iambos: Typologies of Invective and Praise," *Arethusa* 9 (1976), pp. 191–206; *The Best of the Achaeans,* p. 37 n. 5 and pp. 222ff.; Burnett, *The Art of Bacchylides,* especially pp. 44–45 and 57–59 and Gentili, *Poetry and its Public in Ancient Greece,* pp. 107ff.

13. On praise and invective, see Nagy "Iambos: Typologies of Invective and Praise."

14. Both are *dêmiourgoi* 'ones who work for the community' or 'skilled workmen' (Nagy, *The Best of the Achaeans,* pp. 233–234 regarding *Odyssey* 17.381–387).

granted, through his vision of the mythic past, a vision of the present and future as well.[15] But Solon has pointedly dissociated himself from this sort of poetic remembrance.[16] He does not seek knowledge of the future by way of knowledge of the mythic past. He seeks it rather through a precise knowledge of the causal connections between actions and their outcomes. Lines 7–17, for example, establish such a causal connection between modes of acquisition and the fortunes which inevitably result from them:

χρήματα δ᾽ ἱμείρω μὲν ἔχειν, ἀδίκως δὲ πεπᾶσθαι
οὐκ ἐθέλω· πάντως ὕστερον ἦλθε δίκη.
πλοῦτον δ᾽ ὃν μὲν δῶσι θεοί, παραγίγνεται ἀνδρὶ
ἔμπεδος ἐκ νεάτου πυθμένος ἐς κορυφήν·
ὃν δ᾽ ἄνδρες τιμῶσιν ὑφ᾽ ὕβριος, οὐ κατὰ κόσμον
ἔρχεται, ἀλλ᾽ ἀδίκοις ἔργμασι πειθόμενος
οὐκ ἐθέλων ἕπεται, ταχέως δ᾽ ἀναμίσγεται ἄτηι·
ἀρχῆς δ᾽ ἐξ ὀλίγης γίγνεται ὥστε πυρός,
φλαύρη μὲν τὸ πρῶτον, ἀνιηρὴ δὲ τελευτᾶι·
οὐ γὰρ δὴ⟨ν⟩ θνητοῖς ὕβριος ἔργα πέλει,
ἀλλὰ Ζεὺς πάντων ἐφορᾶι τέλος

(Solon 13.7–17)

I desire to have property [*khrêmata*], but I do not wish to acquire it unjustly;
   for justice [*dikê*] comes inevitably afterward.
Wealth [*ploutos*] which the gods give, comes to a man to stay,
   set firm from lowest base to top.
But that which men prize by reckless violence [*hubris*],
   comes not in due order [*kosmos*], but persuaded by unjust deeds,
it follows unwillingly, and swiftly it is mingled with ruin [*atê*];
   its beginning is from a little thing, as is the beginning of a fire,
trivial at first, but in the end grievous;
   for mortals' works of reckless violence [*hubris*] are not long-lived,
but Zeus looks upon the end of all things.

Just acquisition results in abiding wealth; unjust acquisition (by way of *hubris*) results in *atê*.

This view differs from Hesiod's vision of a future in which justice has been neglected, in that Solon minimizes the role of divine forces:

---

15. Burnett, *The Art of Bacchylides*, p. 44.

16. See Chapter 1, p. 14 above.

predictable events result directly from human actions themselves, not from divine responses to them.[17] Hesiod, by contrast, emphasizes a connection between justice among men and justice received from the gods:

εἰ γάρ τίς κ' ἐθέληι τὰ δίκαι' ἀγορεῦσαι
γινώσκων, τῶι μέν τ' ὄλβον διδοῖ εὐρύοπα Ζεύς·
(Hesiod *Works and Days* 280–281)

If one is willing to speak what he sees to be justice, what he knows is the right thing, far-seeing Zeus grants him a blessed life [*olbos*].

Solon focuses, rather, on the instability of human fortunes (for example, Poem 13.9–13, 16ff., 65–66, 75–76) and suggests some lack of correlation between human actions and divine (especially Poem 13.29–32, 67–70). While Hesiod's language is personal, he seems to attempt an impersonal description of personal forces. He is moving toward a sociological view, but his vision is still part-mythological. Solon's conception reduces the significance of the mythological element. His insistence on the direct causal connections between past actions and their inevitable consequences suggests the possibility of predicting, as it were, the future consequences of present actions. This is a function of memory in that it requires the remembrance of past causal relationships. *Mnêmosunê*, moreover, can suggest "call to mind" or "bring, put in mind" and need not refer exclusively to things people have known in the past. This may be why it is the natural province of the Muses, in that they can make people mindful of things to come.

Such a concept of Memory can be of benefit to the *polis* no less than to the individual. It is worth noting that whereas the Muses know τά τ' ἐσσόμενα πρό τ' ἐόντα 'what will be and what was before' (Hesiod *Theogony* 32), and τά τ' ἐόντα τά τ' ἐσσόμενα πρό τ' ἐόντα 'what is and what will be, and what was before' (*Theogony* 38), Dikê 'Justice', in Solon's most extensive discussion of its operation, is a personification of the retribution that knows only τὰ γιγνόμενα πρό τ' ἐόντα 'what is and what was before' (Solon 4.15). The Muses' *Mnêmosunê* may therefore be able to provide something which *Dikê* cannot: knowledge of the future. If so, Solon's emphasis on Memory as the knowledge of cause and effect

---

17. But see A. W. H. Adkins who argues that this difference is not significant (*Poetic Craft in the Early Greek Elegists* [Chicago and London, 1985], p. 117).

is necessary to harmonious political organization, since this knowledge is essential to a sensible guide to conduct.[18]

It is therefore not surprising that Solon's concern for identifying the causal connections between specific human actions and their direct consequences is, perhaps, most marked in Poem 4,[19] the work which most emphasizes his political views. But, as already argued, avoidance of rigid categorization of Solon's poems reveals pervasive thematic parallels between poems as well as between Solon's poetry and that of other poets.[20] Examination of traditional archaic attitudes regarding the Muses, the social function of the poet, and poetic Memory suggests that Poem 13 is about knowledge of causal connections no less than Poem 4. Reference to this theme, in turn, helps to clarify the specific contents of Solon's request in Poem 13 because it underlies his highly individual understanding not only of *Mnêmosunê* but also of *olbos* 'prosperity' and *doxa* 'reputation' as well.

Admittedly, Solon's request in lines 3–6 seems at first glance to express the standard aristocratic conception of happiness. Lines 5–6, Solon's desire to be *glukus* 'sweet' to friends, *pikros* 'bitter' to enemies, certainly express a traditional idea (compare, for example, *Odyssey* 6.184–185 or Sappho 42.6–7). But his request for *olbos* and an *agathê doxa* is more problematic. Why does he ask the Muses for these things? On one level, a connection exists between the address to the Muses and the content of the request, in that by calling upon the Muses as goddesses of poetry Solon is also asking them implicitly for continued prosperity and for the success of his political program, both of which were inextricably connected to his poetry.[21] This may well have been

---

18. In recognizing that Memory may be politically useful, Solon is consistent with contemporary usage. L. Edmunds explains that, in contrast to epic poetry, in elegiac poetry, Memory is at the service of *aretê* 'excellence' or 'virtue', and the principle involved is "usefulness to the *polis*" ("The Genre of Theognidean Poetry," in *Theognis of Megara*, edited by T. J. Figueira, and G. Nagy [Baltimore and London, 1985], pp. 96–97). See also A. Ford, regarding Theognis 769–772 and Theognis' self-depiction as simultaneously the Muses' spokesman and a political envoy ("The Seal of Theognis: The Politics of Authorship in Archaic Greece," in *Theognis of Megara*, pp. 92–93).

19. See Chapter 2, p. 68.

20. See Introduction, p. 6.

21. Gentili, *Poetry and its Public in Ancient Greece*, p. 159. Gentili notes that Fränkel was the first to point out the link between the invocation of the Muses and the request for prosperity.

the audience's first assessment on hearing lines 1–6. One may compare Theognis' invocation which links together the *Kharites* 'Graces' with the Muses (Theognis 15–18).[22]

But in Solon's lines a subtler connection exists as well. One must not conclude, however, that Solon is calling upon the Muses simply in their capacity as goddesses of wisdom.[23] Certainly he never asks for wisdom specifically, and in line 3 he asks not for wisdom but for wealth.[24] But it would seem odd for a poet to ask for *sophiê* 'wisdom, poetic skill' directly. By virtue of being a poet, he already has it. He might possibly ask for a continuation of *sophiê*, but one suspects that if a poet has to ask for it, he risks implying that he has not been sufficiently rewarded by the Muses already. Nevertheless, it is difficult to conclude that *sophiê* is central to the poem since Solon does not dwell on it. To be sure, he (like Theognis) recognizes the Muses as the sources of *sophiê*.[25] It is the poet's province and the gift of the Muses, but a direct request for it, as well as seeming somehow redundant, might also suggest arrogance on the part of the poet.

In Theognis, for example, *sophiê* seems to refer to the poet's ability to create poetry which will be comprehensible only to a select portion of his audience and incomprehensible to the rest. For Theognis, the poet's *sophiê* derives from the Muses and enables him to make false things like true (Theognis 770 and Hesiod *Theogony* 27–28). This ability is explicitly described by the verb *ainissomai* 'to speak in riddles' (Theognis 681).[26] This allusive or riddling language, as, for example, in

---

22. Edmunds maintains that Theognis thereby specializes the function of the Muses, appealing to them as "the ones who can win favor for his poetry in his community" ("The Genre of Theognidean Poetry," pp. 101–102).

23. I cannot agree with A. A. Allen's argument that "the key to the success for which he [Solon] prays is wisdom, by which limits are recognized, injustice avoided, and retribution averted. The elegy is addressed to the Muses as goddesses of wisdom" ("Solon's Prayer to the Muses," *Transactions of the American Philological Association* 80 [1949], pp. 50–65).

24. B. A. van Groningen, *La composition littéraire archaïque grecque* (Amsterdam, 1960), p. 95, n. 1.

25. Edmunds, "The Genre of Theognidean Poetry," pp. 100–101, citing Solon 13.51–52 and Theognis 769–770.

26. Cobb-Stevens, "Opposites, Reversals, and Ambiguities: The Unsettled World of Theognis," p. 166. Similarly, Edmunds, "The Genre of Theognidean Poetry," pp. 106–109, discussing Theognis 713 and Hesiod *Theogony* 27–28.

Theognis' "ship of state" image, is intended to be understandable only to a select few, that is, to the *agathoi* 'noble or good men' to the exclusion of the *kakoi* 'low-born or bad men' (in the moral sense of these terms).[27] The highly partisan poetry of Alcaeus and the riddling verses of Archilochus, too, seem directed at a selected audience.[28] In the seventh century, elegy was the accepted medium for *parainesis* 'exhortation'.[29] To this extent, Solon's elegies may participate in the traditional function of the *ainos* 'praise', 'riddle', or 'fable', but Solon seeks not to appeal only to a small segment of his society, but to unify the *polis* as a whole. Therefore, the riddling element in *sophiê* does not suit his purposes.

Even if *sophiê* would not in itself signify a limited audience or exclusiveness, it might seem arrogant for Solon to suggest that he is himself *sophos* 'wise'. He never calls himself this. His poetry is distinguished by his recognition that his verses must be comprehensible to members of all levels of society, not only to the elite, that he must include everyone in his audience. He does not want to present himself as a member of the select few nor to appear to be making

---

27. Cobb-Stevens, "Opposites, Reversals, and Ambiguities: The Unsettled World of Theognis," p. 166. Similarly G. Nagy, "Theognis and Megara: A Poet's Vision of his City," in *Theognis of Megara*, edited by T. J. Figueira, and G. Nagy (Baltimore and London, 1985), pp. 23–27. Nagy also maintains that *ainos* designates "a mode of poetic discourse that is unmistakably understandable only to its intended audience. To use the terminology of Prague School linguistics: the *ainos* entails one code with at least two messages—the true one for the intended audience and the false or garbled one for all the others" (*The Best of the Achaeans*, pp. 238–242). Pindar and Bacchylides use the formal diction of the *ainos* as well (*The Best of the Achaeans*, pp. 236–238 and 241–242; "Theognis and Megara: A Poet's Vision of his City," p. 26). Nagy further identifies the *ainos* as "an affirmation, a marked speech-act, made by and for a marked social group." In Pindar's traditional diction, the *ainos* specifies listeners who are *sophoi* 'skilled', *agathoi* 'noble', and *philoi* 'near and dear' (*Pindar's Homer*, p. 148). Edmunds explains that the two semantic ranges of *ainos* ('praise' and 'riddle') are linked by the notion of community. The former is "declarative, public, clear," the latter "muted, private, obscure." Both are addressed to a community (Edmunds, "The Genre of Theognidean Poetry," pp. 105–106). See also Chapter 2, p. 95.

28. See Gentili, *Poetry and its Public in Ancient Greece*, p. 42. Gentili, describing a "performance psychology" intended to create an emotional connection between speaker and audience, notes the "esoteric coterie language" used in the allegories of Alcaeus.

29. See G. Else, *The Origin and Early Form of Greek Tragedy* [Cambridge, Mass., 1965], p. 40. Else also provides additional bibliography.

pronouncements. His strategies for inclusion are examined in Chapters 2 and 3. This goal may explain the absence of *ainoi* in the form of animal fables in his poetry. It also may relate to Solon's refusal to ask the Muses for his subject matter, since the Muses can be the direct source of this riddling and exclusive poetry.[30] Instead, Solon seems to hold the more traditional view of *sophiê.* Not composing for a specific or limited audience, he chooses to emphasize a particular aspect of *sophiê,* a type of *Mnêmosunê* 'Memory', namely the knowledge of the direct causal connections between actions and their consequences. This knowledge turns out to be the very element he emphasizes in his request for *olbos* 'prosperity' and *doxa* 'expectation' or 'reputation'.

Solon's desire for *olbos* is not in itself unusual. Praise poetry contains the traditional theme that *olbos* comes from the gods to the righteous and attracts the *phthonos* 'ill-will' or 'envy' of the unrighteous,[31] and the inclusion of a prayer for the poet's future success and prosperity—sometimes expressed as a hope for wealth—is characteristic of Greek hymns.[32]

Nor is Solon's association of *olbos* with the Muses unprecedented. Hesiod explains that

ὃ δ' ὄλβιος, ὅντινα Μοῦσαι
φίλωνται· γλυκερή οἱ ἀπὸ στόματος ῥέει αὐδή.
(Hesiod *Theogony* 96–97)

Blessed [*olbios*] the man who is
loved by the Muses; sweet is the voice that flows from his mouth.

The Homeric Hymn to the Muses makes the same assertion (*Hymn* 25. 4–5). Simonides 519 fr.55(a)8, although too fragmentary to provide any assurance, might contain a similar idea and, arguably, Bacchylides 3.90–92 assumes such an association between *olbos* and the Muses. Other divinities, however, seem to possess the actual power to grant *olbos:* Hekate (Hesiod *Theogony* 420), Ploutos (Hesiod *Theogony* 974), and

---

30. Regarding Theognis 15–18, see Cobb-stevens, "Opposites, Reversals, and Ambiguities: The Unsettled World of Theognis," pp. 172–173 and Edmunds, "The Genre of Theognidean Poetry," pp. 101–102. See also above, Chapter 1, p. 14.

31. Nagy, *The Best of the Achaeans,* pp. 228–229.

32. G. W. Most, *The Measures of Praise* (Gottingen, 1985), p. 120 and n. 111 and n. 112.

Zeus (Hesiod *Works and Days* 281), for example. And yet the latter passage begins to connect *olbos* with knowledge:

εἰ γάρ τίς κ᾽ ἐθέληι τὰ δίκαι᾽ ἀγορεῦσαι
γινώσκων, τῶι μέν τ᾽ ὄλβον διδοῖ εὐρύοπα Ζεύς·
ὃς δέ κε μαρτυρίηισιν ἑκὼν ἐπίορκον ὀμόσσας
ψεύσεται, ἐν δὲ δίκην βλάψας νήκεστον ἀασθῆι,
τοῦ δέ τ᾽ ἀμαυροτέρη γενεὴ μετόπισθε λέλειπται·
ἀνδρὸς δ᾽ εὐόρκου γενεὴ μετόπισθεν ἀμείνων.
(Hesiod *Works and Days* 280–285)

If one is willing to speak what he sees to be justice, what he knows is the right thing, far-seeing Zeus grants him a blessed life [*olbos*].
But if he witnesses falsely and willfully perjures himself, being a liar, a harmer of Justice, incurably blind, he is leaving his family a gloomier future existence.
He who swears truly creates for his family future prosperity.

Hesiod reiterates this point at the end of the *Works and Days*:

τάων εὐδαίμων τε καὶ ὄλβιος ὃς τάδε πάντα
εἰδὼς ἐργάζηται ἀναίτιος ἀθανάτοισιν.
(Hesiod *Works and Days* 826–827)

In his days happy and blessed [*olbios*] is he who knows all this and so works as not to offend the immortal gods.

But it remains for Solon to specify the nature of this knowledge.

This link with knowledge is crucial to understanding the meaning of *olbos* in the poem as a whole. On first hearing line 3, the audience's normal expectation would be that by *olbos* Solon simply means material wealth. But lines 7–13 add a proviso to the poet's opening prayer:

χρήματα δ᾽ ἱμείρω μὲν ἔχειν, ἀδίκως δὲ πεπᾶσθαι
οὐκ ἐθέλω· πάντως ὕστερον ἦλθε δίκη.
πλοῦτον δ᾽ ὃν μὲν δῶσι θεοί, παραγίνεται ἀνδρὶ
ἔμπεδος ἐκ νεάτου πυθμένος ἐς κορυφήν·
ὃν δ᾽ ἄνδρες τιμῶσιν ὑφ᾽ ὕβριος, οὐ κατὰ κόσμον
ἔρχεται, ἀλλ᾽ ἀδίκοις ἔργμασι πειθόμενος
οὐκ ἐθέλων ἕπεται, ταχέως δ᾽ ἀναμίσγεται ἄτηι·
(Solon 13.7–13)

I desire to have property [*khrêmata*], but I do not wish to acquire it unjustly.
for justice [*dikê*] comes inevitably afterward.
Wealth [*ploutos*] which the gods give, comes to a man to stay,

set firm from lowest base to top,
but that which men prize by reckless violence [*hubris*],
comes not in due order [*kosmos*], but persuaded by unjust deeds,
it follows unwillingly, and swiftly it is mingled with ruin [*atê*].

In this way, Solon seeks to specify god-given wealth as wealth combined with justice and to differentiate it from *ploutos* and *khrêmata* in general. The position of each of these words as the first word in its line adds emphasis and encourages comparison.[33] All three words might possibly be mistaken for synonyms, but, unlike *olbos, ploutos* and *khrêmata* are not unequivocally desirable. If not justly acquired, they are unstable and ruinous.

Whether or not Solon is seeking to distinguish *olbos* from *ploutos* or *khrêmata* by giving the former a more restrictive definition, his use of the term here contrasts in important ways with a vaguer use of the term attested elsewhere in archaic poetry, both his own and that of others. The word has a range of uses including 'happiness', 'good fortune', 'prosperity' as well as 'material wealth'. Frequently, either 'material wealth' or something like 'good fortune, happiness' might suit the context. Such ambiguity suggests that the concept is very nearly all-inclusive. Nevertheless, at times *olbos* is virtually indistinguishable from *ploutos* and/or *khrêmata,* that is, from "material wealth" (e.g. Hesiod *Works and Days* 320ff., 379ff.; *Homeric Hymn to Hermes* 379; *Hymns* 30.3–8; Theognis 153–154, 165–166, 383–385, 865–867).[34]

It is not difficult to see, in general, how the identification might occur, since *olbos* may result from *ploutos* (Hesiod *Theogony* 969–974) or lead to it (Pindar *Nemean* 8.17–18), and since *olbos* can be defined in terms of material possessions (*Iliad* 24.543ff.; *Odyssey* 17.420 = 19.76; *Homeric Hymn to Hermes* 461–462, and *Hymn to Demeter* 486–489). Solon's own use of *olbos* and the adjective *olbios* elsewhere in his poetry suggests the same identification. He says:

---

33. In Poem 15, *ploutos* and *khrêmata* are virtually synonymous. Both are contrasted with *aretê* 'excellence'.

34. Most argues that in Pindar the word tends to suggest the expression of divine favor in the form of material possessions (in contrast to *eudaimonia*); e.g. *Pythian* 1.46; *Nemean* 5.19; 8.17; 9.45. But the implication of material wealth is absent in other passages; e.g. *Olympian* 1.56; *Pythian* 2.26; 3.89; 5.55 and 102; *Nemean* 10.13; *Isthmian* 4.58 (*The Measures of Praise*, p. 184 and n.4).

οἱ δ᾽ ἐφ᾽ ἁρπαγῆισιν ἦλθον· ἐλπίδ᾽ εἶχον ἀφνεήν,
κἀδόκ[ε]ον ἕκαστος αὐτῶν ὄλβον εὑρήσειν πολύν
(Solon 34.1–2)

But some came for the purpose of robbery [*harpagai*]; they had rich
[*aphnea*] hope,
and each of them thought that he would find much prosperity
[*polus olbos*].

The context, the close conjunction with *harpagai*, *aphnea*, and, in fact,
with *polus*, suggests that *olbos* here refers to happiness in quite a
material sense. Similarly, Solon asserts that

ὄλβιος, ὧι παῖδές τε φίλοι καὶ μώνυχες ἵπποι
καὶ κύνες ἀγρευταὶ καὶ ξένος ἀλλοδαπός
(Solon 23)

prosperous [*olbios*] is he who has dear children and hooved horses
and hunting dogs and a friend in a foreign land [*xenos allodapos*].

Here Solon appears to define *olbios* in material terms, that is, based upon certain tangible material possessions. A *xenos allodapos* might seem a
bit different, but in a time when material wealth was not particularly
portable, in a largely, if not exclusively, premonetary society, a *xenos
allodapos* would be the equivalent of possessions at home. Again, Solon
insists:

τίκτει γὰρ κόρος ὕβριν, ὅταν πολὺς ὄλβος ἕπηται
ἀνθρώποις ὁπόσοις μὴ νόος ἄρτιος ἦι.
(Solon 6.3–4)

Satiety [*koros*] breeds reckless arrogance [*hubris*], whenever much
prosperity [*polus olbos*] comes
to those men whose mind is not suitable.

Here the word *olbos* must refer to material wealth, for it is unlikely that
in anyone's view *olbos* in a larger sense of "true happiness" could be
responsible for *hubris*. How could such *olbos* possibly contain something
that leads to *atê* 'ruin' (13.11–13), the negation of happiness? The
passage does suggest, however, that *olbos* needs to be accompanied by
something else if it is not to lead to trouble.

It is this additional ingredient which Solon seeks to describe in 13.7–
13. He cannot say "when I ask for *olbos* I do not mean just *olbos*; I mean
real, actual *olbos*," because that would make sense to no one. Solon
wants *olbos* and whatever is required to keep it. He is specific about what
that entails, emphasizing an intellectual distinction based not on the

object(s) but on the means of acquisition. He makes a similar effort to give "wealth" an unmaterialistic dimension in Poems 15 and 24 using the verbal form of *ploutos*. Such a distinction supports the view that the *olbos* Solon seeks from the Muses is in some degree intellectual, rather than exclusively material in nature—particularly since it is in their power to grant the intellectual component directly. Thus, *olbos* (3) is particularized by *pros theôn* 'from the gods' just as *ploutos* (9) is by *hon men dôsi theoi* 'which the gods give'. While Solon's audience would hear his prayer initially with normal expectations regarding the meaning of *olbos*, lines 7–17 stress an additional element—the knowledge of the inevitable consequences of specific actions. This turns out to be not merely an additional element but, in fact, the essential element in true *olbos*.[35]

Solon's request for an *agathê doxa* 'good reputation' employs the same strategy. One might argue that this idea never reappears in the poem and that it probably results from an archaic love of antitheses (i.e. *theôn...anthropôn*).[36] But such a conclusion is not, I think, justified in this case. Consideration of other archaic passages reveals that the desire for an *agathê doxa* is the logical counterpart to *olbos* as Solon defines it, and inextricably related to Solon's understanding of the Muses, Memory, and the poet's craft.

Solon's request for a good *doxa* seems to be, with one possible exception, the earliest attested occurrence of the word in the sense of "reputation." In Homer it is confined to the expression *oud' apo doxês* 'nor other(wise) than one expects',[37] and appears to have some connection with vision or perception, that is, with the accuracy of the vision or perception on which an expectation is based. In its two occurrences, once in the *Iliad*, once in the *Odyssey*, the phrase is used in conjunction with *skopos* 'look-out' or 'spy': Dolon, trying to persuade the Trojans to accept his plan, claims σοὶ δ' ἐγὼ οὐχ ἅλιος σκοπὸς

---

35. G. Nagy (*Pindar's Homer*, pp. 243–249; 276, n.12) explains Solon's view of *olbos* as a transcendent concept, denoting god-given *ploutos* 'wealth' accompanied by *dikê* 'justice', that is, "well-being that is material from the outside and mystical from the inside." This view is communicated directly in Solon's poetry, indirectly in Herodotus' narrative of the meeting between Solon and the Lydian tyrant Croesus (Herodotus 1. 29.1 ff.).

36. Van Groningen, *La composition littéraire archaïque grecque*, p. 96.

37. D. Campbell, *Greek Lyric Poetry* (Basingstoke and London, 1967), p. 235.

ἔσσομαι οὐδ' ἀπὸ δόξης· 'I shall not be a vain spy for you, nor less than your expectation' (*Iliad* 10.324). Echeneos, advising the Phaeacians to accept the advice of their queen Arete, insists

ὦ φίλοι, οὐ μὰν ἧμιν ἀπὸ σκοποῦ οὐδ' ἀπὸ δόξης
μυθεῖται βασίλεια περίφρων·
(*Odyssey* 11.344–345)

Friends, our circumspect queen is not off the mark in her speaking,
nor short of what we expect of her.

These examples might encourage the suspicion that when Solon asks for a good *doxa* he has in mind others' understanding of the accuracy of his perceptions.

Elsewhere in archaic poetry, with certain possible exceptions, the word is used in the same way. In Poem 13, Solon claims:

θνητοὶ δ' ὧδε νοέομεν ὁμῶς ἀγαθός τε κακός τε,
εὖ ῥεῖν ἦν αὐτὸς δόξαν ἕκαστος ἔχει,
πρίν τι παθεῖν· τότε δ' αὖτις ὀδύρεται·
(Solon 13.33–35)

But this is the way we mortals think, both good and bad alike:
each man has confidence in his own expectation [*doxa*]
until he suffers something. Then in turn he wails aloud.

Regardless of how one reads the first words of line 34, *doxa* here can only be interpreted as "expectation."[38] This is also the case when Theognis contrasts *doxa* with *peira* 'trial':

δόξα μὲν ἀνθρώποισι κακὸν μέγα, πεῖρα δ' ἄριστον·
πολλοὶ ἀπείρητοι δόξαν ἔχουσ' ἀγαθῶν.
(Theognis 571–572=1104a–1105a)

Expectation is a great evil for men, trial is best.
Many men without trial have the expectation of good things.

Similarly, Theognis claims:

πολλάκι πὰρ δόξαν τε καὶ ἐλπίδα γίνεται εὖ ῥεῖν
ἔργ' ἀνδρῶν, βουλαῖς δ' οὐκ ἐπέγεντο τέλος.
(Theognis 639–640)

---

38. The manuscripts have ἐνδηνην. For different suggestions as to how to emend this, see the textual apparatus of M. L. West in *Iambi et elegi Graeci*, vol. II.

> Often it happens that, beyond expectation and hope, the works of
> men turn out well,
> While their plans do not come to fulfillment.

Here, too, *doxa* must mean "expectation."

It is only with Pindar that the meaning "expectation" becomes the exception rather than the rule: only at *Olympian* 6.82, 10.63, *Pythian* 1.36, and *Nemean* 11.24. Elsewhere (in 35 other instances of *doxa* or its compound nouns and adjectives with *bathu-*, *epi-*, *eu-*, *megalo-*, and *pan-*),[39] the word has the sense of "fame" or "glory," that is, "good reputation."

There are two passages from archaic poetry, however, in which the word is more problematic. Theognis asserts:

> καὶ σώφρων ἥμαρτε, καὶ ἄφρονι πολλάκι δόξα
> ἕσπετο, καὶ τιμῆς καὶ κακὸς ὢν ἔλαχεν.
> (Theognis 665–666)

> The wise man misses the mark [*hêmarte*], and often expectation
> [*doxa*] keeps pace [*hespeto*] with the fool;
> And although he is worthless, he becomes possessed of honor
> [*timê*].

Here the association with *timê* accords with the meaning "expectation," since *timê* is determined by the sort of thing people expect from the man who possesses it. Nevertheless, since *doxa hespeto* appears to be the opposite of *hêmarte* and can result in *timê*, the word seems to be gliding toward a sense of "success" or "favorable outcome" or perhaps simply "promise," which seems to have a certain built-in positive sense. This is also the case with Theognis' use of the compound adjectives *eudoxos* and *kakodoxos* (195).

Tyrtaeus 10.1–9 may also be somewhat equivocal:

> οὔτ' ἂν μνησαίμην οὔτ' ἐν λόγωι ἄνδρα τιθείην...
> οὐδ' εἰ πᾶσαν ἔχοι δόξαν πλὴν θούριδος ἀλκῆς·
> (Tyrtaeus 12.1 and 9)

> I would not call to mind a man nor take him into account...
> Not if he should have every *doxa* except furious defensive valor [*alkê*].

If *doxa* is translated as "expectation," it refers to the things for which other men look to (expect in) a man, that is, "if people looked to him

---

39. Three additional instances are too fragmentary to be unequivocal.

for every good thing but *alkê*." But Tyrtaeus uses *doxa* to sum up the attributes listed in the preceding lines, and some of the qualities de-scribed in these lines—great size and strength, beauty of form, wealth, nobility—are things visibly present, not abilities or potentialities, and would seem to come directly from the gods, not by way of men.

When Solon asks the Muses to grant him "a good *doxa* from men," he seems, like Tyrtaeus, to be thinking of reputation, but not in terms of actual tangible attributes. He seems to be referring to the perceptions he wishes others to have of him. He is, in effect, using *doxa* in its logically "objective" sense: if one's *doxa* is one's own expectation for the future, then it can also be the expectation others have of one—that is, one's reputation. An archaic audience might well expect him to ask for *kleos* 'glory' not *doxa*. In the praise poetry of Pindar, for example, *kleos* is presented as the ideal opposite of *oneidos* 'reproach' or 'blame', and the righteous man hopes to leave it for his children when he dies.[40] But perhaps *kleos* is not sufficiently future-oriented; It is far too heavily—if not exclusively—posthumous. Solon, simultaneously a poet and a statesman, is unlike an epic hero, for example, who seeks *kleos* from the mouths of future generations. To a poet, *kleos* represents the glories of the past, the subjects for song. It will not help the statesman to surmount present-day obstacles. And, perhaps, too, it has the wrong connotations. If *kleos* is the glory which develops from mouth to mouth and from generation to generation, in contrast to *kudos*, the glory which the gods grant or refuse,[41] it is neither for the Muses to grant nor necessarily based on men's accurate understanding. Elsewhere Solon criticizes his audience for being taken in by what they hear and not accurately observing on their own account:

ὑμέων δ' εἷς μὲν ἕκαστος ἀλώπεκος ἴχνεσι βαίνει,
    σύμπασιν δ' ὑμῖν χαῦνος ἔνεστι νόος·
ἐς γὰρ γλῶσσαν ὁρᾶτε καὶ εἰς ἔπη αἱμύλου ἀνδρός,
    εἰς ἔργον δ' οὐδὲν γιγνόμενον βλέπετε.
                                                    (Solon 11.5–8)

Each one of you steps along in the tracks of the fox,
    but the mind in all of you together is foolish:
For you look to the tongue and the words of a wily man,
    but as to his actual deed you see nothing.

---

40. Nagy, *The Best of the Achaeans*, p. 228, citing *Nemean* 8.34–37.

41. Detienne, *Les maîtres de vérité dans la Grèce archaïque*, p. 20.

Solon's request for a good *doxa* (not for *kleos*) emphasizes the necessary intellectual element that is the province of the Muses and of Memory. A good *doxa* for Solon—other men's favorable expectation of him— must derive from their proper understanding of his previous actions and statements and their consequences. This use of *doxa* suggests that Solon is highly sensitive to differences in perspective, differences between the way in which an individual views himself and his world and the way in which others view that individual.[42] Solon's request for *olbos* and a good *doxa* in effect encompasses both sides of the equation: the former is based on the poet's own knowledge that wealth must be combined with justice, the latter on the audience's knowledge of the truth of the poet's assertions.[43] The essential element in both is that accurate knowledge of the relationship between actions and consequences, that form of Memory which the Muses can bestow. The poet will achieve *olbos* and a good *doxa* if his poem is successful, that is, the gods will grant the former if he says what is true about them, and men will provide the latter if they take his statements to heart and see them borne out by their own experience. The prayer amounts to a request that he

---

42. Gerald Else's view of Solon as the forerunner of Greek tragedy corroborates this point. Else argues that "Greek tragedy, by the peculiarity of its form, is committed to a special kind of double vision: the hero's view of himself and the chorus' view of him" (*The Origin and Early Form of Greek Tragedy*, p. 44). Solon's view of his relationship to his community and his reflections on his own political and poetic activity receive further attention in Poem 36. (See Chapter 3.)

43. As Theognis explains:

χρὴ Μουσῶν θεράποντα καὶ ἄγγελον, εἴ τι περισσὸν
    εἰδείη, σοφίης μὴ φθονερὸν τελέθειν,
ἀλλὰ τὰ μὲν μῶσθαι, τὰ δὲ δεικνύναι, ἄλλα δὲ ποιεῖν·
    τί σφιν χρήσηται μοῦνος ἐπιστάμενος;
                              (Theognis 769–772)

It is necessary that the attendant and messenger of the Muses—if he should know
    anything extraordinary—
not become grudging of his wisdom [*sophiē*].
But rather he must learn some things, teach some, and create some.
For what use is it if one man alone knows?

This reflects the dual nature of the poet's role: he must both know and communicate. Knowledge kept to oneself is sterile; one must be able to express it effectively as well.

See also A. Ford's discussion of this passage ("The Seal of Theognis," in *Theognis of Megara*, pp. 82–95). Ford argues that "this passage is describing not simply a poet but the man who brings the gifts of the Muses to his community" (pp. 92–93).

may both tell the truth about the gods and be persuasive. In this way the prayers for the success of the poet and for that of the city merge.

If Solon's opening address to the Muses is understood as an appeal to that aspect of Memory that is the knowledge of the relationship between actions and consequences, later transitions in the poem seem less abrupt than they might otherwise appear. This aspect of *Mnêmosunê* has been shown to be central to Solon's understanding of *olbos* and *doxa*. It underlies his request for success defined not only in material but also in intellectual terms, and it underlies his request for a good reputation which derives from others' accurate appreciation of his actions (including his poetry) and their consequences.

In addition, Solon's effort to express the causal relationship between human behavior and Zeus' justice, that is, between human nature and human fortunes, depends upon this same understanding of *Mnêmosunê*. The integration of poetry and politics in the opening prayer parallels the divine-human structure of the poem as a whole. Lines 11–32 flow logically from the distinction Solon makes between god-given wealth and wealth wrongfully acquired (7–10), providing an explanation and an extended simile for the workings of Zeus' *tisis* 'vengeance', along with the view that such punishment can fall upon successive generations.[44]

Theognis also voices a similar view, explaining that:

χρῆμα δ' ὃ μὲν Διόθεν καὶ σὺν δίκηι ἀνδρὶ γένηται
καὶ καθαρῶς, αἰεὶ παρμόνιμον τελέθει·
εἰ δ' ἀδίκως παρὰ καιρὸν ἀνὴρ φιλοκερδέι θυμῶι
κτήσεται, εἴθ' ὅρκωι πὰρ τὸ δίκαιον ἑλών,
αὐτίκα μέν τι φέρειν κέρδος δοκεῖ, ἐς δὲ τελευτὴν
αὖθις ἔγεντο κακόν, θεῶν δ' ὑπερέσχε νόος.
ἀλλὰ τάδ' ἀνθρώπων ἀπατᾶι νόον· οὐ γὰρ ἐπ' αὐτοῦ
τίνονται μάκαρες πρήγματος ἀμπλακίας·
ἀλλ' ὁ μὲν αὐτὸς ἔτεισε κακὸν χρέος, οὐδὲ φίλοισιν
ἄτην ἐξοπίσω παισὶν ἐπεκρέμασεν·
ἄλλον δ' οὐ κατέμαρψε δίκη· θάνατος γὰρ ἀναιδὴς
πρόσθεν ἐπὶ βλεφάροις ἕζετο κῆρα φέρων.
(Theognis 197–208)

---

44. Cf. Tyrtaeus 12.30: a pentameter version of *Iliad* 20.308 (Campbell, *Greek Lyric Poetry*, p. 182). If the audience did in fact happen to recall these two passages, they would recognize that Solon has put the line in a new negative context. The effects not of the glorious deeds of the ancestors, but of the unjust ones, are here extending to the progeny.

The possession which comes from Zeus, and to a man who acts
with justice and honestly, is always permanent;
but if a man with a greedy heart acquires it unjustly and beyond
what is proper, or by taking an oath contrary to what is just,
for the moment he thinks to gain some advantage, but in the end
it turns out to be an evil. The mind of the gods prevails.
But these things deceive the minds of men: the blessed gods do not
immediately exact a penalty for things done amiss.
But one man pays the penalty himself for his evil debt,
and does not leave ruin impending for his dear children after him.
Another is not overtaken by Justice; too soon does shameless death
cause his eyes to shut.[45]

But for Theognis, this situation casts grave doubts on the equitability
and validity of divine justice. He objects to Zeus both that sons pay for
the crimes of their fathers (731–742) and that divine rewards and punishments are not contingent on the justice or injustice of human actions (743–752). In contrast, for Solon the insight has a different effect.
The objection that the penalty is often delayed becomes, in Solon's
lines, proof of god's majesty over human irascibility, and the idea that
children may pay the penalty is seen as a guarantee that the deserved
punishment will not fail to appear.[46] This is intended both to prove the
existence of divine justice and to discourage potential malefactors.

The theory may well be an expansion of Hesiod's assertion in the
Works and Days that:

χρήματα δ' οὐχ ἁρπακτά, θεόσδοτα πολλὸν ἀμείνω·
εἰ γάρ τις καὶ χερσὶ βίηι μέγαν ὄλβον ἕληται,
ἢ ὅ γ' ἀπὸ γλώσσης ληίσσεται, οἷά τε πολλὰ
γίνεται, εὖτ' ἂν δὴ κέρδος νόον ἐξαπατήσηι
ἀνθρώπων, αἰδῶ δέ τ' ἀναιδείη κατοπάζηι,

---

45. U. von Wilamowitz-Moellendorff notes that in expressing in the negative the
penalty which children of the wrongdoer may suffer (Theognis 205–206), Theognis
obscures the important point that Solon emphasizes—namely that punishment is entirely
inevitable, even if the wrongdoer *seems* to have escaped it ("Solons Elegie εἰς ἑαυτόν" in
Sappho und Simonides [Berlin, 1966], p. 269).

46. Von Wilamowitz-Moellendorff, "Solons Elegie εἰς ἑαυτόν," p. 264. For the
closeness of Solon's theodicy in this poem to the religious thinking of Aeschylus, see also,
for example, W. Jaeger, *Paideia*, translated by G. Highet, vol. I (New York, 1939), pp. 143–
147; F. Solmsen, *Hesiod and Aeschylus* (New York, 1949), pp. 108–123; Else, *The Origin and
Early Form of Greek Tragedy*, pp. 37–38.

ῥεῖα δέ μιν μαυροῦσι θεοί, μινύθουσι δε οἶκον
ἀνέρι τῶι, παῦρον δέ τ' ἐπὶ χρόνον ὄλβος ὀπηδεῖ.
(Hesiod *Works and Days* 320–326)

Gains not stolen but god-given turn out better by far.
For if one seizes great wealth [*olbos*] for oneself by using sheer force
or gets plunder by means of one's tongue, as frequently happens
when the passion for gain deceives and befuddles the minds of
mortal men, and Shamelessness proves herself stronger than Shame,
easily he is abased by the gods, they ruin the house of
this sort of man, and he is but briefly prosperity's lord.

In Hesiod's formulation, the gods, not the unjust actions themselves, are directly responsible for the dire consequences.[47]

In contrast, Solon's emphasis on the knowledge that specific actions have predictable consequences links lines 7–32 to the request (lines 1–6). The theme also helps to integrate the rest of the poem. Scholars have long been troubled by the abruptness of the transition from lines 7–32 to lines 33–43. The corruption of the text at 34 is particularly unfortunate. Many have sought the theme or themes which can account for the transition and have presented plausible accounts of the poem's structure, but not, perhaps, its content. Wilamowitz, for example, compares the parts of the poem to links in a chain and sees the wish to become rich as the theme which connects the various pieces. For him, the connection between lines 7–32 and 33–43 is the contrast between divine knowledge and power in the first part and human ignorance and inadequacy in the second.[48] Unlike Wilamowitz,

---

47. Solmsen explains that Hesiod's formulation lacks any "intrinsic causal connection between the unjust act itself and the events which Hesiod regards as its punishment." In Poem 4, particularly, Solon identifies the "immanent causality" which links the punishments to the unjust acts. "The precarious balance of the community life" is bound to be disturbed by unjust acquisition and that in itself represents the punishment. Thus, for Solon, natural causality replaces spontaneous divine operation (Solmsen, pp. 112–114). Similarly, C. M. Bowra *Early Greek Elegists* (Cambridge, Mass., 1938), pp. 84ff.; Jaeger, *Paideia*, vol. I, pp. 139ff.; G. Vlastos, "Solonian Justice," *Classical Philology* 41 (1946), pp. 65ff.

48. Von Wilamowitz-Moellendorff, "Solons Elegie εἰς ἑαυτόν," p. 265. For a recent discussion of this question, see, for example, J. Christes, "Solons Musenelegie," *Hermes* 114 (1986), pp. 1–19. In contrast to Wilamowitz, Christes sees the thematic connection between the two parts not in wealth but in Solon's theodicy. Discussing the ring composition of the poem, Christes argues that the striving for riches (described in the center section of the poem), since it is both limitless and irresistible to men, is the form

Richmond Lattimore argues that the elegy is not a series of sections or even two main parts, but "a progression of thought, each subsequent stage being an expansion, or revision, or illustration of a previous stage. It is thus a self-generating series of connected ideas."[49] This basic approach is the least artificial and most fruitful. The poem is seen to develop with an internal logic which may be perceptible without the necessity of recourse to an externally imposed thematic structure. B. A. van Groningen, while agreeing with Lattimore, argues that the poem has a latent structure as well. He maintains that Poem 13 exemplifies a type of archaic composition which he terms "entrelacement." This structure results when the poet is presented simultaneously with a number of inseparable ideas. He presents them, therefore, "entrelacés et combinés." The result is that "il est difficile de constater dans l'ensemble une progression véritable. La composition présente, à première vue, l'aspect d'une improvisation assez déréglée. L'impression est fausse. Le procédé compositionnel est le résultat naturel d'une état d'âme dans lequel la passion, l'émotion ou la conviction sont tellement fortes qu'elles ne se soumettent pas au contrôle ni à la direction d'une pensée ordonnée."[50] Perhaps van Groningen's explanation did not put this question to rest—as one suspects it should have done—because he maintains (as does Wilamowitz) that *olbos* in line 3 encapsulates the subject matter of the poem.[51] Even *olbos* as Solon understands it, *olbos* which includes the knowledge that just and unjust acquisition have predictable consequences, is only part of the picture. If one word is to encapsulate the poem's subject matter, surely it must be *Mnêmosunê*—the particular aspect of Memory, that is, which Solon requires. The fact that this also happens to be the word

---

which god-sent punishment takes (described at the beginning and end of the poem). In rejecting the view of Wilamowitz, Christes points out that for those at the end of the series of professions (the poet, the seer, the physician), most of all it is their good reputation, not material gain, that is at stake (pp. 12–14). But the evidence for his own claim is not entirely persuasive. Christes also, however, provides a good synopsis of the disparate opinions of many different scholars on this question.

49. R. Lattimore, "The First Elegy of Solon," *American Journal of Philology* 68 (1947), p. 162.

50. Van Groningen, *La composition littéraire archaïque grecque*, pp. 94–95.

51. Van Groningen, p. 95.

with which Solon chooses to begin his poem seems consistent with a view of the poem as "a self-generating series of connected ideas" (Lattimore) or as a process of "entrelacement" (van Groningen). Moreover, this argument helps to account for the relationship between lines 1–32 and 33ff. Like Wilamowitz, Lattimore sees the connection between the two main parts of the poem as a contrast of human with divine intelligence. But, he argues, in fact "there is no real break. The essential point has been made that Zeus looks only in the large and toward the end (17, 25–28); this brings us, *via thnêtoi*, to the contrasted human way, which is to look at what is immediate and not to see the end."[52] Unfortunately, this explanation, while not untenable, fails to appreciate much that is unique to Solon's argument. The contrast between divine knowledge and human shortsightedness is, in fact, something of a commonplace in archaic poetry. Undeniably, the contrast is implicit in Solon's verses, but Solon does not choose to emphasize it. By itself, it is unlikely, perhaps, to galvanize people into changing the way that they live.

Therefore, in lines 33–43, it is not the human concern for the here and now, the inability to look to the future, which preoccupies Solon. Instead, it is the utter failure of human beings to perceive the *connection* between present attitudes and actions and future consequences. In these lines, Solon explains that human fortunes do not determine human attitudes. Rather, attitudes—particularly unshakeable optimism and insatiable acquisitiveness—persist undimmed by, even in spite of, actual fortunes. As a result, they are greatly responsible for the form that human fortunes take. The point and its implications become clearer when lines 33–43, which stand precisely at the center of the poem, are seen as an evocation of and even a reply to a particular *topos* 'common-place' or series of related *topoi* fairly frequent in archaic poetry.

In these lines, Solon maintains:

θνητοὶ δ' ὧδε νοέομεν ὁμῶς ἀγαθός τε κακός τε,
    εὖ ῥεῖν ἦν αὐτὸς δόξαν ἕκαστος ἔχει,
πρίν τι παθεῖν· τότε δ' αὖτις ὀδύρεται· ἄχρι δὲ τούτου
    χάσκοντες κούφαις ἐλπίσι τερπόμεθα.
χὤστις μὲν νούσοισιν ὑπ' ἀργαλέηισι πιεσθῆι,
    ὡς ὑγιὴς ἔσται, τοῦτο κατεφράσατο·
ἄλλος δειλὸς ἐὼν ἀγαθὸς δοκεῖ ἔμμεναι ἀνήρ,

---

52. Lattimore, "The First Elegy of Solon," pp. 165–166.

καὶ καλὸς μορφὴν οὐ χαρίεσσαν ἔχων·
εἰ δέ τις ἀχρήμων, πενίης δέ μιν ἔργα βιᾶται,
κτήσασθαι πάντως χρήματα πολλὰ δοκεῖ.
σπεύδει δ᾽ ἄλλοθεν ἄλλος·

(Solon 13.33–43)

But this is the way we mortals think, both good and bad alike:
each man has confidence in his own expectation [*doxa*]
until he suffers something. Then in turn he wails aloud;
but until this, with gaping mouths we take our delight in light hopes.
And whoever is oppressed by painful illness,
considers that he will be healthy;
another who is a coward [*deilos*] thinks that he is a brave man
[*agathos anêr*].
Another, whose form is not charming, considers himself beautiful.
If one is poor, and the effects of poverty constrain him,
he thinks that he is sure to acquire much money.
One rushes off in one direction, another in another [*speudei d' allothen
allos*].

Divided into its component parts, this passage asserts (1) that human beings, regardless of their lineage or character, are optimistic about their present circumstances until they encounter some set-back, at which point they grieve (33–35), and (2) that until this happens we (and Solon includes himself in the assessment) are also optimistic as to future events since we delight in empty hopes (35–37). Examples of (1) are the *deilos* 'coward' who thinks that he is *agathos* 'brave' (39) and the ugly man who thinks that he has a beautiful form (40). Examples of (2) are the grievously sick individual who declares that he will be healthy (37–38) and the desperately poor man who thinks that he will become wealthy (41–42). Certainly, thinking that one is beautiful does not *cause* one to be ugly any more than thinking that one will become healthy causes one to be sick. These examples are, rather, symptomatic of the general human tendency to optimism, even in the face of counter-evidence or experience. The tendency greatly influences the form that human fortunes take because it results in incessant human activity undeterred by thought of disaster. Thus, *speudei d' allothen allos* 'one rushes off in one direction, another in another' (43).

These assertions are part of a thematic tradition which reaches back to Homer. In *Odyssey* 18.130–142, Odysseus asserts:

οὐδὲν ἀκιδνότερον γαῖα τρέφει ἀνθρώποιο
πάντων ὅσσα τε γαῖαν ἔπι πνείει τε καὶ ἕρπει.
οὐ μὲν γάρ ποτέ φησι κακὸν πείσεσθαι ὀπίσσω,

ὄφρ' ἀρετὴν παρέχωσι θεοὶ καὶ γούνατ' ὀρώρηι·
ἀλλ' ὅτε δὴ καὶ λυγρὰ θεοὶ μάκαρες τελέσωσι,
καὶ τὰ φέρει ἀεκαζόμενος τετληότι θυμῶι.
τοῖος γὰρ νόος ἐστὶν ἐπιχθονίων ἀνθρώπων
οἷον ἐπ' ἦμαρ ἄγηισι πατὴρ ἀνδρῶν τε θεῶν τε.
καὶ γὰρ ἐγώ ποτ' ἔμελλον ἐν ἀνδράσιν ὄλβιος εἶναι,
πολλὰ δ' ἀτάσθαλ' ἔρεξα βίηι καὶ κάρτεϊ εἴκων,
πατρί τ' ἐμῶι πίσυνος καὶ ἐμοῖσι κασιγνήτοισι.
τῶι μή τίς ποτε πάμπαν ἀνὴρ ἀθεμίστιος εἴη,
ἀλλ' ὅ γε σιγῆι δῶρα θεῶν ἔχοι, ὅττι διδοῖεν.
(Odyssey 18.130–142)

Of all creatures that breathe and walk on the earth there is nothing
more helpless [akidnoteron] than a man is, of all that the earth fosters;
for he thinks that he will never suffer misfortune in future
days, while the gods grant him courage, and his knees have spring
in them. But when the blessed gods bring sad days upon him,
against his will he must suffer it with enduring spirit.
For the mind in men upon earth goes according to the fortunes
the father of gods and men, day by day, bestows upon them.
For I myself once promised to be a man of prosperity,
but, giving way to force and violence, did many reckless
things, because I relied on my father and brothers. Therefore,
let no man be altogether without the sense of righteousness
but take in silence the gifts of the gods, whatever they give him.

Like Solon's passage, these lines consider human optimism and its
consequences. And yet, they differ markedly from Solon 13.33–43 both
in their assessment of human nature and in their conclusions. Man is
akidnotatos 'most helpless', according to Odysseus, because he never
thinks that he will suffer evil in the future (18.130–132). Solon, as well
as omitting the initial judgement, says the reverse: everyone thinks that
he is doing well (i.e. in the present) until he suffers something. The
inversion is not trivial, for whereas Odysseus' statement suggests the
simple (if myopic) enjoyment of actual, present goods ("while the gods
grant him courage, and his knees have spring"), Solon's suggests rather
an optimism which may or may not have any connection with actual
circumstances. In fact, the examples he supplies—the sick man, the
deilos 'coward', the ugly man, the poor man—strongly suggest the latter.
By contrast, Odysseus claims:

τοῖος γὰρ νόος ἐστὶν ἐπιχθονίων ἀνθρώπων
οἷον ἐπ' ἦμαρ ἄγηισι πατὴρ ἀνδρῶν τε θεῶν τε.
(Odyssey 18.136–137)

For the mind in men upon earth goes according to the fortunes
the father of gods and men, day by day bestows upon them.

That is, Odysseus accepts that men's minds or states of mind are
determined by and in accordance with their fortunes. But Solon
disagrees. He suggests that men's minds are eternally optimistic,
regardless of (or even in spite of) their fortunes.[53]

These different assessments of the human *noos* 'mind' lead to
different solutions. Odysseus concludes:

τῶι μή τίς ποτε πάμπαν ἀνὴρ ἀθεμίστιος εἴη,
ἀλλ' ὅ γε σιγῆι δῶρα θεῶν ἔχοι, ὅττι διδοῖεν.
(*Odyssey* 18.141–142)

Therefore, let no man be altogether without the sense of righteousness
but take in silence the gifts of the gods, whatever they give him.

Solon's lines lack any reference to endurance or forbearance.[54] In fact,

---

53. A. J. Podlecki maintains (in *The Early Greek Poets and Their Times* [Vancouver, 1984]
p. 46) that Archilochus 132—καὶ φρονέουσι τοῖ' ὁποίοις ἐγκυρέωσιν ἔργμασιν 'they
understand such things in accordance with whatever sort of matters they encounter'—
accords with Solon 13.33–36. He remarks that Heraclitus took issue with this view,
responding: οὐ γὰρ φρονέουσι τοιαῦτα πολλοὶ ὁκοίοις ἐγκυρέουσιν,/ οὐδὲ μαθόντες
γινώσκουσιν, ἑαυτοῖσι δὲ δοκέουσι 'for the many do not understand such things in
accordance with whatever sort of things they encounter; nor having learned do they
know, but they think they do' (Clement *Stromateis* ii.8 = fragment 22B17 in H. Diels, *Die
Fragmente der Vorsokratiker*, edited by W. Kranz [Berlin, 1903]).

But Solon's statement says nothing about people learning from experience. He
suggests the contrary, in fact, and does not seem to conflict with Heraclitus' claim.
Arguably, Archilochus here echoes Odysseus' view that people's thoughts and mental
attitudes are determined by their circumstances, whereas Heraclitus supports Solon's
perception that people's thoughts are independent of their circumstances.

54. Contrast Archilochus again: Poem 128 is consistent with the "Odyssean" view.
Archilochus counsels his *thumos* 'heart' not to exult or grieve excessively:

θυμέ, θύμ', ἀμηχάνοισι κήδεσιν κυκώμενε,
†ἀναδευ δυσμενῶν† δ' ἀλέξεο προσβαλὼν ἐναντίον
στέρνον †ἐνδοκοισιν ἐχθρῶν πλησίον κατασταθεὶς
ἀσφαλέως· καὶ μήτε νικέων ἀμφάδην ἀγάλλεο,
μηδὲ νικηθεὶς ἐν οἴκωι καταπεσὼν ὀδύρεο,
ἀλλὰ χαρτοῖσίν τε χαῖρε καὶ κακοῖσιν ἀσχάλα
μὴ λίην, γίνωσκε δ' οἷος ῥυσμὸς ἀνθρώπους ἔχει.

Heart, Heart, disturbed by troubles against which there is no resource,
rise up against the enemy, and ward them off, presenting your chest
against their onslaught, standing hard by and without faltering.
And neither brag openly, if you are victorious,

they offer no explicit advice at all. His emphasis is, perhaps, more psychological than moral. If human nature is as Solon presents it, admonitions will have little effect. Rather, Solon establishes a logical causal connection between this habit of thought he perceives and its consequences—namely that all people expect to make money and pursue wealth in various ways, a view which he then proceeds to elaborate in some detail (lines 43–62). Seen in connection with lines 1–32, Solon's implication must be that, since unjustly acquired advantage is certain to be a source of grief sooner or later, it is not worth seeking—especially since all advantage, justly acquired or not, is either unstable or outright illusion.

Like Homer and Solon, Semonides, too, explores these and similar themes. In Poem 1 his tone is even more didactic than Odysseus' and his observations and conclusions form an intriguing counterpoint with those of both Odysseus and Solon. Even more forcefully than Odysseus, perhaps, Semonides contrasts human short-sightedness with divine control of the ends and outcomes:

ὦ παῖ, τέλος μὲν Ζεὺς ἔχει βαρύκτυπος
πάντων ὅσ᾽ ἐστὶ καὶ τίθησ᾽ ὅκηι θέλει,
νοῦς δ᾽ οὐκ ἐπ᾽ ἀνθρώποισιν, ἀλλ᾽ ἐπήμεροι
ἃ δὴ βοτὰ ζώομεν, οὐδὲν εἰδότες
ὅκως ἕκαστον ἐκτελευτήσει θεός.

(Semonides 1. 1–5)

Child, deep-thundering Zeus holds the end
of all things and brings everything to pass in the way that he wishes.
Mind is not in the power of men, but we live from day to day
like grazing beasts, knowing nothing
of the way in which god will accomplish each thing.[55]

This lament regarding human shortsightedness echoes Odysseus' point that

---

nor fall down in your house and wail, if you are conquered.
Be joyful in welcome circumstances and sorrowful in troubles,
but not overmuch. Know that this sort of rhythm governs our life.

55. D. E. Gerber argues that the context supports Fränkel's claim that ἐπήμεροι here and often elsewhere in early Greek poetry means not "short-lived" but "subject to the changing day" ("Semonides, Fr. 1 West: A Commentary" in *Greek Poetry and Philosophy* edited by D. E. Gerber [Chico, California, 1984], p. 127). I concur with Gerber in rejecting West's emendation of ζώομεν το ζόουσιν (p. 128).

τοῖος γὰρ νόος ἐστὶν ἐπιχθονίων ἀνθρώπων
οἷον ἐπ᾽ ἦμαρ ἄγῃσι πατὴρ ἀνδρῶν τε θεῶν τε.
(*Odyssey* 18.136–1377)

the mind in men upon earth goes according to the fortunes
the father of gods and men, day by day bestows upon them.

In addition, divine control is explicit in the Homeric passage both here and in lines 134, 135, and 142, but the contrast is far more pointed in Semonides' assertion.[56] Solon attributes control of ends and outcomes to Zeus and the gods elsewhere in Poem 13 (lines 17, 63ff.), but in the passage under consideration (lines 33–43) he does not emphasize the contrast. Rather he explores human nature in itself and not in opposition to divine knowledge and power.

Semonides, in contrasting human understanding with divine, accepts—like Odysseus and unlike Solon—that men's minds and states of mind are determined by their immediate circumstances. But whereas Odysseus remarks on the human certainty that present good fortune will not change to bad (*Odyssey* 18.132–133), Semonides, like Solon, acknowledges rather a kind of irrepressible optimism for future improvement, for:

ἐλπὶς δὲ πάντας κἀπιπειθείη τρέφει
ἄπρηκτον ὁρμαίνοντας· οἱ μὲν ἡμέρην
μένουσιν ἐλθεῖν, οἱ δ᾽ ἐτέων περιτροπάς·
νέωτα δ᾽ οὐδεὶς ὅστις οὐ δοκεῖ βροτῶν
Πλούτωι τε κἀγαθοῖσιν ἵξεσθαι φίλος.
(Semonides 1.6–10)

But hope and confidence nurture all those
bent on the unprofitable. Some wait for the day
to come, others the turning of the years;
and there is no mortal who does not think that next year
will come as a friend to wealth and everything good.

Lines 6–7 nicely parallel Solon's claim that χάσκοντες κούφαις ἐλπίσι τερπόμεθα 'with gaping mouths we take our delight in light hopes' (13.36). And yet Semonides makes no mention of the possibility that Solon emphasizes, namely that as well as being susceptible to this kind

---

56. Gerber states that Semonides' use of *telos* (line 1) differs slightly from the Homeric usage. In Homer, Zeus is never explicitly said to have control over the *telos* of all things. Similar to Semonides is Hesiod *Works and Days* 663–669 ("Semonides, Fr. 1 West: A Commentary," p. 126).

of deluded optimism regarding future developments, individuals are also prone to misperceptions regarding their present circumstances (Solon 13.39–40). Such an observation would be particularly inappropriate to Semonides' conclusion:

εἰ δ᾽ ἐμοὶ πιθοίατο,
οὐκ ἂν κακῶν ἐρῶιμεν, οὐδ᾽ ἐπ᾽ ἄλγεσιν
κακοῖς ἔχοντες θυμὸν αἰκιζοίμεθα.
(Semonides 1.22–24)

> If they would be persuaded by me,
> we should not love our troubles, nor torture ourselves
> by holding our heart upon evil griefs.

This recommendation is not unlike Odysseus' at the end of his speech, and both necessarily assume a tidy correlation between individuals' circumstances and their perception of those circumstances. Conversely, therefore, Semonides' or Odysseus' admonition could never follow Solon's assessment of these issues.[57]

Another poem attributed to Semonides by Campbell, doubtfully to Simonides by West (Semonides 29 Campbell, Simonides 8 West), examines the issue of self-delusion from a slightly different perspective. The poet begins by citing:

ἓν δὲ τὸ κάλλιστον Χῖος ἔειπεν ἀνήρ·
"οἵη περ φύλλων γενεή, τοίη δὲ καὶ ἀνδρῶν"·
(Simonides 8.1–2)

> One very beautiful thing which the man of Chios said:
> "As is the generation of leaves, so is that of humanity."

This is a reference to *Iliad* 6.146 and the three lines following, which explain the analogy:

οἵη περ φύλλων γενεή, τοίη δὲ καὶ ἀνδρῶν.
φύλλα τὰ μέν τ᾽ ἄνεμος χαμάδις χέει, ἄλλα δέ θ᾽ ὕλη
τηλεθόωσα φύει, ἔαρος δ᾽ ἐπιγίγνεται ὥρη·
ὣς ἀνδρῶν γενεὴ ἡ μὲν φύει ἡ δ᾽ ἀπολήγει.
(*Iliad* 6.146–149)

---

57. About Semonides' poem, Wilamowitz comments that it all sounds more pessimistic than in Solon's view; there is no thought of divine justice, and, moreover, the practical conclusion from this estimation of life diverges still further from Solon's assessment ("Solons Elegie εἰς ἑαυτόν," p. 273).

As is the generation of leaves, so is that of humanity.
The wind scatters the leaves on the ground, but the live timber
burgeons with leaves again in the season of spring returning.
So one generation of men will grow while another dies.

For "Simonides," this analogy forms the basis of a meditation on human
nature and human understanding. The truth of the analogy is not easily
assimilated, for

παῦροί μιν θνητῶν οὔασι δεξάμενοι
στέρνοις ἐγκατέθεντο·
(Simonides 8.3–4)

Few men upon receiving this with their ears
take it to heart in their breasts.

The gap between reception and actual assimilation of a truth occurs
because hope interferes:

πάρεστι γὰρ ἐλπὶς ἑκάστωι
ἀνδρῶν, ἥ τε νέων στήθεσιν ἐμφύεται.
θνητῶν δ' ὄφρά τις ἄνθος ἔχηι πολυήρατον ἥβης,
κοῦφον ἔχων θυμὸν πόλλ' ἀτέλεστα νοεῖ·
οὔτε γὰρ ἐλπίδ' ἔχει γηρασέμεν οὔτε θανεῖσθαι,
οὐδ', ὑγιὴς ὅταν ἦι, φροντίδ' ἔχει καμάτου.
νήπιοι, οἷς ταύτηι κεῖται νόος, οὐδὲ ἴσασιν
ὡς χρόνος ἔσθ' ἥβης καὶ βιότου ὀλίγος
θνητοῖς.
(Simonides 8.4–12)

For hope is present to each man,
hope which grows naturally in the breasts of the young.
And while a man enjoys the lovely flower of youth,
light-hearted, he imagines many things that will never be
accomplished.
Neither has he the expectation that he will grow old or die,
nor when he is healthy has he any thought of illness.
Fools are they whose mind works like this. They do not know
that the time of youth and life is short
for mortal men.

Unlike Solon, the poet here is examining the relationship of youth and
health to old age, sickness and death. In this way he elaborates on
Solon's assertion that χάσκοντες κούφαις ἐλπίσι τερπόμεθα 'with gaping
mouths we take our delight in light hopes' (13.36) and on Semonides'
observation that ἐλπὶς δὲ πάντας κἀπιπειθείη τρέφει/ ἄπρηκτον
ὁρμαίνοντας 'But hope and confidence nurture all those bent on the

unprofitable' (Semonides 1.6–7). Whereas Semonides 1 details old age, illness, and death as the reason that such hopes will not be realized (1.11–22), here the poet identifies youth and health as the actual source of the vain hopes, the reason that κοῦφον ἔχων θυμὸν πόλλ' ἀτέλεστα νοεῖ 'light-hearted, he imagines many things that will never be accomplished' (Simonides 8.7). Of some additional interest may be the fact that "Simonides" refers to a κοῦφον θυμόν 'light heart', while Solon refers to κούφαις ἐλπίσι 'light hopes'. Although the difference may be merely cosmetic, Solon seems to be criticizing not the one who hopes but the hopes themselves. This would accord with an approach which analyzes rather than criticizes human beings and avoids didactic pronouncements.

Identifying youth and health as the source of deluded optimism, "Simonides" claims, as Odysseus did, that individuals never anticipate future misfortunes: when young a man does not expect to grow old or to die (8); when healthy a man has no thought of sickness (9). One can compare *Odyssey* 18.132–133. This optimism derives from an inability to assimilate things that one may understand but has not yet experienced (3–4). In contrast, Solon approaches the problem from a different perspective: when sick everyone thinks that he will become healthy (Solon 13.37–38), that is, the optimism does not derive from circumstances (youth, good fortune) or, at any rate, not from favorable circumstances; it is a fundamental, unqualified fact of human nature. This contrast receives further emphasis, perhaps, from the fact that for "Simonides," as for Odysseus, human optimism presumes permanence —individuals expect their present condition to continue in the future. For Solon, as in Semonides 1.9–10, human optimism presumes future change, improvement.

As well as differing from Solon on this point, "Simonides," like Odysseus and Semonides (Poem 1), does not consider the possibility that individuals may misperceive or misinterpret their present circumstances.[58] Solon refuses to attribute optimism to good fortune, or to youth, or to health; he recognizes, moreover, that individuals may be mistaken as to their actual circumstances; he understands optimism

---

58. Solon speaks of both *doxa* 'expectation' (13.34–35) and *elpis* 'hope' (13.35–36); the other poets speak only of the latter. V. Leinieks maintains that "*elpis*, unlike *dokei* and *doxa*, refers almost exclusively to future events" ("Ἐλπίς in Hesiod *Works and Days* 96," *Philologus* 128 [1984], p. 1). Leinieks' observation would seem to accord with the verb tenses that Solon uses with each word respectively.

to be not an expectation of permanence but an expectation of change. All of this suggests that he aims at solutions different from the ones offered by other poets. "Simonides" concludes:

ἀλλὰ σὺ ταῦτα μαθὼν βιότου ποτὶ τέρμα
ψυχῆι τῶν ἀγαθῶν τλῆθι χαριζόμενος.
(Simonides 8.12–13)

> But having learned these things toward the end of your life,
> Endure, gratifying your heart with good things.

This admonition, although similar to the advice of Odysseus (*Odyssey* 18.141–142), or of Semonides (1.22–24), is just as incompatible with Solon's understanding of the issues.

These problems are also of great concern to Mimnermus. Like "Simonides," in Poem 2 he takes as his starting point the simile from *Iliad* 6:

ἡμεῖς δ', οἷά τε φύλλα φύει πολυάνθεμος ὥρη
ἔαρος, ὅτ' αἶψ' αὐγῆις αὔξεται ἠελίου,
τοῖς ἴκελοι πήχυιον ἐπὶ χρόνον ἄνθεσιν ἥβης
τερπόμεθα.
(Mimnermus 2.1–4)

> We are like the leaves which the many-flowered season of spring
> brings forth
> when quickly they grow in the rays of the sun.
> Like these we enjoy the blossom of youth for a brief time.

But Mimnermus adapts the simile to his own purposes. In the *Iliad* the point of the comparison is the transience of human life; the seasonal changes of a tree figure the succession of one generation of mankind to another. For Mimnermus the analogy is between the brevity of youth and the swift growth and decay of leaves.[59] This comparison may be implicit in "Simonides" 8 as well. Indeed, Mimnermus' analogy echoes "Simonides'" claim ὡς χρόνος ἔσθ' ἥβης καὶ βιότου ὀλίγος / θνητοῖς 'that the time of youth and life is short for mortal men' (Simonides 8.11–12). According to Mimnermus, not only do we delight in youth for a brief time: we do so

πρὸς θεῶν εἰδότες οὔτε κακὸν
οὔτ' ἀγαθόν·
(Mimnermus 2.4–5)

---

59. Campbell, *Greek Lyric Poetry*, p. 226.

knowing neither evil nor good
from the gods.

The phrase is perplexing. Campbell suggests that "Mimnermus must mean that since bliss is unmixed in our youth we do not distinguish then between good and bad fortune,"[60] but this risks implying that we are pretty dim, and other possibilities exist. Perhaps Mimnermus means that in enjoying the pleasures of youth we do not necessarily recognize good and bad fortune for what they are—that is, perhaps, like Solon, Mimnermus is sensitive to the possibility that individuals may misinterpret their own fortunes. The *deilos* 'coward' may think that he is *agathos* 'brave', the ugly man may think that he is beautiful. If so, Mimnermus, unlike Solon, attributes this possibility not to human nature in general but to youthful human nature. Alternatively, perhaps Mimnermus' statement means that while we are enjoying the pleasures of youth we do not think about the source of these pleasures, fail to recognize that the fortunes we are enjoying are from the gods. To be sure, both Odysseus (*Odyssey* 18.134, 135, 137, 142) and Semonides (1.1–5) consider this point worth emphasizing in addressing these themes. But the simplest and most plausible explanation may be that the young, lacking the knowledge which only age and experience can bring, never realize how well off they are and, as a result, fail to use to the fullest the advantages of youth. The problem is not quite an inability to distinguish good from bad fortune (as Campbell suggests) but, rather, an inability to appreciate the degrees. This point, like *Odyssey* 18.136–137 and Semonides 1.1–5, is a criticism of the human propensity to appreciate only the here and now, and, like "Simonides" 8.7, Mimnermus attributes this shortcoming to the inexperience of youth.

Having listed old age, illness, death in war, at sea, and by suicide, Semonides grimly laments

οὕτω κακῶν ἄπ' οὐδέν, ἀλλὰ μυρίαι
βροτοῖσι κῆρες κἀνεπίφραστοι δύαι
καὶ πήματ' ἐστίν.
(Semonides 1.20–22)

Thus nothing is apart from evils, but there are thousands
of dooms for mortals and countless griefs
and pains.

Similarly, Mimnermus paints a grim picture of future evils, claiming:

---

60. Campbell, p. 227.

Κῆρες δὲ παρεστήκασι μέλαιναι,
ἡ μὲν ἔχουσα τέλος γήραος ἀργαλέου,
ἡ δ᾽ ἑτέρη θανάτοιο· μίνυνθα δὲ γίνεται ἥβης
καρπός, ὅσον τ᾽ ἐπὶ γῆν κίδναται ἠέλιος.
αὐτὰρ ἐπὴν δὴ τοῦτο τέλος παραμείψεται ὥρης,
αὐτίκα δὴ τεθνάναι βέλτιον ἢ βίοτος·
πολλὰ γὰρ ἐν θυμῶι κακὰ γίνεται· ἄλλοτε οἶκος
τρυχοῦται, πενίης δ᾽ ἔργ᾽ ὀδυνηρὰ πέλει·
ἄλλος δ᾽ αὖ παίδων ἐπιδεύεται, ὧν τε μάλιστα
ἱμείρων κατὰ γῆς ἔρχεται εἰς Ἀίδην·
ἄλλος νοῦσον ἔχει θυμοφθόρον· οὐδέ τίς ἐστιν
ἀνθρώπων ὧι Ζεὺς μὴ κακὰ πολλὰ διδοῖ.
(Mimnermus 2.5–16)

    The black Keres stand near, one having the
       power of grievous old age,
the other of death. The harvest of youth is short-lived
as the rays that the sun spreads over the land.
And when the end of this period is past,
       then it is better to be dead than alive;
for many sorrows [*polla kaka*] arise in one's spirit; sometimes one's substance
is consumed, and the effects of poverty [*erga peniês*] are painful.
One man longs for children, and still desiring them keenly,
       goes down under the earth to Hades;
Another suffers life-destroying illness [*thumophthoros nousos*];
       nor is there anyone to whom Zeus does not give many sorrows.

Such pessimism is not far from the sentiments expressed in *Odyssey* 18.130–142, Semonides 1, and "Simonides" 8. Odysseus and Semonides advise silent forbearance, grim endurance (*Odyssey* 18.141–142, Semonides 1.22–24). "Simonides" recommends indulging in good fortune while one can ("Simonides" 8.12–13). With the choice between grievous old age and death, Mimnermus contends that death is preferable to suffering the *polla kaka* 'many sorrows' which assail men once the brief season of youth is past. Of these evils he specifies *erga peniês* 'effects of poverty' (Mimnermus 2.12), unsatisfied longing for children (2.13–14), and *thumophthoros nousos* 'life-destroying illness' (Mimnermus 2.15). In another passage Mimnermus reiterates:

ἀλλ᾽ ὀλιγοχρόνιον γίνεται ὥσπερ ὄναρ
ἥβη τιμήεσσα· τὸ δ᾽ ἀργαλέον καὶ ἄμορφον
γῆρας ὑπὲρ κεφαλῆς αὐτίχ᾽ ὑπερκρέμαται,
ἐχθρὸν ὁμῶς καὶ ἄτιμον, ὅ τ᾽ ἄγνωστον τιθεῖ ἄνδρα,
βλάπτει δ᾽ ὀφθαλμοὺς καὶ νόον ἀμφιχυθέν.
(Mimnermus 5.4–8)

> Short-lived as a dream
> is man's precious youth; Painful [*argaleon*] and formless [*amorphon*]
> old age hangs immediately over one's head.
> Equally hateful and dishonoured, it makes a man unrecognizable.
> It ruins his eyes and mind when it has seeped in.

Youth is brief. Old age is *argaleon* 'painful' and *amorphon* 'formless'. In contrast, Solon seems to reject this standard pessimism as psychologically inaccurate. He is perhaps questioning not the grim assessment of human existence so much as the value of the traditional advice. Since human attitudes are more responsible for human fortunes than fortunes are for attitudes, the traditional view that youth and aging are the major sources of misfortune—the former as the source of optimism and self-delusion, the latter as the source of illness, feebleness, and misery—is unacceptable. His statements in Poem 13.33–43 sound almost like a reply to the advice of these other poets and to Mimnermus in particular. Such advice is not useful, Solon seems to suggest, because human beings never lose hope. The poor man thinks that he will become rich; the sick man thinks that he will become healthy. Solon thus specifically refers to two of the three ills Mimnermus bemoans, *erga peniês* 'effects of poverty' (Solon 13.41) and *nousoi* 'illnesses' (Solon 13.37). Moreover, human beings cannot or will not always even perceive their own condition accurately. The man with an ugly *morphê* 'form' thinks that he is *kalos* 'beautiful' (13.40). What motivating impact could there be in the identification of *gêras* 'old age' as *amorphon* 'formless'?

Solon's response to Mimnermus on this point is consistent with his correction of this poet in Poem 20, where he rejects Mimnermus' claim that sixty years is a sufficient length of life (Mimnermus 6), insisting:

> ἀλλ' εἴ μοι καὶ νῦν ἔτι πείσεαι, ἔξελε τοῦτο—
> μηδὲ μέγαιρ', ὅτι σέο λῶιον ἐπεφρασάμην —
> καὶ μεταποίησον Λιγυαιστάδη, ὧδε δ' ἄειδε·
> "ὀγδωκονταέτη μοῖρα κίχοι θανάτου."
>
> (Solon 20)

> But if even now you will still listen to me, take this out —
>   and do not begrudge the fact that I have concluded better than you—
> and change it, Ligyaistades, and sing this:
> "would that the fate of death might overtake me at eighty years."[61]

---

61. According to Plutarch, Solon also corrected Mimnermus in another context. See Poem 21.

This view is also reminiscent, perhaps, of Achilles' response to Odysseus in *Odyssey* 11:

μὴ δή μοι θάνατόν γε παραύδα, φαίδιμ' Ὀδυσσεῦ.
βουλοίμην κ' ἐπάρουρος ἐὼν θητευέμεν ἄλλωι,
ἀνδρὶ παρ' ἀκλήρωι, ὧι μὴ βίοτος πολὺς εἴη,
ἢ πᾶσιν νεκύεσσι καταφθιμένοισιν ἀνάσσειν.
                              (*Odyssey* 11.488–491)

O shining Odysseus, never try to console me for dying.
I would rather follow the plow as thrall to another
man, one with no land allotted him and not much to live on,
than be a king over all the perished dead.

Solon seems to share Achilles' attitude toward the supreme value of life—even at its least appealing.[62]

He explores some of these issues in another poem as well. Poem 27, Solon's "Ages of Man" poem, has received relatively little attention, but here, too, he is consistent in his departure from traditional views. This poem notably lacks any expression of the view that hope is associated with youth or that the young are unable to acknowledge the inevitability of sickness, old age, and death. One might well expect such sentiments in this context. Solon's omission of them in Poem 27 may underscore his divergence from other poets on this point. Fränkel comments that artistically the poem is dry and of little interest, but that what is remarkable is Solon's calm objectivity in accepting natural human development in its rise and decline:[63]

---

62. Regarding Solon 13.37, cf. *Iliad* 13.667 (Campbell, *Greek Lyric Poetry*, p. 237). This Homeric parallel is a reference to the choice of Euchenor, for whom it was prophesied either to go to Troy with the Achaeans and be killed by a Trojan, or to die at home of grievous illness. Euchenor chose to go to Troy. In contrast, Solon's phrase may reveal something about his attitude toward the heroic code (as evidenced in Euchenor's choice—which presages Achilles'—and in Sarpedon's speech in *Iliad* 12). It is as if Solon were suggesting that this is all very well *in theory*, since we all do know that we are going to die eventually, and who would not prefer to die heroically? But in reality this may not effectively motivate average individuals to heroic conduct if, as verses 13.37–38 maintain, even the grievously ill person expects that he will recover, that is, if in some blind, deluded way, we cannot expect that we will not live forever. If so, in Solon's view, the choice for every political man, that is, for every man in the *polis*, must be not "How will you choose to die?" (the choice for the epic hero) but, rather, "How will you choose to live?" In this Solon's attitude may be similar to Socrates' in Plato's *Apology* which is often misinterpreted as merely fearlessness in the face of death.

63. Fränkel, *Dichtung und Philosophie des frühen Griechentums*, p. 306.

παῖς μὲν ἄνηβος ἐὼν ἔτι νήπιος ἕρκος ὀδόντων
φύσας ἐκβάλλει πρῶτον ἐν ἕπτ᾽ ἔτεσιν.
τοὺς δ᾽ ἑτέρους ὅτε δὴ τελέσηι θεὸς ἕπτ᾽ ἐνιαυτούς,
ἥβης †δὲ φάνει† σήματα γεινομένης.
τῆι τριτάτηι δὲ γένειον ἀεξομένων ἔτι γυίων
λαχνοῦται, χροιῆς ἄνθος ἀμειβομένης.
τῆι δὲ τετάρτηι πᾶς τις ἐν ἑβδομάδι μέγ᾽ ἄριστος
ἰσχύν, ἧι τ᾽ ἄνδρες πείρατ᾽ ἔχουσ᾽ ἀρετῆς.
πέμπτηι δ᾽ ὥριον ἄνδρα γάμου μεμνημένον εἶναι
καὶ παίδων ζητεῖν εἰσοπίσω γενεήν.
τῆι δ᾽ ἕκτηι περὶ πάντα καταρτύεται νόος ἀνδρός,
οὐδ᾽ ἔρδειν ἔθ᾽ ὁμῶς ἔργ᾽ ἀπάλαμνα θέλει.
ἑπτὰ δὲ νοῦν καὶ γλῶσσαν ἐν ἑβδομάσιν μέγ᾽ ἄριστος
ὀκτώ τ᾽· ἀμφοτέρων τέσσαρα καὶ δέκ᾽ ἔτη.
τῆι δ᾽ ἐνάτηι ἔτι μὲν δύναται, μαλακώτερα δ᾽ αὐτοῦ
πρὸς μεγάλην ἀρετὴν γλῶσσά τε καὶ σοφίη.
τὴν δεκάτην δ᾽ εἴ τις τελέσας κατὰ μέτρον ἵκοιτο,
οὐκ ἂν ἄωρος ἐὼν μοῖραν ἔχοι θανάτου.

(Solon 27)

A child not yet a youth, having grown his first set of teeth as an infant,
   loses them in his first seven years.
When god accomplishes another seven years,
   he shows signs of his coming youthful prime.
In the third seven-year period, while his limbs are still growing,
   his chin grows hairy, the flower of his changing skin.
In the fourth seven years every man is at his best by far [meg' aristos]
   in regard to his physical strength [iskhus] which men hold as the
      achievement of excellence [aretê].
In the fifth it is the right time for a man to be mindful of marriage
   and to seek children, the race to come after him.
In the sixth, the mind [noos] of a man is fully trained concerning all
      things,
   nor does he still wish equally to do things to which he cannot put
      his hands.
In the seventh period of seven years and also in the eighth, his mind
   [noos]
   and his tongue [glôssa] are at their best by far [meg' aristos]
      —fourteen years for both.
In the ninth, he is still capable, but his tongue [glôssa] and sound
      judgement [sophiê]
   are somewhat weaker in regard to great excellence [aretê].
But if he should complete the full measure of ten seven-year periods,
   not untimely would he encounter the fate of death.

Consistent with Poem 13 in omitting the traditional view that aging is a major source of human misfortune, this poem emphasizes development over decline and does not lament the effects of the aging process.

In doing so, however, Poem 27 is more awkward than Solon's other poems (which may account, in part, for scholars' coolness toward it). In contrast to Solon's other poems, the language here often seems metrically determined, and the poem may be intended simply as a rationale for actual practice in Athens and other cities.[64] Arguably, Poems 27 and 20 may be part of the same poem in answer to Mimnermus—as if Solon, having begun in this way, then proceeded: "No, let me go further. Even seventy years isn't enough. I want to live eighty."[65] If these divisions represent stages customarily accepted in Athens and elsewhere, it is reasonable to suppose that Solon would seek to base his argument on accepted premises. But again Solon's strategy of subtle emphases may be at work, because, by the end of the poem, whether of the poem as it stands or with the addition of Poem 20, these "accepted premises" have come under review.

The first six lines of the poem are unexceptionable, even tedious, in their description of the stages of human physical maturation. But at lines 7–8 comes the first indication of critical evaluation:

τῆι δὲ τετάρτηι πᾶς τις ἐν ἑβδομάδι μέγ' ἄριστος
ἰσχύν, ἧι τ' ἄνδρες πείρατ' ἔχουσ' ἀρετῆς.
(Solon 27.7–8)

In the fourth seven years every man is at his best by far [*meg' aristos*]
in regard to his physical strength [*iskhus*], which men hold as the
achievement of excellence [*aretê*].

Perhaps the Homeric line ending (*meg' aristos*) is a subtle reminder that Homeric *aretê* 'excellence' entailed more than just strength? At any rate, the reference is to a popular opinion which it is not at all clear that Solon shares. Lines 11–16 emphasize *noos* 'mind' (11, 13), *glôssa* 'tongue' (13, 16) and *sophiê* 'intelligence' (16). These are the central values of adult life—from age thirty-five onward. There is, perhaps, the suggestion that youth may be a cause of misjudgement and delusion in lines 11–12:

64. Adkins, *Poetic Craft in the Early Greek Elegists*, p. 132.

65. Van Groningen, *La composition littéraire archaïque grecque*, pp. 136–137.

τῆι δ' ἔκτηι περὶ πάντα καταρτύεται νόος ἀνδρός,
οὐδ' ἔρδειν ἔθ' ὁμῶς ἔργ' ἀπάλαμνα θέλει.
(Solon 27.11–12)

In the sixth, the mind [*noos*] of a man is fully trained concerning all
things,
nor does he still wish equally to do things to which he cannot put
his hands [*apalamna*].[66]

But the point is hardly stressed. It is enlisted, primarily, in support of
the poem's central proposition that aging is a positive phenomenon. It
is phrased, therefore, as an example of positive development: by age
thirty-five, men no longer seek to attempt the impossible.

In presenting the aging process as a positive phenomenon, however,
lines 11–12 appear to suggest that intellectual development is simply
the result of a natural chronological progression rather than derived
from individual experience. These lines seem to indicate that people
naturally grow wiser as they grow older. This is undeniably the implicit
corollary to the view that the young are prone to misperceptions and
misjudgements, and it is certainly a soothing perspective. But surely it is
not Solon's. If it were, he would have little need for the criticisms he
levels at Athenians elsewhere in his poetry for their lack of intellectual
development. One can see this, for example, at 4.9–10, 9.3–4, and 11.5–
8. He may, it is true, be talking in purely relative terms, acknowledging
that a fool is always a fool, but less foolish when old than when young,
but such a point would hardly be worth emphasizing. Solon appears, instead, to have shifted from describing actual development to describing
potential for development. At the same time, his description of the
stages of development emphasizes that which is most important in human existence: the capacity for intellection and communication. Lines
13–14, therefore, far from being an awkward lumping together of the
seventh and eighth seven year periods, help rather to highlight the importance of *noos* 'mind' and *glôssa* 'tongue'. The phrase *meg' aristos* (13)

---

66. Campbell, notes that while L.S.J. gives "lawless" as the translation of *apalamna*, it
might equally mean "impossible." He cites *Iliad* 5.597, Hesiod *Works and Days* 20, and
Simonides 542.34 which use the word of "shiftless" men, and concludes that the word
might have been used (like *amēkhanos*) of impossible things (*Greek Lyric poetry*, p. 248).
Gentili understands *apalamnos* in Simonides 542 as "incompetent" (in A. T. Cole's
translation). He points out the word's connection with *palamē*, which designates the
dexterity and skillfulness of the hand, and, by extension, a person's ability in general
(*Poetry and its Public in Ancient Greece*, p. 255, n. 21).

is thus, perhaps, a deliberate, pointed repetition of the phrase uttered skeptically in line 7, and ἀμφοτέρων τέσσαρα καὶ δέκ' ἔτη 'fourteen years for both' (14) is not, one suspects, "mere padding," as Campbell maintains,[67] but a reminder of the brief amount of time in which a man may perfect these two most important skills. With its implicit criticism of the popular emphasis on *iskhus* 'physical strength' as the central element in *aretê* 'excellence',[68] and its explicit rejection of the conventional condemnation of aging, the poem presents a hierarchy of values. For Solon, the significant fact about the aging process is not the physical deterioration which may accompany it, but the opportunity it provides for intellectual development. As he explains in another poem:

γηράσκω δ' αἰεὶ πολλὰ διδασκόμενος
(Solon 18.1)

As I grow old I am always learning many things.

One might contrast this assertion with, for example Theognis' statement:

—μή με δίδασκ'· οὔτοι τηλίκος εἰμι μαθεῖν.
(Theognis 578)

Do not instruct me; indeed I am not of such an age as to learn.

Poem 27 is thus more than merely descriptive; it is something of an invitation and a challenge.

The rejection, in Poem 27, of the traditional negative view of aging helps to explain the absence of this sentiment in Poem 13 and distinguishes Solon from Theognis as well. Whereas the ill effects of aging (and the ignorance of youth) are not, for Solon, determinative factors, Theognis is still eager to reassert the traditional sentiments, offering at different times the advice of Odysseus, Semonides, "Simonides," and Mimnermus. He laments repeatedly the coming of old age and the brevity of youth, crying, for example:

ὤ μοι ἐγὼν ἥβης καὶ γήραος οὐλομένοιο,
τοῦ μὲν ἐπερχομένου, τῆς δ' ἀπονισομένης.
(Theognis 527–528)

---

67. Campbell, *Greek Lyric Poetry*, p. 248.

68. C. M Bowra explains that Solon's conception is wider than Tyrtaeus', for example, in that Solon believes man is capable of excelling in more than one way (*Early Greek Elegists*, p. 102).

Alas for youth and alas for miserable old age,
the one for coming, the other for going away.

and again:

ἐμπίομαι· πενίης θυμοφθόρου οὐ μελεδαίνω,
οὐδ' ἀνδρῶν ἐχθρῶν, οἵ με λέγουσι κακῶς.
ἀλλ' ἥβην ἐρατὴν ὀλοφύρομαι, ἥ μ' ἐπιλείπει,
κλαίω δ' ἀργαλέον γῆρας ἐπερχόμενον.
(Theognis 1129–1132)

I'll drink my fill; I do not have a care for life-destroying poverty,
nor for my enemies who speak badly of me.
But I bewail my lovely youth which is leaving me,
and I weep at old age approaching.

His response to this inevitable fact of existence is not unlike the hedonism expressed by "Simonides." With an evocative simile, Theognis maintains:

ἡμεῖς δ' ἐν θαλίηισι φίλον καταθώμεθα θυμόν,
ὄφρ' ἔτι τερπωλῆς ἔργ' ἐρατεινὰ φέρηι.
αἶψα γὰρ ὥστε νόημα παρέρχεται ἀγλαὸς ἥβη·
οὐδ' ἵππων ὁρμὴ γίνεται ὠκυτέρη,
αἵ τε ἄνακτα φέρουσι δορυσσόον ἐς πόνον ἀνδρῶν
λάβρως, πυροφόρωι τερπόμεναι πεδίωι.
(Theognis 983–988)

Let us give our heart over to festivities,
while lovely activities still bring delight.
For, as quickly as a thought, shining youth passes by;
not swifter is the rush of horses
which carry a lord furiously to the labor of the spear,
while they delight in the wheat-bearing plain.

He reiterates this view a number of times in response not only to the fact of aging but also to the inevitability and finality of death as, for example, in lines 567–570, 973–978, and 1007–1012.[69]

Elsewhere, Theognis advises endurance and forbearance in much

---

69. The emphasis on the finality of death is itself a popular *topos* for a number of poets. Campbell, noting this theme in Anacreon 395, lists also *Iliad* 9.408–409, Hesiod *Theogony* 770–773, Aeschylus *Persians* 668–670, Theocritus 17.120, Philetas fr. 6 Powell, Catullus 3.11–12, Virgil *Aeneid* 6.126–129, and Horace *Odes* 1.24.15–18 (*Greek Lyric Poets*, p. 326). One might also add to this list Alcaeus 38.

the same vein as Odysseus (*Odyssey* 18.141–142) and Semonides (1.22–24):[70]

τολμᾶν χρὴ τὰ διδοῦσι θεοὶ θνητοῖσι βροτοῖσιν,
   ῥηϊδίως δὲ φέρειν ἀμφοτέρων τὸ λάχος,
μήτε κακοῖσιν ἀσῶντα λίην φρένα, μήτ' ἀγαθοῖσιν
   τερφθῇς ἐξαπίνης πρὶν τέλος ἄκρον ἰδεῖν.
                                             (Theognis 591–594)

It is necessary to endure the things which the gods give to mortal men,
   and to bear easily either lot,
neither being excessively vexed in your mind at bad things, nor at
   good
be delighted precipitously, before you see the complete end.

Such equanimous endurance is characteristic of nobility for,

μηδὲν ἄγαν χαλεποῖσιν ἀσῶ φρένα μηδ' ἀγαθοῖσιν
   χαῖρ', ἐπεὶ ἔστ' ἀνδρὸς πάντα φέρειν ἀγαθοῦ.
                                             (Theognis 657–658)

Neither be excessively vexed in your mind at difficulties, nor at good
   things
   rejoice excessively, since it is the part of a good man [*agathos anêr*]
   to bear all things.

Theognis expresses the same views also in lines 441–446 (=1162a–1162f).

In still another passage, however, Theognis concurs with Mimnermus that in some circumstances—namely, for Theognis, poverty—death is preferable, for

ἄνδρ' ἀγαθὸν πενίη πάντων δάμνησι μάλιστα,
   καὶ γήρως πολιοῦ Κύρνε καὶ ἠπιάλου·
ἣν δὴ χρὴ φεύγοντα καὶ ἐς μεγακήτεα πόντον
   ῥιπτεῖν καὶ πετρέων Κύρνε κατ' ἠλιβάτων.
καὶ γὰρ ἀνὴρ πενίηι δεδμημένος οὔτέ τι εἰπεῖν
   οὔτ' ἔρξαι δύναται, γλῶσσα δέ οἱ δέδεται.
χρὴ γὰρ ὁμῶς ἐπὶ γῆν τε καὶ εὐρέα νῶτα θαλάσσης
   δίζησθαι χαλεπῆς Κύρνε λύσιν πενίης.
τεθνάμεναι φίλε Κύρνε πενιχρῶι βέλτερον ἀνδρὶ
   ἢ ζώειν χαλεπῆι τειρόμενον πενίηι.
                                             (Theognis 173–182)

---

70. Archilochus 13 and 128 might also be added to this list.

Of all things, poverty overcomes a good man most,
    more than grizzled old age, Kyrnos, or ague;
For one fleeing poverty, it is necessary even to fall into the sea
    that yawns with mighty hollows, Kyrnos, or down from high rocks.
For a man overcome by poverty is able neither to say nor to do anything,
    and his tongue is bound.
It is necessary equally both on land and on the broad back of the sea,
    to seek a release, Kyrnos, from harsh poverty.
For an impoverished man, my Kyrnos, it is better to be dead
    than to live oppressed by harsh poverty.

Thus, Theognis, unlike Solon, appears to accept the traditional assessments of human existence and how best to cope with it.

Solon's assertions on these matters are unlikely to be entirely independent of the statements of his predecessors and contemporaries. Viewed in the context of these passages of Homer, Semonides, "Simonides," Mimnermus, and Theognis, Solon's views, and, moreover, his placement of these views as the centerpiece of his long elegy to the Muses, may be more easily understood. In lines 7–29 of this poem, Solon defines human prosperity by describing the fruits of god-given *ploutos* and of *ploutos* acquired through *hubris*. He emphasizes the inevitability of punishment for wrongdoing and recognizes that even the innocent are not exempt from suffering. The passage could serve comfortably as a preamble to any of the traditional assessments of human existence in comparison to divine, of human shortsightedness, of human optimism. The audience might well expect that Solon is leading up to an admonition, like that in *Odyssey* 18.141–142 or Semonides 1.22–24, to endure with equanimity both good and bad fortune, or perhaps to the hedonistic advice of "Simonides" or Theognis to enjoy prosperity while one has it and while one is healthy and young enough to take pleasure in it, or even to Mimnermus' despairing assertion that death is preferable to aging, illness, and misfortune.

Solon does not accept, however, that human optimism is determined by good fortune, by god-given *aretê* 'excellence', by youth, by health. He does not reassert that human life is transient, that youth is short-lived and followed only by suffering. Solon's concern is not the existential but the ethical problem of human life. Moreover, whereas other poets criticize human optimism, Solon accepts it as a fact of human nature. All of the other poets appear to want to criticize or even change their audience's emotional responses toward youth, old age, sickness, misfortune, death—even as they recognize the inability of individuals to assimilate things that they have not yet experienced. In contrast,

Solon's approach seems designed to be more practical: why keep repeating the tired old saw that human beings see only the here and now while gods look to the ends? Why keep urging forebearance, endurance, moderation, circumspection when individuals so obviously remain unmoved? What is needed, rather, is an accurate diagram of predictable connections between actions and consequences, and that, in effect, is what Solon provides.

His observations in lines 33–43 are new and unexpected: human beings are optimistic by their very nature. They grieve at misfortune but do not anticipate it. They believe things about themselves both in the present and in the future which have no basis in fact. The significant fact of human nature is not that people enjoying good fortune expect that it will endure; rather it is that people suffering misfortune are eternally optimistic about the possibility of change. People even mistake present misfortune for good fortune (13.39–40). These are the facts of human nature which result in the ceaseless activity of human beings in all its diverse forms. Solon thus identifies the way in which human activity contributes to the form that human fortunes take.

By attributing incessant human activity to a fundamental fact of human nature, Solon indicates that human beings no less than gods are responsible for human fortunes. Therefore, although Solon does contrast human ignorance and powerlessness with divine knowledge and control over outcomes, this does not appear to be the focal point of the poem. Solon seems, perhaps, less interested in contrasting human power with divine than in emphasizing how intertwined the two are.[71] Nearing the end of his poem, Solon returns to the question of ends and outcomes and its relation to human actions, asserting:

> Μοῖρα δέ τοι θνητοῖσι κακὸν φέρει ἠδὲ καὶ ἐσθλόν,
> δῶρα δ᾽ ἄφυκτα θεῶν γίγνεται ἀθανάτων.
> πᾶσι δέ τοι κίνδυνος ἐπ᾽ ἔργμασιν, οὐδέ τις οἶδεν
> πῆι μέλλει σχήσειν χρήματος ἀρχομένου·
> ἀλλ᾽ ὁ μὲν εὖ ἔρδειν πειρώμενος οὐ προνοήσας
> ἐς μεγάλην ἄτην καὶ χαλεπὴν ἔπεσεν,
> τῶι δὲ κακῶς ἔρδοντι θεὸς περὶ πάντα δίδωσιν
> συντυχίην ἀγαθήν, ἔκλυσιν ἀφροσύνης.
> (Solon 13.63–70)

---

71. In this Solon possibly anticipates Aeschylus, in whose tragedies the view of human causality intertwined with divine is more fully developed and intensely problematic. See, for example, *Persians* 742: ἀλλ᾽, ὅταν σπεύδηι τις αὐτός, χὠ θεὸς συνάπτεται 'But, when a man strives eagerly, the god also joins in'.

Fate brings to mortals both evil and good,
and the gifts of the immortal gods are not to be shunned.
There is danger in all actions, nor does anyone know
where he will make land, after a thing is begun [*khrêmatos
arkhomenou*].
But one trying to do well [*eu erdein peirômenos*], through failure of
foresight,
may fall into great and harsh ruin,
while to one who acts badly [*kakôs erdonti*], god gives good fortune
concerning all things, a release from his folly.

The assertion that failure and success may be independent of human deliberation and circumstances (13.67–70) now follows Solon's analysis of the deluded optimism of human beings and his lengthy description of the diverse forms of human activity which derive from it. The themes cannot be disentangled; lines 63–70 cannot be severed from the knowledge Solon has already conveyed—namely that human beings also contribute to their own fortunes. The latter view, as Solon was perhaps the first to recognize, is necessary for the survival of a community. He is most emphatic on this point in Poem 4, which will be discussed in the following chapter. He emphasizes the compatibility of the two views by placing his long exploration of human nature and activity—that is, of human causality (13.33–62)—between assertions of divine causality: descendants may suffer for the misdeeds of their ancestors (13.29–32), and human fortunes are variable, unpredictable, and determined by the gods (13.63–70).

But Solon is not merely reiterating the epic conception in which divine and human motivation are intertwined. For him, they are not two equally simple ways of explaining the same thing. Rather, he perceives a single, more complex way involving elements of both. Prior to Solon, divine capriciousness and human folly appear as more or less interchangeable explanations for the course of events. Solon suggests that the will of human beings is somewhat more free than epic poetry presents it. He does not reach the point of seeing it in conflict with divine will, but he suggests that human beings do have *some* control. He thus provides something of a break from the earlier notion of double motivation.

Recognition of the variability and unpredictability of human fortunes is not unique to Solon. Both Homer and Semonides express this in the passages already discussed, and Theognis 585–590 is almost identical to Solon 13.65–70:

πᾶσίν τοι κίνδυνος ἐπ' ἔργμασιν, οὐδέ τις οἶδεν
πῆι σχήσειν μέλλει πρήγματος ἀρχομένου·
ἀλλ' ὁ μὲν εὐδοκιμεῖν πειρώμενος οὐ προνοήσας
εἰς μεγάλην ἄτην καὶ χαλεπὴν ἔπεσεν·
τῶι δὲ κακῶς ποιεῦντι θεὸς περὶ πάντα τίθησιν
συντυχίην ἀγαθήν, ἔκλυσιν ἀφροσύνης.
(Theognis 585–590)

There is danger in all actions, nor does anyone know
    where he will make land, after a thing is begun [*prêgmatos
    arkhomenou*];
but one trying to be of good repute [*eudokimein peirômenos*], through
    failure of foresight,
    may fall into great and harsh ruin;
while to one who acts badly [*kakôs poieunti*], the god gives good fortune
concerning all things, a release from his folly.

While this may be simply a different redaction of Solon's statement,[72] the variations could be instructive. It would be helpful to know the connotations for Solon of *eu erdein* (vs. *eu poiein*), but, unfortunately the phrase does not occur elsewhere in his extant verses. Although *prêgmatos* and *khrêmatos* may merely be synonyms, nevertheless, Theognis' substitution of the former may not be trivial. Perhaps he, unlike Solon, does not choose to identify *khrêmata* (more specifically: 'property') precisely as the source of the problem. The point is necessary to Solon's argument in that his assertions of divine causality apply most specifically to the acquisition of wealth: wealth justly acquired is secure; wealth unjustly acquired is a source of retribution. Between and outside this polar opposition lies the vast area of human experience to which the observations of lines 33ff. apply.

In another passage, Theognis again emphasizes the instability of human fortunes and the fact that gods, not human beings, are in control. He asserts:

οὐδ' ὀμόσαι χρὴ τοῦθ', ὅτι "μήποτε πρῆγμα τόδ' ἔσται"·
θεοὶ γάρ τοι νεμεσῶσ', οἷσιν ἔπεστι τέλος.
κἄπρηξαν μέντοί τι· καὶ ἐκ κακοῦ ἐσθλὸν ἔγεντο

---

72. In citing these two passages, Wilamowitz argues that one should not attribute the alterations to scribal errors, since that simply obscures the difference between intentional and unintentional alterations and destroys any possibility of appreciating differences between versions ("Solons Elegie εἰς ἑαυτόν," p. 270).

καὶ κακὸν ἐξ ἀγαθοῦ · καί τε πενιχρὸς ἀνὴρ
αἶψα μάλ' ἐπλούτησε, καὶ ὃς μάλα πολλὰ πέπαται
ἐξαπίνης †ἀπὸ πάντ' οὖν† ὤλεσε νυκτὶ μιῆι.
(Theognis 659–664)

It is necessary that one not swear this: "This thing will never be."
For the gods feel just resentment (*they* control the end),
and of course they accomplish a thing. And good may come from bad
and bad from good; a poor man may become rich very quickly,
and one who has very many possessions
suddenly may lose everything in one night.

Archilochus also expresses this idea:

τοῖς θεοῖς †τ' εἰθεῖάπαντα · πολλάκις μὲν ἐκ κακῶν
ἄνδρας ὀρθοῦσιν μελαίνηι κειμένους ἐπὶ χθονί,
πολλάκις δ' ἀνατρέπουσι καὶ μάλ' εὖ βεβηκότας
ὑπτίους, κείνοις ⟨δ'⟩ ἔπειτα πολλὰ γίνεται κακά,
καὶ βίου χρήμηι πλανᾶται καὶ νόου παρήορος.
(Archilochus 130)

All things are easy for the gods. Often they set upright from troubles
men lying upon the black earth,
but often they overturn onto their backs
even those set very firmly on their feet,
and then there are many evils for a man like this,
and he wanders in need of livelihood and out of his mind.

But whereas in these two passages Archilochus and Theognis contrast
the reversals of men in unfavorable circumstances with those of men
initially in favorable ones, Solon contrasts ὁ μὲν εὖ ἔρδειν πειρώμενος 'a
man trying to do well' (13.67) with τῶι δὲ κακῶς ἔρδοντι 'one acting
badly' (13.69), that is, Solon contrasts intentions, rather than actual
favorable circumstances, with actual unfavorable circumstances, since
the latter phrase says nothing about intentions. This is also the case in
Theognis 587–590 above. By choosing to discuss intentions, Solon emphasizes not merely the variability of human fortunes, but also the
apparent irrelevance of human intentions and efforts and the arbitrari-
ness of divine rewards and punishments.[73] This seems to argue against

---

73. I follow Wilamowitz' paraphrase of lines 65ff.: 'It is not done with our power and
our intelligence; for all of us, things turn out as for the physician, sometimes good,
sometimes bad, not in proportion to our merit and our expectation' ("Solons Elegie εἰς
ἑαυτόν," p. 266).

the view that Solon is attempting to convey a modern sense of moral responsibility, but does little to weaken a claim that he recognizes a logic of cause and effect in human actions and their outcomes. The difficulty is that the results of human actions are unlikely to be the ones intended or anticipated. Indeed, in these lines both Solon and Theognis suggest that misfortune is closely connected to ignorance, claiming:

τῶι δὲ κακῶς ἔρδοντι θεὸς περὶ πάντα δίδωσιν
συντυχίην ἀγαθήν, ἔκλυσιν ἀφροσύνης.
(Solon 13.69–70)

while to one who acts badly [*kakôs erdonti*], the god gives good fortune concerning all things, a release from his folly.

and

τῶι δὲ κακῶς ποιεῦντι θεὸς περὶ πάντα τίθησιν
συντυχίην ἀγαθήν, ἔκλυσιν ἀφροσύνης.
(Theognis 589–590)

while to one who acts badly [*kakôs poieunti*], the god gives good fortune concerning all things, a release from his folly.

This sense of the relationship between human actions and their outcomes informs the concluding lines of Solon's poem. Solon asserts:

πλούτου δ᾽ οὐδὲν τέρμα πεφασμένον ἀνδράσι κεῖται·
οἳ γὰρ νῦν ἡμέων πλεῖστον ἔχουσι βίον,
διπλάσιον σπεύδουσι· τίς ἂν κορέσειεν ἅπαντας;
κέρδεά τοι θνητοῖς ὤπασαν ἀθάνατοι,
ἄτη δ᾽ ἐξ αὐτῶν ἀναφαίνεται, ἣν ὁπότε Ζεὺς
πέμψηι τεισομένην, ἄλλοτε ἄλλος ἔχει.
(Solon 13.71–76)

But of wealth there lies no limit visible for men,
    for those of us who now have the most property,
    strive with double zeal; who can satisfy [*korennumi*] all?
    Indeed, the immortals give gains [*kerdea*] to mortals,
    but from them [*ex autôn*] ruin [*atê*] appears plainly, which one man
        has at one time
    another at another [*allote allos ekhei*], whenever Zeus sends it as
        retribution [*teisomenên*].

Lattimore explains that *autôn* refers to *kerdea* and that 13.74–76 is a development of the point that Solon made in lines 9–13. And yet, Lattimore finds the connection vague. Solon seems to mean here that all wealth, good or bad, may lead to *atê*, whereas in 9–13 only wealth obtained by *hubris* is problematic.[74] But Solon seems to be reiterating the views expressed in 7–13 now combined with the knowledge of human nature conveyed in lines 33–62. Perhaps Solon's point is that given human nature as it is—unshakeably optimistic, incessantly active—*atê* is always a possibility from *kerdea*. After all, man's relationship to *ploutos* is inherently problematic since πλούτου δ' οὐδὲν τέρμα πεφασμένον ἀνδράσι κεῖται 'of wealth there lies no limit visible to men' (71). The verb *korennumi* (73), too, returns the discussion to the initial theme of the unjust (because insatiable) pursuit of wealth. To put it mildly, there is, perhaps, the implication that there may be more valuable things to strive after.

Theognis 227–229 is virtually identical to Solon 13.71–73 with the substitution of *anthrôpoisin* (227) for *andrasi keitai* (13.71). But Theognis follows this observation with the claim that

> χρήματά τοι θνητοῖς γίνεται ἀφροσύνη,
> ἄτη δ' ἐξ αὐτῆς ἀναφαίνεται, ἣν ὁπότε Ζεὺς
> πέμψηι τειρομένοις, ἄλλοτε ἄλλος ἔχει.
> (Theognis 230–232)

> Indeed, possessions [*khrêmata*, perhaps more specifically: 'property'] become folly for mortals.
> and from folly, ruin [*atê*] appears plainly,
> which one man has at one time, another at another, whenever Zeus sends it to ones who are distressed [*teiromenoi*].

The absoluteness of the statement may result from a problem with the text at line 230. (The first word, χρήματά, should perhaps be χρήμασί.) Still, while Solon explains that κέρδεά τοι θνητοῖς ὤπασαν ἀθάνατοι 'the immortals give gains [*kerdea*] to mortals' (74), and sees *atê* as *teisomenê* 'avenging' (75), Theognis notes that Zeus sends *atê* but neglects to mention that the gods also send *kerdea* and sees the recipients of *atê* as simply *teiromenoi* 'distressed'. With these alterations, Theognis omits both the idea that divine justice is at work and that *kerdea* in general, and not only *khrêmata*, are themselves problematic.[75] In fact, elsewhere Theognis seems to contrast *kerdos* with *kakon* in stating:

---

74. Lattimore, "The First Elegy of Solon," p. 178.

75. But see Nagy's comment that in Theognis 46, 50, and 835, *kerdos* is a correlate of *hubris* ("Theognis and Megara: A Poet's Vision of his City," p. 45, n.1).

αὐτίκα μέν τι φέρειν κέρδος δοκεῖ, ἐς δὲ τελευτὴν
αὖθις ἔγεντο κακόν, θεῶν δ' ὑπερέσχε νόος.
(Theognis 201–202)

For the moment he thinks to gain some advantage [*kerdos*], but in the
end
it turns out to be an evil [*kakon*]. The mind of the gods prevails.

This seems far from Solon's recognition that *atê* results from *kerdea* (74–
75), that is, that *kerdos* can in effect be *kakon.* Hesiod, too, expresses the
latter view in maintaining:

μὴ κακὰ κερδαίνειν· κακὰ κέρδεα ἶσ' ἄτηισι.
(Hesiod *Works and Days* 352)

Get not gains that are evil; evil gains equal disaster.

These statements can also be juxtaposed with Theognis' assertion
that

οὐδεὶς Κύρν' ἄτης καὶ κέρδεος αἴτιος αὐτός,
ἀλλὰ θεοὶ τούτων δώτορες ἀμφοτέρων·
οὐδέ τις ἀνθρώπων ἐργάζεται ἐν φρεσὶν εἰδὼς
ἐς τέλος εἴτ' ἀγαθὸν γίνεται εἴτε κακόν.
πολλάκι γὰρ δοκέων θήσειν κακὸν ἐσθλὸν ἔθηκεν,
καί τε δοκῶν θήσειν ἐσθλὸν ἔθηκε κακόν.
οὐδέ τῶι ἀνθρώπων παραγίνεται, ὅσσ' ἐθέλησιν·
ἴσχει γὰρ χαλεπῆς πείρατ' ἀμηχανίης.
ἄνθρωποι δὲ μάταια νομίζομεν, εἰδότες οὐδέν·
θεοὶ δὲ κατὰ σφέτερον πάντα τελοῦσι νόον.
(Theognis 133–142)

No one, Kyrnos, is himself the cause of ruin [*atê*] and gain [*kerdos*],
    but the gods are the givers of both of these things;
nor does anyone act knowing in his heart
    whether the end he works toward is good or bad [*kakon*].
For often thinking he will produce a bad result he produces a
    good,
and thinking he will produce a good result he produces a bad.
Nor does any mortal get as much as he wishes.
For the boundaries of harsh helplessness are prohibitive.
We mortals think vain thoughts, knowing nothing;
    but the gods accomplish everything according to their mind.

In these lines Theognis combines awareness of the variability of human
fortunes and awareness of human ignorance of outcomes with the view
that human beings are in no way responsible for their own *kerdos* or

atê.[76] In contrast, Solon seems to suggest otherwise. By combining in lines 71–76 a reference to *ploutos* and *atê* (recalling *ploutos* and *atê* in lines 7–13) and a reference to human activity and zeal (*diplasion speudousi* [73] recalling *speudei d' allothen allos* [43]), with the view that *kerdea* themselves lead to *atê* (a connection Theognis fails to express), Solon emphasizes that while *atê* does indeed come from the gods (74), it comes by way of human actions, by *hubris* (11).

The last phrase of the poem, ἄλλοτε ἄλλος ἔχει (*allote allos ekhei*) 'one has at one time, another at another', recalls the sense of *Mnêmosunê* 'Memory' with which Solon began. If the future is largely unknowable because uncertainty is inherent in all human affairs, it is also partially knowable, to the extent that certain actions and attitudes may result in predictable consequences. Given the variability of human fortunes, it is essential to recollect accurately the causal connections between specific actions and their outcomes. Archilochus 13.5–9 provides a useful contrast. For Archilochus, the variability of human fortunes is a comforting concept. He takes solace in the fact that human suffering is dispersed, maintaining:

> ἀλλὰ θεοὶ γὰρ ἀνηκέστοισι κακοῖσιν
> ὦ φίλ' ἐπὶ κρατερὴν τλημοσύνην ἔθεσαν
> φάρμακον. ἄλλοτε ἄλλος ἔχει τόδε· νῦν μὲν ἐς ἡμέας
> ἐτράπεθ', αἱματόεν δ' ἕλκος ἀναστένομεν,
> ἐξαῦτις δ' ἑτέρους ἐπαμείψεται.
>
> (Archilochus 13.5–9)

> But against incurable troubles, friend, the gods
> have placed strong endurance as a healing medicine.

---

76. Theognis is not entirely consistent on this point. Lines 833–836 seem to conflict with the attribution in 133–142 of divine rather than human responsibility for *atê* and *kerdos*:

πάντα τάδ' ἐν κοράκεσσι καὶ ἐν φθόρωι· οὐδέ τις ἥμιν
αἴτιος ἀθανάτων Κύρνε θεῶν μακάρων,
ἀλλ' ἀνδρῶν τε βίη καὶ κέρδεα δειλὰ καὶ ὕβρις
πολλῶν ἐξ ἀγαθῶν ἐς κακότητ' ἔβαλεν.
(Theognis 833–836)

All these things have gone to the ravens and to ruin;
    nor is any one of the blessed immortals the cause of it for us, Kyrnos,
but the violence of men and their miserable profits and their reckless
    arrogance
have thrown us from much good into evil.

One has trouble at one time, another at another [*allote allos ekhei*].
    Now it has turned
toward us, and we groan aloud over the bloody wound.
At another time it will come in turn to others.

In contrast, placed at the end of Solon's Poem 13, the phrase *allote allos ekhei* holds a dire warning. Knowledge of the variability of human fortunes now reinforces the recognition that certain causal relationships are inevitable, specifically, the relationship between wealth and *atê*.[77]

In this elegy Solon does not offer any prescriptive advice or simple solutions. If his opening address to the Muses is understood as an appeal to *Mnêmosunê* in the sense of knowledge of the future through an understanding of the logic of cause and effect, the poem's interest lies not so much in the originality of Solon's conclusions as in the subtleties of his arguments. In urging people to modify their desires, Solon attempts to enlist in support of the empirically weak proposition that evildoers are inevitably punished, the stronger, more readily accepted proposition that all things in life are uncertain. The ambiguity of lines 65–66 (οὐδέ τις οἶδεν / πῆι μέλλει σχήσειν χρήματος ἀρχομένου 'nor does anyone know/ where he will make land, after a thing is begun') and 71 (πλούτου δ' οὐδὲν τέρμα πεφασμένον ἀνδράσι κεῖται 'of wealth there lies no limit visible to men') provide the pivot points for this effort, in that neither passage distinguishes between uncertainty of limit and limitlessness. The point must be that, given that all things in life are uncertain, how foolish to ignore this one certainty, namely that the desire for wealth has no known terminus. The implication that anyone who understood correctly the logical consequences of unjust actions would necessarily refrain from indiscriminate acquisitiveness reveals a tremendous faith in the potential powers of the intellect.[78] In this Solon seems to presage the Socratic paradox that no one willingly

---

77. See also Solon 15.4 in which he argues that the instability of *khrêmata* 'property' makes *aretê* 'excellence' preferable to *ploutos* 'wealth'.

78. A. A. Allen maintains that Solon understands wisdom solely in terms of recognition of limits and that he implies that *atê* can be avoided entirely by means of such wisdom ("Solon's Prayer to the Muses," pp. 50–65). This overlooks Solon's point that people can suffer for the wrongdoing of their ancestors, and fails to appreciate much of the poem's message. By emphasizing that human beings no less than gods are responsible for human fortunes, Solon does not so much stress that individuals must recognize their limits as reveal a greatly expanded vision of human capabilities and potential.

does evil. His emphasis on the causal connections between human nature, human activities, and human fortunes, serves to supplement his acceptance of divine causality in that he adds to it a recognition of human participation and the possibility of making that participation deliberate rather than inadvertent.[79]

---

79. Contrast Bowra, who considers that in this poem Solon is insisting that men are at the mercy of Fate (*Early Greek Elegists*, p. 98).

Chapter Two

Poem 4: Poetry and Community

The themes that Solon emphasizes in Poem 13 occur elsewhere in his extant poetry and are perhaps particularly visible in the two next largest poems, 4 and 36. Scholars have been reluctant to view Poem 4 in the same light as Poem 13, considering the former "later" in Solon's career,[1] and "political" rather than purely "ethical."[2] And yet, as already suggested, given the scarcity of Solon's extant poetry, such distinctions, although not untenable, may obstruct rather than promote clear understanding of his views. Undue emphasis on distinctions between the two poems may impede recognition of themes stressed in both.[3] Although poem 4 treats Solon's political ideology more exhaustively than poem 13, Athenian literature is more or less always occupied with the problem of political organization.[4] Moreover, consideration of Poem 4 as "political" has led scholars to identify important Hesiodic parallels and one striking Homeric precursor, but may have contri-

1. E.g. M. Croiset, "La morale et la cité dans les poésies de Solon," *Académie des Inscriptions et Belles Lettres*, Comptes Rendus (1903), pp. 583ff.

2. E.g. F. Solmsen, *Hesiod and Aeschylus* (Ithaca, N.Y., 1949), p. 112. W. Jaeger thinks that both Poem 13 and Poem 4 must date from an early period in Solon's life, but argues that Poem 4 is in a middle position between "those poems which are political in a narrower sense (where Solon takes a stand against the disastrous behavior of the political factions and leaders of his native city or where he justifies his own official line of action), and the pure reflection of the 'Prayer to the Muses'" ("Solon's Eunomia," in *Five Essays*, translated by A. M. Fiske [Montreal, 1966], p. 81).

3. Jaeger does acknowledge that "although he does not say so explicitly, all his words and deeds give the impression that his whole political effort was inspired by a religio-political philosophy of life" ("Solon's Eunomia", p. 81).

4. A. Masaracchia, *Solone* (Florence, 1958), p. 246.

buted to the neglect of other archaic parallels which provide the necessary context for Solon's views. Poem 4 shares with both epic poetry and the genre of praise-blame poetry its pre-occupation with the problem of consumption and the requirement of society that it be regulated. Examination of Poem 4 in this context reveals Solon's awareness that the traditional language and imagery no less than the traditional solutions offered by other poets are inadequate. Where these are inherently exclusionary, Solon recognizes that his poetry, like his *polis*, needs to include all members of society. In attempting to resolve the political conflict in Athens, Solon was battling not only political realities but poetic conventions as well.

Important thematic similarities exist betweeen Poem 4 and Poem 13. Both, for example, stress the value of intellectual understanding. Just as in Poem 13, in his conception of success and good reputation for an individual, Solon includes the knowledge of the causal connections between specific actions and their consequences, so, too, in Poem 4 he emphasizes the necessity of this knowledge for the well-being of a community. The troubles threatening the survival of the *polis* are the result of intellectual failings on the part of the inhabitants.[5] The *astoi*

---

5. In this context, one may contrast Theognis 833–836:

πάντα τάδ' ἐν κοράκεσσι καὶ ἐν φθόρωι· οὐδέ τις ἥμιν
   αἴτιος ἀθανάτων Κύρνε θεῶν μακάρων,
ἀλλ' ἀνδρῶν τε βίη καὶ κέρδεα δειλὰ καὶ ὕβρις
   πολλῶν ἐξ ἀγαθῶν ἐς κακότητ' ἔβαλεν.

All these things have gone to the ravens and to ruin,
   nor is any one of the blessed immortal gods the cause of it for us, Kyrnos,
but the violence of men and their miserable profits and reckless arrogance
   have thrown us from much good into evil.

Both Solon and Theognis attribute the cause of the destruction to men in contrast to gods, but whereas Theognis describes a *fait accompli*, Solon is detailing a future possibility: that is, the hope remains that destruction may still be averted. Moreover, Theognis blames the *biê* 'violence', *kerdea* 'profits', and *hubris* 'reckless arrogance' of men. In contrast, Solon blames *aphradia* 'folly', *khrêmata* 'property', and *hubris* 'reckless arrogance'. The second and third terms are parallel, but the first are not. Solon is emphasizing the intellectual limitations of human beings. (He continues: οὐ γὰρ ἐπίστανται 'for they do not understand'.) The problem is not *biê* by and of itself but the way in which it is used. Compare, for example, Solon's claim in Poem 36 that:

'citizens' are willing to destroy the city *aphradiêsin* 'by folly' (4.5–6), and δήμου θ' ἡγεμόνων ἄδικος νόος 'the mind of the leaders of the people is unjust' (4.7). The difficulty is that

οὐ γὰρ ἐπίστανται κατέχειν κόρον οὐδὲ παρούσας
εὐφροσύνας κοσμεῖν δαιτὸς ἐν ἡσυχίηι
(Solon 4.9–10)

they do not know how to restrain their greed [*koros*], nor
    how to order their present festivities in the peacefulness of the
    banquet.

In contrast, *Dikê* 'Justice' is characterized by her knowledge for

ἣ σιγῶσα σύνοιδε τὰ γιγνόμενα πρό τ' ἐόντα
(Solon 4.15)

silent, she knows about what is happening and what has happened.

Solon seems to share the traditional archaic view which considers as intellectual deficiencies what we might term "moral" failings.[6]

ταῦτα μὲν κράτει
ὁμοῦ βίην τε καὶ δίκην ξυναρμόσας
ἔρεξα
(Solon 36.15–17)

I did these things
by my power, joining together force [*biê*] and justice [*dikê*].

6. See, for example, W. S. Barrett regarding *Hippolytus* 377–381. Barrett explains that "Greek usage does not distinguish the intellectual from the moral and volitional faculties of the mind, and commonly describes moral attitudes, etc. in the same words that it uses for intellectual ones: e.g. γνώμη here, 427, 1304; γιγνώσκω 380; ἐπίσταμαι 380, 996; φρονεῖν 378, 920; νοῦς 920" (Euripides, *Hippolytus*, edited by W. S. Barrett [Oxford, 1964], pp. 227–228). See also E. R. Dodds regarding the archaic "habit of explaining character or behavior in terms of knowledge." Dodds maintains that, as a consequence, "the so-called Socratic paradoxes, that 'virtue is knowledge,' and that no one does wrong on purpose,' were no novelties, but an explicit generalized formulation of what had long been an ingrained habit of thought" (*The Greeks and the Irrational* [Berkeley, 1951], pp. 16–17).

In emphasizing the importance of intellectual understanding, Poem 4, like Poem 13, acknowledges the extent to which human beings contribute to the form that their own fortunes may take, stressing the knowledge of predictable and direct relationships between specific actions and their consequences.[7] As discussed in Chapter 1 above, Poem 13 explores in some detail the way in which human beings participate in the shaping of their own destiny, and in Poem 4, responsibility is transferred emphatically from gods to men.[8]

Both poems also perceive optimism and insatiability as elements of human nature. In Poem 13, Solon suggests that human optimism is independent of actual circumstances and leads to incessant human activity in all its diverse forms as σπεύδει δ' ἄλλοθεν ἄλλος 'one rushes off in one direction, another in another' (13.43). Moreover, the desire for wealth is insatiable, since

πλούτου δ' οὐδὲν τέρμα πεφασμένον ἀνδράσι κεῖται·
οἳ γὰρ νῦν ἡμέων πλεῖστον ἔχουσι βίον,
διπλάσιον σπεύδουσι· τίς ἂν κορέσειεν ἅπαντας;
(Solon 13.71–73)

Of wealth no limit lies visible for men;
    for those of us who now have the most property
strive with double zeal; who could satisfy all?

In Poem 4 Solon also links the optimism and insatiability of human nature, maintaining that

αὐτοὶ δὲ φθείρειν μεγάλην πόλιν ἀφραδίηισιν
ἀστοὶ βούλονται χρήμασι πειθόμενοι
(Solon 4.5–6)

But the citizens themselves, persuaded by money, are willing
to destroy this great city by their folly,

and that

οὔθ' ἱερῶν κτεάνων οὔτέ τι δημοσίων
φειδόμενοι κλέπτουσιν ἀφαρπαγῆι ἄλλοθεν ἄλλος
(Solon 4.12–13)

---

7. Specifically: unjust actions and the dire consequences which result directly from the actions themselves, not through divine intervention.

8. H. Fränkel, *Dichtung und Philosophie des frühen Griechentums* (New York, 1951), p. 293.

sparing neither possessions that are sacred nor those belonging to
the public,
they steal rapaciously from every direction.

In their ignorance and, by implication, their optimism, the citizens of
the *polis* are unaware of the danger they are risking, and Solon must
insist that δημόσιον κακὸν ἔρχεται οἴκαδ᾿ ἑκάστωι 'the public evil comes
homeward to each man' (4.26).

Such thematic similarities between Poem 4 and Poem 13 indicate
that rigid categorization of the former as part of Solon's "political"
poetry is unhelpful. The label "political" itself adds little to one's understanding of the poem. Poem 4 has been called "the program of a
reformer,"[9] but as political theory the poem is remarkably vague. Thus,
for example, *astoi* 'citizens' (6), *khrēmasi peithomenoi* 'persuaded by
money' or 'trusting in money' (6), *ēluthe* 'comes' (18), *doulosunēn*
'slavery' (18), and *hē* 'which' (19), are all ambiguous in their reference.[10] The poem's lack of specificity as political theory encourages
one to seek archaic antecedents which scholars have neglected,
passages with comparable themes, emotional overtones, and social
function.

Many have noted similarities between Poem 4 and passages of
Homer and Hesiod. Several compare the opening lines of Solon's
poem with Zeus' speech in the first book of the *Odyssey* (1.32–43).[11]
Arguably, the antithesis between *theoi* 'gods' and *autoi* 'themselves', that
is, *anthrōpoi* 'men', and the assertion of human rather than divine
responsibility for human fortunes recalls Zeus' speech, and perhaps the
causal motif of the passage in the *Odyssey* was Solon's model.[12]

---

9. U. Von Wilamowitz-Moellendorff, *Aristoteles und Athen*, vol. II (Berlin, 1893), p. 307.

10. A. W. H. Adkins, noting these examples, explains that "the pervasive, deliberate
ambiguities are produced by linguistic skill, not ineptitude." He concludes that the poem
is neither history nor political theory, but rather "a work of rhetoric concerned to
persuade *via* emotive language, not to convey precise information" (*Poetic Craft in the Early
Greek Elegists* [Chicago and London, 1985], pp. 113–124).

11. Jaeger, "Solon's Eunomia," pp. 82–84. See also: Fränkel, *Dichtung und Philosophie
des frühen Griechentums*, pp. 293–294; C. M. Bowra, *Early Greek Elegists* (Cambridge, Mass.,
1939), p. 78; Adkins, *Poetic Craft in the Early Greek Elegists*, p. 113.

12. Jaeger, "Solon's Eunomia," pp. 82–84. Jaeger also stresses the importance of
foreknowledge in both passages, which makes the human individual responsible.

Hesiodic elements in Solon's poem have received even more attention. The opening language of the poem seems to show Homeric influence, but the succeeding lines resemble more closely Hesiod's warning to Perses and his account of the nobles' wrongdoing.[13] And, indeed, Solon's description of the function of *Dikê* does seem to echo Hesiod.[14] The formal structure of Solon's praise of *Eunomiê* recalls the proem of the *Works and Days*, and Hesiod's lines may well have been Solon's model.[15] But now the same praise is applied not to the gods but to good social order (*Eunomiê*).[16]

The formal structure of the entire poem, in fact, appears to be Hesiodic. The first thirty-one lines present an analysis of the trouble the city faces, and lines 32–39 propose a solution. This diptych structure may recall the contrast between the just and the unjust city in the *Works and Days*.[17] And Hesiod's combination of dire warnings against unjust actions, and advice on good, may have provided Solon with a structural model for his own elegy.[18]

Considerations of formal structure aside, however, thematic echoes in Poem 4 suggest other early parallels to Solon's poem. Both epic and praise-blame poetry recognize as problematic the relationship between individual satisfaction and communal harmony. Just as in Poem 13 Solon's invocation to the Muses simultaneously recalls and re-evaluates conventional attitudes regarding the poet and the social function of his poetry, so, too, in Poem 4, Solon's concern for the survival of his *polis* and his criticism of immoderate consumption reveal both his indebtedness to and his departure from archaic tradition.

In the opening lines of the poem, Solon is attempting to evoke for his audience the immense horror of the imminent destruction of their

---

13. D. Campbell, *The Golden Lyre: The Themes of The Greek Lyric Poets* (London, 1983), p. 92.

14. Jaeger, "Solon's Eunomia," p. 89; E. A. Havelock, *The Greek Concept of Justice* (Cambridge, Mass., 1978), p. 260; Adkins, *Poetic Craft in the Early Greek Elegists*, p. 117.

15. Jaeger, "Solon's Eunomia," p. 96.

16. Fränkel, *Dichtung und Philosophie des frühen Griechentums*, p. 295.

17. Jaeger, "Solon's Eunomia," pp. 88–89.

18. Bowra, *Early Greek Elegists*, p. 78.

city. Destruction of the form Solon envisions, a devastation originating from within the city, is without exact precedent in earlier poetry. But precedent of a sort exists in the form of discussion of countless (celebrated) cities destroyed by external enemies. The most famous example in extant archaic poetry of a city haunted by the specter of imminent destruction is Troy in the *Iliad.* And Solon's initial lines must owe a debt to Homer.

Solon begins his poem by saying:

ἡμετέρη δὲ πόλις κατὰ μὲν Διὸς οὔποτ᾽ ὀλεῖται
  αἶσαν καὶ μακάρων θεῶν φρένας ἀθανάτων·
τοίη γὰρ μεγάθυμος ἐπίσκοπος ὀβριμοπάτρη
  Παλλὰς ᾽Αθηναίη χεῖρας ὕπερθεν ἔχει·
(Solon 4.1–4)

But our city will never be destroyed by the dispensation of Zeus
  and the intentions of the blessed immortal gods;
for such a great-hearted guardian [*episkopos*], daughter of a mighty
    father,
  is Pallas Athene who holds her hands over it [*kheiras huperthen ekhei*].

Scholars are not in agreement as to whether these lines actually began the original poem. Demosthenes may have only cited part of the poem.[19] It might seem implausible, however, that an orator would fail to cite the opening lines of a well-known work, the lines which make an elegy recognizable and memorable to an audience. If so, we may, in fact, have the entire poem with the exception of the lacunae at lines 10, 11, and 25.[20] But this argument would be more convincing if Demosthenes were giving only a brief citation of the poem rather than invoking such a large amount of text. The presence of δέ in line 1 does seem to suggest that the initial part of the poem has been lost, and if the particle is given its clearly antithetical value, one might suspect preliminary mention of one or several cities destroyed by divine will. Troy would certainly seem to be a well-known example.[21]

---

19. Von Wilamowitz-Moellendorff, *Aristoteles und Athen*, pp. 305–306.

20. Masaracchia, *Solone*, pp. 247–248.

21. B. A. van Groningen, *La composition littéraire archaïque grecque* (Amsterdam, 1960), pp. 131–132. One might, perhaps, compare Simonides 531, in which the discussion of the dead at Thermopylae may form the culmination of a discussion of the transience of most types of achievement.

Whether or not the analogy was explicit, in any case, the opening of the poem as we have it does begin to suggest the analogy between Athens with its internal troubles and a city at risk from external enemies. The assertion that Athena is Athens' divine protector (*episkopos*) serves to emphasize the contrast between divine and human responsibility for the fortunes of the *polis*. But it serves another purpose as well: it enables Solon both to identify the striking fact that the devastation threatening Athens originates not from outside the city but from within it, and, at the same time, to produce in his audience the emotional reaction appropriate to the more familiar threat of utter destruction by external enemies.

To be sure, other archaic passages refer to gods' roles as protectors or guardians of particular cities, although they do not use the term *episkopos*. In *Iliad* 4.30–67, for example, Zeus, Athena, and Hera discuss their respective attachments to particular cities and their occupants, and Hera admits to Zeus:

> ἤτοι ἐμοὶ τρεῖς μὲν πολὺ φίλταταί εἰσι πόληες,
> Ἄργος τε Σπάρτη τε καὶ εὐρυάγυια Μυκήνη·
> τὰς διαπέρσαι ὅτ' ἄν τοι ἀπέχθωνται περὶ κῆρι·
> τάων οὔ τοι ἐγὼ πρόσθ' ἵσταμαι οὐδὲ μεγαίρω.
> εἴ περ γὰρ φθονέω τε καὶ οὐκ εἰῶ διαπέρσαι,
> οὐκ ἀνύω φθονέουσ', ἐπεὶ ἦ πολὺ φέρτερός ἐσσι.
> (*Iliad* 4.51–56)

Of all cities there are three that are dearest to my own heart:
Argos and Sparta and Mykenai of the wide ways. All these,
whenever they become hateful to your heart, sack utterly.
I will not stand up for these against you, nor yet begrudge you.
Yet if even so I bear malice and would not have you destroy them,
in malice I will accomplish nothing, since you are far stronger.

The implication of the statement is that cities dear to a particular god will not be destroyed unless a stronger god wills their destruction. Tyrtaeus 2.12–13 seems to offer similar reassurance:

> αὐτὸς γὰρ Κρονίων καλλιστεφάνου πόσις Ἥρης
> Ζεὺς Ἡρακλείδαις ἄστυ δέδωκε τόδε
> (Tyrtaeus 2.12–13)

For Zeus himself, the son of Kronos, husband of beautifully-garlanded Hera,
has given this city to the descendants of Herakles.

And elsewhere Tyrtaeus encourages his countrymen:

ἀλλ᾽, Ἡρακλῆος γὰρ ἀνικήτου γένος ἐστέ,
θαρσεῖτ᾽· οὔπω Ζεὺς αὐχένα λοξὸν ἔχει·
(Tyrtaeus 11.1–2)

But, since you are all of the race of invincible Herakles,
take courage; Zeus does not yet hold his neck aslant [i. e. has not
yet averted his eyes, is still sympathetic].

In all three of these passages, the danger facing the city comes in the form of assault from outside. But Athens is not threatened by external enemies, nor is the city endangered by a god stronger than Athena. In addition, Solon's point is, of course, the opposite of reassuring. In spite of the fact that Athens has a divine protector,

αὐτοὶ δὲ φθείρειν μεγάλην πόλιν ἀφραδίηισιν
ἀστοὶ βούλονται
(Solon 4.5–6)

The citizens themselves, by their folly, are willing
to destroy this great city.

Solon's collocation is both disturbing and unusual. The expected assertion would be *either* that the gods are providing protection, and, therefore there is no need to worry, *or* that the gods are not to blame, but we are destroying ourselves. Solon himself makes the latter assertion in Poem 11.1–4. Solon's formulation is unHomeric: in the Homeric epics if someone's destruction is imminent, the implication is that he has been abandoned, deservedly or undeservedly, by the gods. Thus, for example, in *Iliad* 22, when Hektor recognizes that he is about to die, he acknowledges that Zeus and Apollo have withdrawn their protection (22.296–303). Solon suggests, rather, some limitation on divine power, and, in a way, makes men more powerful than gods. His statement raises an essential question: in what does the city consist? What is it that the god is protecting? What is it that we are destroying?

If Athena cannot protect Athens from destruction from within, in what sense can Solon claim that she is the city's *episkopos*? When a god or goddess chooses to protect a city, this is usually because the people of that city are dear to the god. This seems explicit, for example, in *Iliad* 4.40–41 and 44–47 and implicit in Tyrtaeus 2.12–13. But Athenians are not behaving as a unified people. They are not united, for example, against an external enemy. They do not acknowledge an identity of interest among themselves. When Solon claims that the city risks destruction in spite of the fact that Athena is its *episkopos*, he begins to suggest that somehow the *polis* itself is a separate entity from its inhabitants. Athena's role as *episkopos* of the *polis* cannot prevent the people from destroying one another. But what *is* a city if not the people in it? Perhaps Solon's implicit answer is that the relations between the people, not merely the people themselves, are the city. One Homeric use of *episkopos* suggests this as a possible answer. At *Iliad* 22.255, Hektor refers to the gods as *marturoi* and *episkopoi harmoniaôn* 'witnesses and guardians of agreements'. One may speculate that Solon has this objective genitive in mind when he refers to Athena as the *episkopos* of Athens, that is, as the guardian and protector not of the people themselves but of a kind of tacit civic bond.[22]

Perhaps, then, Solon is thinking of a city not simply as a collection of individuals but as a compact or agreement between individuals. In any case, the use of the epithet *episkopos* encourages the identification of Athens' plight with Troy's. Nowhere else in extant epic or lyric poetry is a god called the *episkopos* of a city. In a fragmentary passage, Hesiod appears to refer to Hermes as *episkopos* of shepherds.[23] Simonides addresses Kleio as

---

22. Achilles' response to Hector's proposal emphasizes the difficulty of establishing such bonds:

"Εκτορ, μή μοι, ἄλαστε, συνημοσύνας ἀγόρευε·
ὡς οὐκ ἔστι λέουσι καὶ ἀνδράσιν ὅρκια πιστά,
οὐδὲ λύκοι τε καὶ ἄρνες ὁμόφρονα θυμὸν ἔχουσιν,
ἀλλὰ κακὰ φρονέουσι διαμπερὲς ἀλλήλοισιν,
ὣς οὐκ ἔστ' ἐμὲ καὶ σὲ φιλήμεναι, οὐδέ τι νῶϊν
ὅρκια ἔσσονται, πρίν γ' ἢ ἕτερόν γε πεσόντα
αἵματος ἆσαι ῎Αρηα, ταλαύρινον πολεμιστήν.
(*Iliad* 22.261–267)

Hektor, argue me no agreements. I cannot forgive you.
As there are no trustworthy oaths between men and lions,
nor wolves and lambs have spirit that can be brought to agreement
but forever these hold feelings of hate for each other,
so there can be no love between you and me, nor shall there be
oaths between us, but one or the other must fall before then
to glut with his blood Ares the god who fights under the shield's guard.

Solon focuses on this difficulty with particular poignancy in Poem 36. (See Chapter 3.)

23. Fr. 217.2–4:

[ ] σὺν ῾Ερμῆι Μαιάδος υἱεῖ
[ ] ἐπίσκοπος ἠδὲ νομήων
[ ] ι δώματα καλά

ἀγνᾶν ἐπίσκοπε χερνίβων
(Simonides 577(b)1)

episkopos of pure water vessels.

And Pindar refers to the Graces as

παλαιγόνων Μινυᾶν ἐπίσκοποι
(Pindar *Olympian* 14.4)

episkopoi of the Minyans born of old.

The latter reference is close to the identification of a divinity as *episkopos* of a particular city, but it is worth noting that Pindar does not call the Graces *episkopoi* of Orkhomenus.

The word also occurs five times in Homer, once in the *Odyssey*, and three more times in the *Iliad* in addition to its use in *Iliad* 22 mentioned above. In *Odyssey* 8, Euryalos taunts Odysseus, telling him that he does not look like an athlete but rather like a merchant, one who

φόρτου τε μνήμων καὶ ἐπίσκοπος ἦισιν ὁδαίων
κερδέων θ᾿ ἁρπαλέων·
(*Odyssey* 8.163–164)

careful of his cargo and grasping for profits,
goes carefully on his way.

In *Iliad* 10, the word seems to have the sense of 'spy' rather than 'guardian' or 'protector', as Menelaus asks Agamemnon

ἦ τιν᾿ ἑταίρων
ὀτρυνέεις Τρώεσσιν ἐπίσκοπον;
(*Iliad* 10.37–38)

Is it some one of your companions
you are stirring to go and spy on the Trojans?

And Odysseus, speculating about Dolon's intentions, comments

οὐκ οἶδ᾿ ἦ νήεσσιν ἐπίσκοπος ἡμετέρηισιν,
ἦ τινὰ συλήσων νεκύων κατατεθνηώτων
(*Iliad* 10.342–343)

I do not know whether he comes to spy on our vessels
or to strip some one of the perished corpses.

Aside from Solon's use of the word, the only other passage in extant epic or lyric poetry in which *episkopos* refers to the guardian of a city occurs in *Iliad* 24, where the word refers to Hektor as *episkopos* of Troy. Grieving over Hektor's corpse, Andromache foresees the destruction of

Troy. She herself has been left a widow, and her son will never reach manhood:

πρὶν γὰρ πόλις ἥδε κατ' ἄκρης
πέρσεται· ἦ γὰρ ὄλωλας ἐπίσκοπος, ὅς τέ μιν αὐτὴν
ῥύσκευ, ἔχες δ' ἀλόχους κεδνὰς καὶ νήπια τέκνα
(*Iliad* 24.728–730)

for before then head to heel this city
will be sacked, for you, its defender [*episkopos*] are gone, you who guarded
the city, and the grave wives and innocent children.

Solon's use of the term *episkopos* suggests that Athens is facing troubles not only comparable to the ones Troy faced but even worse. The loss of its human *episkopos* will lead to the destruction of Troy, whereas the presence of a divine *episkopos* will not serve to protect Athens; a human being might defend his city against external enemies, whereas even a goddess cannot defend hers against internal ones.

The phrase χεῖρας ὕπερθεν ἔχει 'holds her hands above it' (4. 4) also encourages the identification of Athens with Troy. It is a variation of an epic phrase which uses a form of ὑπερέχω and χεῖρα. This phrase occurs once in Hesiod, four times in the *Iliad*, and once in the *Odyssey* in connection with a god or goddess' protection of someone or some thing. It is used of Athena's protection of the oven used in baking pottery (Hesiod fr. 302.2), and the protection of individuals by Zeus or τις θεῶν 'some god' (*Iliad* 4.249, and 24.374; *Odyssey* 14.184). In *Iliad* 9, Achilles angrily advises the Greeks to go home, claiming that

οὐκέτι δήετε τέκμωρ
Ἰλίου αἰπεινῆς· μάλα γὰρ ἔθεν εὐρύοπα Ζεὺς
χεῖρα ἑὴν ὑπερέσχε
(*Iliad* 9.418–420)

No longer shall you find any term set
on the sheer city of Ilion, since Zeus of the wide brows has strongly
held his own hand over it.

The statement recurs at 9.685- 687 when Odysseus repeats Achilles' words to Agamemnon. But Achilles is mistaken. Troy does fall, and Zeus' protection does not prevent it. Strictly speaking, Zeus withdraws his protection. In the same way, Athena's protection cannot be counted upon to prevent the destruction of Athens.

While the opening lines of Poem 4 derive emotional power from the suggestion of parallels in epic poetry, the rest of the poem contains themes and images which find enlightening parallels in praise-blame poetry. For Solon, immoderate consumption poses the essential threat to Athens' stability. Both epic and praise-blame poetry recognize the social necessity of regulating individual consumption. But Solon's analysis of the problem is subtler than that of other poets, and the solutions he articulates reflect both this more accurate assessment of the problem and a novel vision of the social purposes of his poetry. Solon claims:

οὐ γὰρ ἐπίστανται κατέχειν κόρον οὐδὲ παρούσας
εὐφροσύνας κοσμεῖν δαιτὸς ἐν ἡσυχίηι
(Solon 4.9–10)

they do not know how to restrain their greed [*koros*], nor how to order their present festivities in the peacefulness of the banquet [*dais*].

In this passage, he is simultaneously acknowledging and criticizing other poets' depictions of the problem. In criticizing the Athenians for their inability to control their *koros* and to feast in an orderly manner, Solon is employing a traditional archaic analogy.

Potentially devastating, unrestrained, and improper consumption is a central theme in archaic poetry.[24] In the Homeric epics, improper consumption characterizes the threat to Troy and to Ithaca respectively. In *Iliad* 24, for example, Apollo, describing Achilles, says that

λέων δ' ὣς ἄγρια οἶδεν,
ὅς τ' ἐπεὶ ἄρ μεγάληι τε βίηι καὶ ἀγήνορι θυμῶι
εἴξας εἶσ' ἐπὶ μῆλα βροτῶν, ἵνα δαῖτα λάβηισιν·
(*Iliad* 24.41–43)

his purposes are fierce, like a lion
who, when he has given way to his own great strength and his haughty spirit, goes among the flocks of men, to devour them [*daita labêisin*].[25]

---

24. For a discussion of of the symbolic association between the orderly distribution of meat and the social order of the *polis*, see G. Nagy, *Greek Mythology and Poetics* (Ithaca and London, 1990), pp. 269–275.

25. In addition, Hekabe describes Achilles as *ômêstês* 'eating raw flesh, savage' (24.207). This adjective and the synonym *ômophagos* do not refer to human beings anywhere else in epic or lyric poetry. In Homer, both words occur only in the *Iliad* and only in reference to undomesticated animals (with the exception of Hekabe's statement). Birds (11.454), dogs (22.67), and fish (24.82) are *ômêstai*; lions (5.782; 7.256; 15.592), jackals (11.479), and wolves (16.157) are *ômophagoi*. In Hesiod, the monsters Echidna (*Theogony* 300) and Cerberus (*Theogony* 311), in Alcaeus Dionysos (129.9), and in

In the *Odyssey*, the suitors' shameless consumption of the absent Odysseus' livelihood threatens Odysseus' marriage and household and the stability of Ithaca.[26] In praise-blame poetry, greed is a traditional target for blame, and the expression of that blame typically uses the imagery of the greedy consumption of food, particularly of meat.[27]

The converse, orderly, controlled eating, serves to represent peace and political tranquility. In the *Iliad*, the accord between Achilles and Priam is sealed and life is resumed when the two feast together. The meal is emblematic of the restoration of order and the return to proper consumption. Achilles' companions prepare it εὖ κατὰ κόσμον 'according to good order' (*Iliad* 24.622), and the formulaic description of the meal contrasts markedly with Apollo's description of Achilles noted above:

> λέων δ' ὣς ἄγρια οἶδεν,
> ὅς τ' ἐπεὶ ἄρ μεγάληι τε βίηι καὶ ἀγήνορι θυμῶι
> εἴξας εἶσ' ἐπὶ μῆλα βροτῶν, ἵνα δαῖτα λάβηισιν ·
> (*Iliad* 24.41–43)

Bacchylides a lion (13.46) are all *ômêstês*. In the Homeric Hymns, *thêres* 'beasts' are *ômophagoi* (*Hymn to Aphrodite* 124), as are fish in Ibycus (321.4), and Centaurs in Theognis (542). Using an adjective appropriate to beasts or monsters, Hekabe thus powerfully emphasizes Achilles' inhuman and unnatural voraciousness and lack of restraint. Achilles' behavior only leads to more inhuman and unnatural voraciousness. Still speaking of Achilles, Hekabe maintains:

> τοῦ ἐγὼ μέσον ἧπαρ ἔχοιμι
> ἐσθέμεναι προσφῦσα· τότ' ἂν τιτὰ ἔργα γένοιτο
> παιδὸς ἐμοῦ,
> (*Iliad* 24.212–214)

> I wish I could set teeth
> in the middle of his liver and eat it. That would be vengeance
> for what he did to my son.

26. G. Nagy argues that the story of Iros and Odysseus in *Odyssey* 18 emphasizes that "one is not entitled to feel *phthonos* 'en· ʃ, jealousy' about things that are not one's own (18.16–18)." He explains that "the suitɔrs merit their death—and Iros, his beating—not for eating the food of Odysseus but for actually denying it to him" (*The Best of the Achaeans: Concepts of the Hero in Archaic Greek Poetry* [Baltimore, 1979], p. 230). But one suspects that this contention is a bit extreme. Surely in part the suitors and Iros must be culpable for actually consuming Odysseus' possessions.

27. Nagy, *The Best of the Achaeans*, pp. 223–229 and 287. Nagy explains that in the diction of praise poetry, gluttony is a prime characteristic of *phthonos*.

    his purposes are fierce, like a lion
who when he has given way to his own great strength and his haughty
spirit, goes among the flocks of men, to devour them [*daita labêisin*].

Achilles and Priam eat to repletion, and for this Homer has the
formulaic phrase

αὐτὰρ ἐπεὶ πόσιος καὶ ἐδητύος ἐξ ἔρον ἔντο
(*Iliad* 24.628)

but when they had put aside their desire for eating and drinking.

The analogy is evident in the poetry of Theognis as well. When
Theognis seeks divine protection for Megara, he prays:

Ζεὺς μὲν τῆσδε πόληος ὑπειρέχοι αἰθέρι ναίων
    αἰεὶ δεξιτερὴν χεῖρ᾽ ἐπ᾽ ἀπημοσύνηι
ἄλλοί τ᾽ ἀθάνατοι μάκαρες θεοί· αὐτὰρ Ἀπόλλων
    ὀρθώσαι γλῶσσαν καὶ νόον ἡμέτερον·
φόρμιγξ δ᾽ αὖ φθέγγοιθ᾽ ἱερὸν μέλος ἠδὲ καὶ αὐλός·
    ἡμεῖς δὲ σπονδὰς θεοῖσιν ἀρεσσάμενοι
πίνωμεν χαρίεντα μετ᾽ ἀλλήλοισι λέγοντες,
    μηδὲν τὸν Μήδων δειδιότες πόλεμον.
                    (Theognis 757–764)

May Zeus who dwells in the upper air always hold his right hand
    over this city to make it safe [*hupeirekhoi kheira*]
and the other blessed immortal gods; and may Apollo
    set straight our tongue and our mind;
and may the lyre and the pipe sound out a holy song;
    and let us pour a libation to the gods and drink,
speaking gracious things among one another,
    fearing not at all the war with the Medes.

Throughout the Theognidea, the descriptions of communal eating and
drinking parallel the descriptions of the *polis*, that is, the *polis* is
described in terms of a symposium, and the symposium is described in
terms of a *polis*.[28] In lines 757–764, Theognis' implication is that,
protected from external enemies, the citizens are able to enjoy the
pleasures of the symposium. Unlike Solon, Theognis does not define
the *polis* geographically. Rather, for him it is equivalent to a collection
of "right-thinking" people, that is, his political party. (So, too, for
Alcaeus.)

---

28. D. B. Levine, "Symposium and the Polis," in *Theognis of Megara*, edited by. T. J.
Figuiera and G. Nagy (Baltimore and London, 1985), pp. 176–196.

But if Theognis' language suggests that the symposium is a micro-cosm of the state,[29] Solon's usage reveals that the analogy is flawed. To be sure, both Solon 4.5–10 and Theognis employ the same terminology,[30] but Solon's criticism reveals the inadequacy of the aristocratic symposium as a paradigm for political organization. Both aim at harmony and proper order, but attaining this is more difficult in a political context.[31] The Athenians *already have* divine protection, and this does not enable them to enjoy communal harmony. Solon's criticism recognizes a fundamental flaw in the analogy: the appetite for food is not, in fact, parallel to the appetite for wealth. The former has an inherent physiological limit; the latter has none. This difference is reflected in Solon's use of the word *koros* 'satiety, surfeit'.

Solon appears to differ from Homer and Hesiod in acknowledging an inherent interrelationship between satiety and insatiability. Both epic poets use the noun *koros* and verb *korennumi* in the same way to

---

29. Levine, "Symposium and the Polis," p. 194. Levine also discusses the paradigmatic function of eating and drinking in Aristophanes' *Acharnians* and Plato's *Laws*. He maintains that Aristophanes "treats the peaceful *polis* as though it were a banquet," and that Plato, insisting on the close association between community and common eating and drinking, "makes the symposium a model for the establishment of an ideal community." The *Republic*, too, Levine notes, contains a "metaphorical description of an intemperate democracy (562d)" which Plutarch also repeats (*Greek Questions* [*Moralia* 295 c–d]). Both Plato and Plutarch "treat citizens who have had too much freedom in the *polis* as banqueters who have indulged excessively in wine. The intemperance of their political actions is compared to overindulgence at a banquet, much like the intemperate leaders of the *dêmos* in Solon 4.9–10" (Levine, pp. 194–196).

30. Levine explains that in lines 5–10, Solon "dramatizes the destruction of a city by a reference to the citizens' excesses and inability to behave themselves properly at a banquet." He notes that both Solon and Theognis use *kosmos* and its derivatives to describe the ordering of both a symposium and a *polis* or lack of *kosmos* for improper ordering of both a symposium and a *polis* ("Symposium and the Polis," pp.185–186). Adkins comments that in the *Iliad* the verb *kosmein* is used only of marshalling men and chariots. In the *Odyssey* it is used for the arranging of a meal for Nausikaa. In Solon's lines, "the full sense of 'order, rule, discipline' must be present" (*Poetic Craft in the Early Greek Elegists*, pp. 114–115). The Homeric usage may thus reveal the seeds of the analogy.

31. W. Donlan recognizes that the symposium is not in fact a satisfactory descriptive or prescriptive analogy for political organization, but he suggests that this is because of the rigid rules in effect at symposia and because discord in this context is of comparatively little consequence. He maintains that while the *polis* should be like a properly ordered symposium, it fails to be ("Πιστὸς φίλος ἑταῖρος," in *Theognis of Megara*, edited by. T. J. Figuiera and G. Nagy [Baltimore and London, 1985], pp. 237–238).

describe a condition of satisfaction or sufficiency and one in which the component of restraint or cessation is inherent. They reserve the adjective *akorêtos* for the sense of insatiability or incessant desire. Hesiod contrasts *koros* with οὐλομένη πενίη 'accursed poverty' when he claims that women are willing to share the former but not the latter with their men (*Theogony* 593). He uses *korennumi* in the positive sense of 'fill up, satisfy, have one's fill' when, for example, he describes the pleasures of sitting in the shade, drinking wine and κεκορημένον ἦτορ ἐδωδῆς 'my desire for food completely satisfied' (Hesiod *Works and Days* 593). Similarly, he uses the verb to refer to 'filling up' or 'being filled' with grain (*Works and Days* 33), wine (*Works and Days* 368) and a meal (fr. 274.2). It is not *koros* but the adjective *akorêtos* which has the sense of 'insatiate, unable to be satisfied'. It occurs only in the *Shield*, three times in the phrase ἀκόρητος ἀυτῆς 'insatiate of the war-cry' (*Shield* 346, 433, 459).

Homeric poetry, too, uses both verb and noun in a positive sense to describe the condition of satisfaction and satiety. In the *Iliad* the verb refers to satiety of eating in both human beings and animals (8.379, 13.831, 17.241, 11.562, 16.747, 19.167, 22.509), satiety of work (11.87), war (13.635), being confined (18.287), and weeping and lamentation (22.427). The noun occurs twice, in reference to sleep, love-making, music, and dancing (13.636–637) and to combat (19.221). The implication of all these passages is that when one has *koros* of a thing, one wants no more of it. The adjective *akorêtos* indicates the inability to achieve satisfaction, the inability to stop wanting more of something. People are described as *akorêtos* 'insatiable' *mothou* 'of battle-din' (7.117), *polemou* 'of war' (12.335), *autês* 'of the war-cry' (13.621), *makhês* 'of battle' (13.639; 20.2), and *apeilaôn* 'of threats' (14.479). One passage in particular illustrates the way all three of these words are used in the poem. Menelaos describes the Trojans,

> τῶν μένος αἰὲν ἀτάσθαλον, οὐδὲ δύνανται
> φυλόπιδος κορέσασθαι ὁμοιίου πτολέμοιο.
> πάντων μὲν κόρος ἐστί, καὶ ὕπνου καὶ φιλότητος
> μολπῆς τε γλυκερῆς καὶ ἀμύμονος ὀρχηθμοῖο,
> τῶν πέρ τις καὶ μᾶλλον ἐέλδεται ἐξ ἔρον εἶναι
> ἢ πολέμου· Τρῶες δὲ μάχης ἀκόρητοι ἔασιν.
> (*Iliad* 13.634–639)

whose fighting strength is a thing of blind fury, nor can they ever be glutted full [*korennumi*] of the close encounters of deadly warfare. Since there is satiety [*koros*] in all things, in sleep, and love-making,

in the loveliness of singing and the innocent dance. In all these
things a man will strive sooner to win satisfaction
than in war; but in this the Trojans cannot be glutted [*akorêtoi easin*].

Odysseus similarly associates *koros* with cessation—or at least respite—
from battle, for he insists:

αἶψά τε φυλόπιδος πέλεται κόρος ἀνθρώποισιν,
ἧς τε πλείστην μὲν καλάμην χθονὶ χαλκὸς ἔχευεν,
ἄμητος δ᾽ ὀλίγιστος, ἐπὴν κλίνηισι τάλαντα
Ζεύς, ὅς τ᾽ ἀνθρώπων ταμίης πολέμοιο τέτυκται.
(*Iliad* 19.221–224)

When there is battle men have suddenly their fill [*koros*] of it
when the bronze scatters on the ground the straw in most numbers
and the harvest is most thin, when Zeus has poised his balance,
Zeus, who is administrator to men in their fighting.

In the *Odyssey*, *koros* and *korennumi* are used in the same way, and the
suggestion that the condition of *koros* leads to cessation is even more
explicit. The adjective *akorêtos* does not appear, but the verb is used to
refer to satiety of grief (4.541, 10.499), food (10.411, 14.28, 14.456,
18.372), food and music (8.98), food and wine (14.46), and contests
(23.350). When one has reached the point of satiety, as described by
the verb, one stops the particular activity. All but two of these passages
proceed to mention the new activity which then follows. The same is
true of the noun, which only occurs once in the poem. Menelaos makes
clear the connection between *koros* and cessation when he explains:

πολλάκις ἐν μεγάροισι καθήμενος ἡμετέροισιν
ἄλλοτε μέν τε γόωι φρένα τέρπομαι, ἄλλοτε δ᾽ αὖτε
παύομαι· αἰψηρὸς δὲ κόρος κρυεροῖο γόοιο.
(*Odyssey* 4.101–103)

many a time when I am sitting here in our palace
I will indulge my heart in sorrow, and then another time
give over, for surfeit [*koros*] of gloomy lamentation comes quickly.

Here, *koros* of lamentation causes Menelaos to stop grieving. The two
instances in the *Homeric Hymns* seem consistent with Homeric and
Hesiodic usage. In the *Hymn to Demeter*, the verb seems to indicate
repletion in a favorable sense. The daughters of Celeus are described

ὥς τ᾽ ἢ ἔλαφοι ἢ πόρτιες ἤαρος ὥρηι
ἄλλοντ᾽ ἂν λειμῶνα κορεσσάμεναι φρένα φορβῆι,
(Hymn to Demeter 174–175)

as deer or young heifers in the time of spring
leap throughout a meadow, sated [*korennumi*] in their hearts with
    pasture.

In the hymn to Aphrodite, the adjective *akorêtoi* is used of *pardalies*
'leopards' to convey the sense of 'instatiate' (*Hymns* 5.71).
But Solon's usage seems semantically different. He does appear to
use the verb in the same sense as Homer and Hesiod in maintaining:

οἳ γὰρ νῦν ἡμέων πλεῖστον ἔχουσι βίον,
διπλάσιον σπεύδουσι· τίς ἂν κορέσειεν ἅπαντας;
                              (Solon 13.72–73)

   for those of us who now have the most property
   strive with double zeal; who could satisfy [*korennumi*] all?

But the noun, rather than having the positive, favorable connotation of
satiety or satisfaction, with cessation of the pursuit as an inherent
component, takes on, in Solon's usage, the negative, dangerous sense
of insatiability, excessiveness, incessant greed for more. Solon
admonishes the wealthy citizens:

ὑμεῖς δ᾽ ἡσυχάσαντες ἐνὶ φρεσὶ καρτερὸν ἦτορ,
οἳ πολλῶν ἀγαθῶν ἐς κόρον [ἠ]λάσατε,
ἐν μετρίοισι τίθεσθε μέγαν νόον· οὔτε γὰρ ἡμεῖς
πεισόμεθ᾽, οὔθ᾽ ὑμῖν ἄρτια τα[ῦ]τ᾽ ἔσεται.
                              (Solon 4c.1–4)

   But you who have pushed to a surfeit [*koros*] of good things,
      quieting the strong heart in your breast,
   place your great mind in order; for we will not
      be persuaded, nor will these things be suitable for you.

The context suggests that *koros* is a dangerous thing. This implication is
strengthened by the claim that

τίκτει γὰρ κόρος ὕβριν, ὅταν πολὺς ὄλβος ἔπηται
ἀνθρώποις ὁπόσοις μὴ νόος ἄρτιος ᾖι.
                              (Solon 6.3–4)

   Satiety [*koros*] breeds reckless violence [*hubris*], whenever much
      prosperity comes
   to men whose mind is not suitable.

This claim contrasts markedly with Homeric usage, in which not only
does *koros* never produce *hubris*: it is the *lack* of *koros* which is associated
with *hubris*. Menelaos refers to

ὑβριστῇισι,
Τρωσίν, τῶν μένος αἰὲν ἀτάσθαλον, οὐδὲ δύνανται
φυλόπιδος κορέσασθαι ὁμοιίου πτολέμοιο.
(*Iliad* 13.633–635)

these outrageous people [*hubristai*], these Trojans
whose fighting strength is a thing of blind fury, nor can they ever
be glutted full [*korennumi*] of the close encounters of deadly warfare.

The alleged *hubris* of the Trojans is, in this statement, coincident with
their inability to be sated with war, their inability to have *koros*—which
would, presumably, cause them to stop fighting. If *koros,* in Solon's view,
produces *hubris,* it must be checked. The difficulty is that οὐ γὰρ
ἐπίστανται κατέχειν κόρον 'they do not know how to restrain their *koros*'
(Solon 4.9). Solon identifies *Eunomiê* 'Good Order' as the remedy for
hubris because it stops *koros* (Solon 4.34). Thus, while for Homer and
Hesiod the component of restraint is inherent in the condition of *koros*
itself, for Solon the condition is one which *requires* restraint if cessation
is to occur.

In lyric poetry, *koros* often retains its Homeric and Hesiodic sense of
satiety leading inevitably to cessation of the activity in question. A few
passages are too fragmentary to be of use, but others are more helpful.
Tyrtaeus admonishes the Spartans for their unwillingness to continue
fighting or fleeing the enemy, asserting

ὦ νέοι, ἀμφοτέρων δ' ἐς κόρον ἠλάσατε.
(Tyrtaeus 11.10)

Young men, you have reached a surfeit [*koros*] of both.

The Spartans have *koros* of both flight and pursuit, that is, they want no
more of it. Alcman seems to use *koros* in the the sense of 'sufficiency' or
'abundance' in the *Partheneion*:

οὔτε γάρ τι πορφύρας
τόσσος κόρος ὥστ' ἀμύναι.
(Alcman 1.64–65)

nor is their any surfeit [*koros*] of purple dye
sufficient to defend us.

In another lyric fragment the phrase τὰν ἀκόρεστον αὐάταν 'insatiate
ruinous folly' uses the adjective *akorestos* for the sense of 'insatiate'.[32]

---

32. *Fragmenta adespota* 973 in D. L. Page *Poetae melici Graeci* (Oxford, 1962). Another
fragment refers to *koros* as satiety of food and drink followed immediately by the
conclusion of the meal (*Melici minores* 836(b)39) in *Poetae melici Graeci.*

But if the pursuit of *koros* has a terminus for Homer and not for Solon, this may largely reflect the fact that epic poetry is praise poetry of a certain type and gives relatively little emphasis to faults which stem from heroic excess.[33] In the praise poetry of Pindar, too, *koros* retains its Homeric sense of a condition with a built-in limit. But although Pindar's usage is semantically close to that found in epic poetry, his perspective is different than Homer's. Whereas Homer describes the condition from the perspective of the consumer, Pindar examines it from the viewpoint of the producer. For both poets, *koros* contains its own inherent limit, but for Pindar, as a performer, satiety in his audience is a bad thing since it will lead them to want no more of his song. Pindar retains the Homeric notion that *koros* leads to cessation (at least temporarily):

> ἀλλὰ γὰρ ἀνάπαυ-
> σις ἐν παντὶ γλυκεῖα ἔργωι· κόρον δ' ἔχει
> καὶ μέλι καὶ τὰ τέρπν' ἄνθε' Ἀφροδίσια.
> (*Nemean* 7.52–53)

But in every matter
　　　　　　intermission is sweet:
　　even honey
　　and the flowers of Aphrodite
　　bring satiety.

He also uses the absence of *koros*, that is, *akoros* for the sense of 'insatiable' or 'ceaseless' in the statement

> εἰρεσία δ' ὑπεχώρη-
> σεν ταχειᾶν ἐκ παλαμᾶν ἄκορος.
> (*Pythian* 4.202)

Under their swift hands then the oar blades
　　dipped insatiably.

But in contrast to Homer, Pindar takes a dim view of *koros*. He refers to it as *aianês* 'wearisome' (*Pythian* 1.82, and *Isthmian* 3/4.2), and *plagios* 'treacherous' (*Nemean* 1.64–65), maintains that it is *barus* 'burdensome' to encounter (*Nemean* 10.19–20), and appears to contrast it with *aretê* 'excellence' (Fragment 169a.15). Pindar's condemnation derives from his position as a peformer: he denounces *koros* not joined with *dikê*

---

33. One notable recipient of blame is the figure of Thersites in the *Iliad*. (See Nagy, *The Best of the Achaeans*, pp. 253ff.)

'justice' for attacking *ainos* 'praise' (*Olympian* 2.95),[34] and suggests that it might cause irritation if a singer goes on too long, explaining:

εἰμὶ δ᾽ ἄσχολος ἀναθέμεν
πᾶσαν μακραγορίαν
λύραι τε καὶ φθέγματι μαλθακῶι,
μὴ κόρος ἐλθὼν κνίσηι.

(*Pythian* 8.29–32)

> But I am without leisure
>   to set the whole story down
>   in melody and lyrics.
> Tedium [*koros*] would surely come
>   and chafe my audience.

One can compare the Homeric passage cited above in which *koros* of song is one of several natural and, by implication, desirable limits. Menelaos describes the Trojans,

τῶν μένος αἰὲν ἀτάσθαλον, οὐδὲ δύνανται
φυλόπιδος κορέσασθαι ὁμοιίου πτολέμοιο.
πάντων μὲν κόρος ἐστί, καὶ ὕπνου καὶ φιλότητος
μολπῆς τε γλυκερῆς καὶ ἀμύμονος ὀρχηθμοῖο,
τῶν πέρ τις καὶ μᾶλλον ἐέλδεται ἐξ ἔρον εἶναι
ἢ πολέμου· Τρῶες δὲ μάχης ἀκόρητοι ἔασιν.

(*Iliad* 13.634–639)

> whose fighting strength is a thing of blind fury, nor can they ever
> be glutted full [*korennumi*] of the close encounters of deadly warfare.
> Since there is satiety [*koros*] in all things, in sleep, and love-making,
> in the loveliness of singing and the innocent dance. In all these
> things a man will strive sooner to win satisfaction
> than in war; but in this the Trojans cannot be glutted [*akorētoi easin*].

Only Pindar's claim that *koros* led Zeus to curse Tantalus (*Olympian* 1.55–56) seems to require an understanding of the word that is similar to Solon's. In this passage, *koros* preceeds *atê*. Although *hubris* is not mentioned, clearly that was Tantalus' sin. His desire to share the gift of immortality with others results in the sort of disaster that comes not from 'fulness' but from 'over-fulness'. It may not, perhaps, be surprising that this Solonian interpretation occurs in a modernizing of the myth by Pindar. Like Solon, too, Pindar proclaims the necessity of restraining *koros*:

---

34. Regarding *ainos* see also Chapter 1, p. 20 and note 27.

εἴ τις ἀνδρῶν εὐτυχήσαις ἢ σὺν εὐδόξοις ἀέθλοις
ἢ σθένει πλούτου κατέχει φρασὶν αἰανῆ κόρον,
ἄξιος εὐλογίαις ἀστῶν μεμίχθαι.
                                        (*Isthmian* 3/4.1–3)

If a man, fortunate in the enjoyment
    of glorious prizes or the might of wealth,
        keeps his thoughts above restless ambition [*koros*],
    then he deserves
the praise of his fellow citizens.[35]

In this passage, *koros* could be translated as 'excess', and so, too in
Olympian 13.10 (ὕβρις κόρου ματέρα '*hubris*, mother of *koros*'), but the
reversal of Solon's genealogy in the latter passage suggests that Pindar
is thinking of the way a singer's arrogance and insensitivity might
cause his audience to be sated with him. And the *koros* that is checked
in *Isthmian* 3/4.1–3 may be the same satiety rather than the victor's
own excess. However the passages are interpreted, *koros* continues to
be, by and large, the same thing for Pindar as for Homer. It is
something that contains its own inherent limit, and, as such, is from
Pindar's perspective (as the supplier rather than the consumer)
undesirable.

The view that Pindar's genealogy was the prevalent formulation and
Solon's something of an unaccepted variant is supported by additional
passages from Herodotus and Sophocles. Herodotus cites an oracle
which has *koros* as the child of *hubris* (Herodotus 8.77). The reference is
to the *koros* and *hubris* of the Persians who have every expectation of
destroying the Greeks at Salamis, but, according to the oracle, *Dikê*
'Justice' will grant victory to the Greeks. The story of Xerxes (and of
Croesus, too, for that matter) suggests the Solonian idea that *hubris* has
its origin in insatiability and excess. That Herodotus, nevertheless,
makes *hubris*, and not *koros*, the engendering agent, may reflect the
continuing influence of a pre-Solonian formula. Sophocles, too, seems
to accept the un-Solonic view when the Chorus, chilled by Oedipus'
relentlessness and Jocasta's rejection of the validity of prophecies,
laments:

---

35. Compare Solon 4.9: οὐ γὰρ ἐπίστανται κατέχειν κόρον 'they do not know how to
restrain their *koros*'.

ὕβρις φυτεύει τύραννον
(Oedipus Tyrannus 873)

hubris breeds the absolute ruler.[36]

Vegetal imagery is traditional in the representation of these concepts,[37] and Solon employs it, too, when he maintains that *Eunomié*

αὐαίνει δ' ἄτης ἄνθεα φυόμενα
(Solon 4. 35)

withers the blooming flowers of ruinous folly [*atê*].[38]

But Solon's identification of *koros* as the engendering agent (Solon 6.3) may be a reversal of the traditional imagery.[39] His formulation is more specific: the root of the problem is not *hubris* in general but, specifically, greed, greed without any inherent limit which therefore needs to be controlled from outside.

The earliest trace of an attitude toward greed and insatiability roughly comparable to Solon's occurs in Theognis. Like Pindar and Solon, he criticizes *koros*, but his criticism begins to distinguish between *koros* in general and *koros* of wealth in particular. Like other poets, Theognis uses the verb in the sense of 'to satisfy' (for example, 1.229, 2.1249, 2.1269), but maintains, with Solon, that *koros* can produce *hubris* (1.152). He claims, moreover, that *koros* is highly destructive (1.693), more destructive than *limos* 'hunger' (1.605), in fact, and refers to it as *leugaleos* 'baneful' (1.1174) and the worst evil for mortals (1.1175). But Theognis indicates that *koros* in general is not the problem: rather it is

---

36. This reading has been disputed, but Blaydes' alternative, ὕβριν φυτεύει τυραννίς, accepted by R. D. Dawe (*Sophoclis tragoediae* [Leipzig, 1975–1979]), for example, has not remained popular. H. Lloyd-Jones and N. G. Wilson (*Sophoclea: Studies in the Text of Sophocles* [Oxford, 1990]), among others, accept the manuscript reading.

37. A. Michelini. "'Ύβρις and plants," *Harvard Studies in Classical Philology* 82 (1978), pp. 35–44.

38. Nagy explains that "Greek botanical lore recognizes that plants are capable of indefinite expansion, and thus the growth of plants is for the Greeks appropriate for visualizing *hubris*: like some exuberant plant, *hubris* keeps advancing until it is checked by an external force" ("Theognis and Megara: A Poet's Vision of his City," in *Theognis of Megara*, edited by T. J. Figuiera and G. Nagy [Baltimore and London, 1985], p. 61).

39. B. L. Gildersleeve maintains that such a reversal of the genealogy is irrelevant since "according to Greek custom, grandmother and granddaughter often bore the same name. It is a mere matter of *hubris—koros—hubris*" (*Pindar: The Olympian and Pythian Odes* [New York, 1979], pp. 229–230), but this seems to trivialize the issue.

the pursuit of the unattainable *koros* of wealth, specifically, which is so destructive. This is because:

πλὴν πλούτου παντὸς χρήματός ἐστι κόρος.
(Theognis 596)

There is *koros* of every thing except wealth.

This corroborates the claim attributed both to him and to Solon that

οἳ γὰρ νῦν ἡμῶν πλεῖστον ἔχουσι βίον,
διπλάσιον σπεύδουσι. τίς ἂν κορέσειεν ἅπαντας;
(Theognis 228–229 = Solon 13.72–73)

for those of us who now have the most property, strive with double zeal. Who would satisfy all?

Because Theognis begins to distinguish between *koros* in general and *koros* of wealth in particular, his use of the verb in connection with wealth begins to take on the sense of 'to glut' or 'to oversatisfy'. Otherwise, if there can be no *koros* of wealth (596), he could not assert that someone ὑβρίζηι πλούτωι κεκορημένος 'commits outrage, having been glutted with wealth' (751). The phrase indicates that the verb can be used negatively as leading to *hubris*. In another passage, however, Theognis seems to adhere to the Homeric usage in suggesting that the problem is that over-satisfaction is not perceptible to the individual:

οὔτε γὰρ ἂν πλούτου θυμὸν ὑπερκορέσαις·
(Theognis 1158)

for one cannot oversatisfy [*huperkorennumi*] the heart with wealth.

The compound form of the verb suggests that *koros* itself is good, but excessive *koros* (*huper-*) is bad. The implication of these examples is not simply that, where wealth is concerned, one cannot get enough, but, rather, that one cannot get enough without getting too much.

The close verbal parallels between Theognis and Solon suggest that at least one of the authors of the Theognidean corpus was familiar with Solon's poetry. Alternatively, it is possible that at a later date than Solon, other poets were thinking along the same lines as he. Since, however, nothing in the Theognidean corpus is demonstrably earlier than Solon, the former possibility seems not unlikely. In any case, Theognis' statements indicate that Solon is not unique in his concern about the delicate relationship between satiety and insatiability. But Solon recognizes the threat that this issue poses to the community. For Homer, there is no delicate balance between satiety and insatiability;

when one reaches satiety, one stops. But Solon suggests that the condition of satiety as perceived by the individual may only become apparent once the point has been reached—and passed. Moreover, in the view of others, an individual may appear to have reached satiety when the individual himself still feels unsatisfied. Pindar, recognizes this difference in perspective in the situation of the performer who may feel that he has not said enough when others think that he has. But Solon is thinking more of the acquisitive individual whose greed for wealth remains unsatisfied even though in the view of others he may seem to possess more than enough. For peaceful coexistence within a community, this disparity is all-important. In Solon's view, the collective (if not the individual's own good sense) must be able to determine—and control—when an individual has enough. If this is left to the individual, perception of the point of satiety may never occur.[40] In fact, the more one has, the more one wants. This is particularly true where the pursuit of wealth is concerned. Other activities—eating, sleeping, working, fighting—seem to have built-in physiological limits. One may not stop until one has passed the point of satiety and become over-sated, but one must, eventually, stop. This is not the case with wealth. There is no inherent physiological limit to its acquisition (πλούτου δ' οὐδὲν τέρμα πεφασμένον ἀνδράσι κεῖται 'of wealth no limit lies visible for men' [Solon 13.71]),[41] and for the community this difference can

---

40. Solon's focus on *koros* contrasts with Hesiod's emphasis on *limos* 'hunger'. Solmsen notes that Hesiod mentions hunger more frequently than any other evil (*Hesiod and Aeschylus*, p. 89). Hesiod, too, is concerned with the problem of sufficiency, but he views it from the perspective of insufficiency rather than that of over-sufficiency (e.g. *Works and Days* 366–367). *Koros* might be seen as the antithesis of *limos*—although *koros*, as Solon understands it, like *limos*, also leads to desire for more. But unlike *koros*, *limos* appears to be a purely subjective emotion. One has hunger when one feels hunger. There is not the same possibility for self-deception; it is impossible for someone to have hunger and not know it. In contrast, Solon argues that the rich have satiety and do not know it.

41. One thinks, too, of Solon's comment in Poem 16:

γνωμοσύνης δ' ἀφανὲς χαλεπώτατόν ἐστι νοῆσαι
μέτρον, ὃ δὴ πάντων πείρατα μοῦνον ἔχει.

It is very difficult to perceive the unseen measure of good judgement
which alone holds the ends of all things.

Solmsen interprets this as a reference to the difficulty of finding where to draw the line between the rights of one group and the next (*Hesiod and Aeschylus*, pp. 122–123). But very possibly the statement also relates to the internal counterpart of this problem: the individual himself cannot even determine when he has had enough or too much.

be devastating. When Solon claims that Εὐνομίη...παύει κόρον *'Eunomiê* stops *koros'* (4.32–34), he is asserting the need for communal, rather than individual, regulation of individual consumption and acquisition. And yet, who comprises that community? In recognizing that the process of eating is not actually parallel to the process of acquiring wealth, Solon identifies a central flaw in the symposium paradigm as a model for, and means of encouraging, social order. But there is another, perhaps greater, flaw. In the poetry of Theognis, for example, the symposium is the ideal place of education and a microcosm of the larger community, in that it is the place to associate exclusively with *agathoi* 'noble or good men' and avoid *kakoi* 'low-born or bad men'.[42] In contrast, Solon recognizes that the paradigm fails to account for the fact that, in the *polis*, members of all levels of society will necessarily be present, not only the aristocrats. His criticism of ἡγεμόνες δήμου 'the leaders of the people' for their inability to control their *koros* or to regulate properly the manner of their feasting is, therefore, both a criticism of the failure of aristocratic political organization to achieve social harmony in the *polis* and a criticism of the exclusivity of symposiastic praise-blame poetry.

As already noted, for the symposiastic praise-blame poet, the purposes of poetic *sophiê* are potentially exclusive.[43] Praise is inherently aristocratic, intended to be acceptable to the few.[44] As specified in the

---

42. Levine, "Symposium and the Polis," pp. 179–180.

43. See Chapter 1, pp. 20–21.

44. M. Detienne, *Les maîtres de vérité dans la Grèce archaïque* (Paris, 1981), p. 21, quoting Pindar *Pythian* 3.112–115:

Νέστορα καὶ Λύκιον Σαρπηδόν᾽, ἀνθρώπων φάτις,
.ἐξ ἐπέων κελαδεννῶν, τέκτονες οἷα σοφοὶ
ἅρμοσαν, γιγνώσκομεν. ἁ δ᾽ ἀρετὰ κλειναῖς ἀοιδαῖς
χρονία τελέθει. παύροις δὲ πράξασθ᾽ εὐμαρές.

We know of Nestor and Lykian Sarpedon
from resonant words, such as skilled craftsmen of songs
have welded together.
It is radiant poetry
that makes virtue long-lived,
but for few is the making easy.

Similarly, A. P. Burnett, *The Art of Bacchylides* (Cambridge, Mass., 1985), p. 41.

poetry of Pindar and Bacchylides, praise-blame poetry has as its social function praise of the noble (*kalôn epainos*) and blame of the base (*aiskhrôn psogos*).[45] But in the ideology of praise poetry, only the *sunetoi* 'intelligent men' can deliver or understand the message of praise, that is, praise poetry is correctly interpreted only by the man who is *phronôn* 'wise'. Epic poetry, too, expresses this sentiment.[46] The purpose of this exclusivity is to strengthen the bonds of *philotês* 'friendship' within a select portion of the community.[47] Even if some critics object that this argument may be too narrowly based on etymology, the point remains that occasional poetry, unlike epic, often required the exercise of a certain tact or etiquette depending on the composition of the audience. Thus Alcaeus, for example, in his "ship of state" image, (Alcaeus 326), avoids naming specific names. Such veiled language reflects the potentially exclusive nature of occasional poetry, depending upon the presence or absence in the audience of the objects of praise or blame.

Solon perceives, however, that an elitist, exclusionary conception of society is unable to unify the *polis* precisely because it requires the exclusion of a large part of the population. When he does use veiled language, he does so not with a specific audience in mind but with an understanding of the difficulty of the material and the subtlety of the ideas he wishes to express. If, as Nagy maintains, "the *euphrosunê* 'festivity' of the audience is an emblem of social cohesion," and, further, if *euphrosunê* is, in fact, a "programmatic word traditionally used in *ainos* to designate the occasion of the *ainos*,"[48] Solon's comment at 4.9–10 acquires some specificity:

---

45. Nagy, *The Best of the Achaeans*, pp. 222–223.

46. Nagy, *The Best of the Achaeans*, p. 240; "Iambos: Typologies of Invective and Praise," *Arethusa* 9 (1976), p. 197. This "built-in ideology of exclusiveness" is a feature of *ainos* as the programmatic word for designating both praise poetry specifically and more generally "an allusive tale containing an ulterior purpose" (*The Best of the Achaeans*, pp. 237–239). For more on *ainos* see also Chapter 1, p. 20.

47. Nagy, "Iambos: Typologies of Invective and Praise," pp. 197–199; *The Best of the Achaeans*, pp. 240–241; "Theognis and Megara: A Poet's Vision of his City," pp. 24–27; similarly (regarding Theognis), L. Edmunds, "The Genre of Theognidean Poetry," in *Theognis of Megara*, edited by. T. J. Figuiera and G. Nagy (Baltimore and London, 1985), pp. 101–102; V. Cobb-Stevens, "Opposites, reversals, and Ambiguities: The Unsettled World of Theognis," in *Theognis of Megara*, p. 173.

48. Nagy citing *Odyssey* 9.3–11 (*The Best of the Achaeans*, p. 92). See also his p. 236 and n. 5, and "Theognis and Megara: A Poet's Vision of his City," p. 27, n. 2.

οὐ γὰρ ἐπίστανται κατέχειν κόρον οὐδὲ παρούσας
εὐφροσύνας κοσμεῖν δαιτὸς ἐν ἡσυχίηι
(Solon 4.9–10)

they do not know how to restrain their greed [*koros*], nor
how to order [*kosmein*] their present festivities [*euphrosunai*] in the
peacefulness of the banquet [*dais*].

The inability to restrain *koros* parallels the inability to order or regulate (*kosmein*) the *euphrosunai* of the *dais*. The linking of excessive, unrestrained consumption to lack of *euphrosunê* seems a direct criticism of partisan poetry for its failure to achieve a proper—that is, socially cohesive—form of *euphrosunê*.

Solon's poetry is, therefore, distinguished by the recognition that it must be, potentially at least, acceptable to everyone, not just a select few. As noted in Chapter 1, this helps to account for the fact that he does not ask the Muses to give him his subject matter in Poem 13. It also may explain the absence of *ainoi* in the form of animal fables in his poetry (although, as will be discussed in Chapter 3, he does draw upon the conventional connotations of animal imagery). In addition, many of his comments seem overtly designed to *include* rather than *exclude* his listeners.

In rejecting the use of stratagems which might make his verses opaque for a significant segment of his audience, Solon employs a number of counter-strategies. One approach is the careful specification of the meanings of the words he employs. We have seen this strategy at work in Chapter 1 with regard to his use of *mnêmosunê*, *olbos*, and *doxa* in Poem 13. Specifying meaning in this way seems to be the opposite of employing a riddling language, since it seeks to ensure that everyone understands the same things by the same words. Another strategy will be examined in Chapter 3: Solon's use of the socially and poetically necessary scapegoat, which he adapts to suit his own purposes. But perhaps the most striking difference between Solon and other poets is his effort to minimize distinctions between *kakoi* 'low-born or bad men' and *agathoi* 'noble or good men' in his poetry.

The contrast betweeen Solon and Theognis on this point is instructive, particularly if, as seems probable, the figure of Theognis is not a single individual poet.[49] Theognis' poetry is directed toward the

---

49. T. J. Figueira and G. Nagy (in their introduction to *Theognis of Megara*, edited by T. J. Figuiera and G. Nagy [Baltimore and London, 1985], p. 2) argue that Theognis "represents a cumulative synthesis of Megarian poetic tradition."

agathoi to the exclusion of the *kakoi* and intended to be understandable to the *sophoi* 'wise men'.[50] This orientation can be seen, for example, in his claim that:

τίκτει τοι κόρος ὕβριν, ὅταν κακῶι ὄλβος ἕπηται
ἀνθρώπωι καὶ ὅτωι μὴ νόος ἄρτιος ἦι.
(Theognis 153–154)

Satiety [*koros*] breeds wanton violence [*hubris*], whenever much prosperity [*olbos*] comes
to a bad [*kakos*] man whose mind is not suitable [*artios*].

This statement is by no means the same as Solon's assertion that:

τίκτει γὰρ κόρος ὕβριν, ὅταν πολὺς ὄλβος ἕπηται
ἀνθρώποις ὁπόσοις μὴ νόος ἄρτιος ἦι.
(Solon 6.3–4)

Satiety [*koros*] breeds wanton violence [*hubris*], whenever much prosperity [*olbos*] comes
to men whose mind is not suitable [*artios*].[51]

Theognis' introduction of *kakôs* adds a "natural" or ethical condemnation of the ill-fated possessor of *olbos* ("natural" if *kakos* = 'low-born'; ethical if *kakos* = 'coward, evil man'). Solon's lines maintain that *hubris* results if *olbos* is present and a certain intellectual development is lacking. Unlike Theognis, he accepts that a person's mind could be *not artios* regardless of whether this person is *kakos* or *agathos*, and leaves open the possibility that this same person's mind could become *artios*. Theognis accepts neither the possibility that the mind of an *agathos* could be not *artios* nor that the mind of a *kakos* could become *artios*. Solon does not veer away from either possibility. If

---

50. Nagy, "Theognis and Megara: A Poet's Vision of his City," pp. 24–25; Cobb-Stevens, "Opposites, reversals, and Ambiguities: The Unsettled World of Theognis," p. 166. See also Edmunds, "The Genre of Theognidean Poetry," pp. 105–106 regarding Theognis 681.

51. Nagy notes that such discrepancies may be meaningful, and not merely textual variations, arguing that "such patterns of phraseological convergence and divergence in parallel passages ascribed to different poets, or even textual variants of the same poem, are a reflex of the workings of oral poetry." He maintains that such differences "reflect for the most part not editorial deterioration in one direction or another, but formulaic versatility corresponding to different compositional needs" ("Theognis and Megara: A Poet's Vision of his City," pp. 46–51). And see also Chapter 1, note 72 above regarding the view of Wilamowitz.

olbos here is equivalent to material wealth, Theognis' claim that καὶ γάρ τοι πλοῦτον μὲν ἔχειν ἀγαθοῖσιν ἔοικεν,/ ἡ πενίη δὲ κακῶι σύμφορος ἀνδρὶ φέρειν 'it is fitting for the *agathoi* to have wealth, and poverty is suitable for the *kakoi* to endure' (Theognis 525–526) may highlight the difference between him and Solon on this point. For Solon the issue is purely one of intellectual understanding or lack of it. Unlike Theognis, he recognizes that wealth can be dangerous for everyone. It may well be that the Theognidean idea is the earlier, and that Solon is applying to all society norms which aristocrats once prescribed for the *kakoi*.

Elsewhere, too, Solon seems to minimize differences between *kakoi* and *agathoi*. Distinction between them is notably absent in Poem 27, discussed in Chapter 1, which contains no suggestion that the potential for intellectual development is in any way dependent upon one's status as *agathos* or *kakos*. Similarly, in Poem 13, Solon claims:

θνητοὶ δ' ὧδε νοέομεν ὁμῶς ἀγαθός τε κακός τε
(Solon 13.33)

this is the way we mortals think, both *agathos* and *kakos* alike.

One suspects that this statement would have been something of a shock to any audience conditioned to the elitism and exclusivity of the praise-blame genre, that is, to a poetry traditionally asserting rigid distinctions between *kakoi* and *agathoi*.[52]

To be sure, the categories of *kakoi* and *agathoi* were undoubtedly in flux throughout this period. Whereas the terms originally connoted high or low birth, Theognis uses them on occasion as ethical categories ('noble' or 'base') in reference to intrinsic worth rather than birth.[53] If this linguistic shift represents an ongoing struggle for political power,[54]

---

52. Bacchylides, too, maintains that hope deceives high and low alike (3.74; 9.18; cf. 13.157). Burnett comments that *gnômai* such as this, being true for all mankind, have a leveling function and serve to make the praise song less exclusive (Burnett, *The Art of Bacchylides*, pp. 50–51). But whereas Pindar and Bacchylides use this to avoid "the envy of the excluded" (see Burnett, pp. 48ff.), Solon seems to have a more constructive social purpose, namely, political unity.

53. Nagy, "Theognis and Megara: A Poet's Vision of his City," p. 54.

54. Cobb-Stevens argues that "the reversal in position of the *kakoi* and *agathoi*" is "the very substance of the turmoil of a *polis*, that those who were *agathoi* by birth become morally or economically *kakoi*, and that those who were *kakoi* by birth come into power above those who were by birth (and sometimes morally) *agathoi*" ("Opposites, reversals, and Ambiguities: The Unsettled World of Theognis," pp. 159–165).

Solon seems less concerned with this issue than with a pragmatic solution. Accordingly, he insists that:

θεσμοὺς δ᾽ ὁμοίως τῶι κακῶι τε κἀγαθῶι
εὐθεῖαν εἰς ἕκαστον ἁρμόσας δίκην
ἔγραψα.
(Solon 36.18–20)

I wrote laws for the base and the noble alike,
awarding each man his just due.

His purpose is not to negate the categories, nor even to reevaluate them. He did not intend, for example, to equalize the distribution of property, since it did not please him:

πιεί[ρ]ης χθονὸς
πατρίδος κακοῖσιν ἐσθλοὺς ἰσομοιρίην ἔχειν.
(Solon 34.8–9)

[it is not desirable that] the base have an equal
share of the rich fatherland with the noble.

Distinguishing between equality of possessions and equality of political rights, Solon acknowledges that failure to do so, failure to differentiate between economic equality and political equality, is an impediment to political unity.

As a result, the ambiguities in Solon's verses serve a different purpose than the ambiguities in the verses of Theognis. Theognis uses ambiguity to convey an aristocratic message. His ultimate hope is the resumption of political power by the *agathoi*. To this end, his poetry is directed toward them and is entirely preoccupied with deceiving and avoiding being deceived.[55]

In contrast, the ambiguities in Solon's poetry do not distinguish between members of his audience; they are equally ambiguous to all. Poem 4 provides numerous examples. As noted above, *astoi* 'citizens' (6), *khrêmasi peithomenoi* 'persuaded by money' (6), *hêgemonôn* 'leaders' (7), *êluthe* 'comes' (18), *doulosunên* slavery', and *hê* 'which' (19) are all

---

55. Levine, "Symposium and the Polis," p. 186. Cobb-Stevens explains that, for Theognis, "persuasion must take the form of wily words (*haimulioi logoi* [704]), words that can make deceitful things be like genuine (713). Yet it must be a persuasiveness at all times opposed to the ploys of the many, whose deceptions need not be even remotely like the truth" ("Opposites, reversals, and Ambiguities: The Unsettled World of Theognis," pp. 172–175).

ambiguous in their reference.[56] Similarly, in lines 21–23, the precise identity of 'friends' and 'enemies' is impossible to ascertain, and *en dêmôi* (23) might mean 'among the common people' or 'in the land'. No doubt, such ambiguity is excellent rhetoric in a political speech designed to reach and persuade two different groups.[57]

As a result, far from employing deception (*haimulioi logoi* 'wily words' in Theognis), Solon criticizes the *dêmos* 'the people'[58] for being taken in by the words of a *haimulos* 'wily' man:

εἰ δὲ πεπόνθατε λυγρὰ δι' ὑμετέρην κακότητα,
μὴ θεοῖσιν τούτων μοῖραν ἐπαμφέρετε·
αὐτοὶ γὰρ τούτους ηὐξήσατε ῥύματα δόντες,
καὶ διὰ ταῦτα κακὴν ἔσχετε δουλοσύνην.
ὑμέων δ' εἷς μὲν ἕκαστος ἀλώπεκος ἴχνεσι βαίνει,
σύμπασιν δ' ὑμῖν χαῦνος ἔνεστι νόος·
ἐς γὰρ γλῶσσαν ὁρᾶτε καὶ εἰς ἔπη αἱμύλου ἀνδρός,
εἰς ἔργον δ' οὐδὲν γιγνόμενον βλέπετε.

(Solon 11.1–8)

If you have suffered miseries through your own baseness,
  do not ascribe this fate to the gods;
for you yourselves have strengthened these men, giving them protections,
  and on account of these things you have evil slavery.

---

56. See note 10 above.

57. Adkins, *Poetic Craft in the Early Greek Elegists*, pp. 113 ff. B. Gentili points out that while both Theognis and Solon use the same mode of expression and nearly identical language (Solon 4.6–11 and Theognis 39–50), their intentions differ: Theognis contrasts citizens (*astoi*) and leaders (*hêgemones*); Solon criticizes both (*Poetry and its Public in Ancient Greece*, translated by A. T. Cole [Baltimore, 1988], p. 62). In Solon's lines, *astoi* might refer to the whole body politic, to the nobles, or to prominent citizens, and *khrêmasi peithomenoi* might mean 'persuaded by (someone else's) great wealth' or 'persuaded by (their own) great wealth' (Adkins, *Poetic craft*, p. 113). Nagy argues (in disagreement with West) that *hêgemones* means not 'popular leaders' but 'the elite of society' in the description of the coming of the *euthuntêr* 'corrector' (Nagy, "Theognis and Megara: A Poet's Vision of his City," p. 43). Masarracchia explains that regardless of who Solon means by *astoi*, they are like the *dêmou hêgemones* in their greed for wealth, which is destroying the city (Masarracchia, *Solone*, pp. 253ff., 267ff.). Similar ambiguity occurs in Poem 36, in which the identity of contending parties is also unclear (36.22–25). (See Chapter 3, note 34.)

58. D. L. Page notes that Homer, Hesiod, Alcman, and Alcaeus use the word to signify the entire populace of the state in contrast to the rulers (*Sappho and Alcaeus* [Oxford, 1955], p. 177). Solon seems to use the word in the same way to refer to those without political power.

Each one of you steps along in the tracks of the fox,
but the mind in all of you together is foolish;
for you look to the tongue and the words of a wily man,
but as to his actual deed you see nothing.

In criticizing the *dêmos* for being taken in by the man who says one thing and does another, Solon is objecting to precisely the kind of aristocratic deception advised and employed by Theognis. Theognis actually advises saying one thing and doing another, as, for example, when he urges:

εὖ κώτιλλε τὸν ἐχθρόν· ὅταν δ᾽ ὑποχείριος ἔλθηι,
τεῖσαί μιν πρόφασιν μηδεμίαν θέμενος.
ἴσχε νόωι, γλώσσηι δὲ τὸ μείλιχον αἰὲν ἐπέστω·
δειλῶν τοι τελέθει καρδίη ὀξυτέρη.
(Theognis 363–366)

beguile your enemy with fair words; but when he comes under your hand,
take vengeance on him without pretext.
Be firm in your mind, but let gentleness always be upon your tongue;
the heart of cowards, you know, is rather quick to anger.

Solon is, in a sense, "squealing" by urging the *dêmos* not to allow themselves to be deceived any longer, and by explaining how, in fact, the deception occurs: it is a disjunction between word and deed, that is, a deception not simply on the level of language, but, more importantly, on the level of actions. More often elsewhere, the distinction is between saying one thing and *thinking* another (as, for example, in *Iliad* 9.312–313; *Odyssey* 8.165–167; Theognis 91–92, 93–94, 95–96, 365–366), but it is characteristic of Solon to look to the *effect* of such deceitful thinking. One thinks of his concern to identify the direct consequences of specific actions in Poems 13 and 4.

Solon's attitude toward the *dêmos* in Poem 11 is consistent with his explanation of his actions in Poem 5: in which he claims:

δήμωι μὲν γὰρ ἔδωκα τόσον γέρας ὅσσον ἐπαρκεῖν
(Solon 5.1)

To the *dêmos* I gave as much privilege [*geras*] as was sufficient.

In this statement he pointedly reverses the traditional relationship as it is understood in Homer. In the world of the *Odyssey* it is the collective which gives *geras* 'privilege' to the ruler. Odysseus speaks of the γέρας θ᾽ ὅ τι δῆμος ἔδωκεν 'the rights the people have given' to Alkinoos (*Odyssey* 7.150). For Hesiod, *geras* refers to divine privilege; it is never the possession of mortals (*Works and Days* 126; *Theogony* 393, 396, 427). In Homer, however, *geras* is something accorded mortals—certain mortals, that is. It can be a prize awarded an individual warrior (*Iliad* 1.123 and 276; *Odyssey* 7.10 and 11.534) or servant (*Odyssey* 20.297), rites due to the dead (*Iliad* 23.9; *Odyssey* 24.190 and 296), privileges of old men (*Iliad* 4.323) or grieving mortals (*Odyssey* 4.197), or the rights and powers of a king in his homeland (*Odyssey* 11.175, 184; 15.522). *Geras* in Homer is a mark of distinction. It differentiates certain individuals from other individuals. The conferral of *geras* on the *dêmos*—the distinction of a collection of mortals—is, therefore, a startling inversion of a Homeric concept. It underscores Solon's effort to distinguish the *dêmos* as an actor in the political process.

The realization that the symposium is an inadequate paradigm for political organization, the avoidance of the exclusivity of praise-blame poetry, and the rejection of aristocratic deception in the desire to include all listeners in a community of those who will understand derive from Solon's perception of the problem of consumption and over-consumption and his concern for the relationship between public and private. When he criticizes the citizens of Athens, it is not only for their lack of restraint but also for their inability, or unwillingness, to distinguish public from private:

οὔθ᾽ ἱερῶν κτεάνων οὔτέ τι δημοσίων
φειδόμενοι κλέπτουσιν ἀφαρπαγῆι ἄλλοθεν ἄλλος
(Solon 4.12–13)[59]

---

59. The nouns *harpaktêr* 'robber' and *apharpagê* or *harpagê* 'robbery, rapacity, rape' are not common in epic or lyric poetry, and are extant only in Solon, Hesiod, and Homer. In addition to *apharpagêi* (or *eph' harpagêi*) here at Solon 4.13, Solon also reproaches his critics for indulging in *harpagê* in Poem 34.1. Hesiod says *harpakta* 'stolen', which he criticizes in contrast to *theosdota* 'god-given' (*Works and Days* 320), and *harpaktos,* referring to a seizure of sailing opportunity without thought of possible consequences (*Works and Days* 684). In this passage Hesiod also connects such improper seizure with intellectual limitations, claiming that men do this *aidreiêisi nooio* 'through ignorance' (*Works and Days* 682–685). When Priam castigates his surviving sons, he calls them *harpaktêres epidêmioi* 'plunderers of their own people in their land' (*Iliad* 24.262). The adjective *epidêmios* is also not common in epic or lyric poetry. It occurs only three other times in Homer, and elsewhere, not at all. In the *Odyssey* it seems to mean 'in the country' or 'at home', referring to Odysseus' presence in Ithaca (*Odyssey* 1.194 and 233). In the *Iliad* Nestor uses it of war among one people, as opposed to war between different peoples, in asserting:

ἀφρήτωρ ἀθέμιστος ἀνέστιός ἐστιν ἐκεῖνος
ὃς πολέμου ἔραται ἐπιδημίου ὀκρυόεντος.
(*Iliad* 9.63–64)

> sparing neither possessions that are sacred nor those belonging to
> the public,
> they steal with rapacity [*apharpagē*] from every direction.

Solon's metaphorical use of *helkos* 'wound' also reflects this concern for the relationship between public and private, because while distinctions can and must be made in the *polis* between public and private property, public and private fortunes are inevitably interrelated. Having described the avenging function of *Dikē* 'Justice', Solon insists:

τοῦτ' ἤδη πάσηι πόλει ἔρχεται ἕλκος ἄφυκτον
(Solon 4.17)

> This comes immediately upon every city as an inescapable wound
> [helkos].

In Solon's metaphor, the city itself receives a wound as if it were a warrior on a battlefield.[60] The martial metaphor seems to recall the opening lines of the poem in suggesting again a city under siege by external enemies.[61]

> Out of all brotherhood, outlawed, homeless shall be that man
> who longs for all the horror of fighting among his own people.

Priam's combination of the two uncommon words is thus quite striking. His phrase, *harpaktēres epidēmioi* suggests, as do Solon's lines, the dangers of uncontrolled consumption and the confusion of public with private.

60. Adkins notes that "those who portray Solon as a political theorist render *helkos* as 'sore' or 'sickness' resulting from the disease of injustice in the city. But *helkos* at this period is used of wounds inflicted from without by persons or animals (*Iliad* 2.723, 4.217, 5.361, 11.267, etc.). It never means 'disease' or 'sickness', and its first appearance in the sense of 'sore' seems to be in Thucydides 2.49.5" (*Poetic Craft in the Early Greek Elegists*, p. 118).

61. And again there may be a parallel to Troy. The reference to *helkos* might recall the wounds of any number of warriors throughout the *Iliad* or even, more specifically, Hektor's wounds at 24.420. But the suggestion that one wound (or one man's wounds) can affect an entire city is, perhaps, pre-figured in *Iliad* 24. When Kassandra sees Hektor's corpse, she cries out πᾶν κατὰ ἄστυ 'to the entire city' (24.703), and recalls that, while alive, Hektor μέγα χάρμα πόλει τ' ἦν παντί τε δήμω 'was a great joy to his city, and all his people' (24.706). Solon's suggestion that one wound can affect the whole may recall the way that the wounds of one warrior affect the survival of Troy in *Iliad* 24.

And, as is the case with a besieged city, here, too, the stakes are not trivial, for

ἐς δὲ κακὴν ταχέως ἤλυθε δουλοσύνην,
ἣ στάσιν ἔμφυλον πόλεμόν θ' εὕδοντ' ἐπεγείρει,
ὃς πολλῶν ἐρατὴν ὤλεσεν ἡλικίην·
(Solon 4.18–20)

it swiftly comes to evil slavery,
which wakens intestine discord and sleeping war,
that destroys the lovely youth of many.

The emotional overtones are unmistakable: slavery is the punishment that external enemies inflict on the inhabitants of a city they have defeated.[62]

But Solon also intends this reference to slavery quite literally. He explains that

τῶν δὲ πενιχρῶν
ἱκνέονται πολλοὶ γαῖαν ἐς ἀλλοδαπὴν
πραθέντες δεσμοῖσί τ' ἀεικελίοισι δεθέντες
(Solon 4.23–25)

many of the poor
are wandering in a foreign land
having been sold and enslaved in shameful bonds.

In addition, the mention of slavery evokes the dire prospect that the entire city may come under the rule of a tyrant. Solon thus not only draws upon the familiar, emotionally charged theme of the inevitable enslavement inflicted by external enemies, but also refers to specific contemporary circumstances which his audience would recognize.

Although not further elaborated in this poem, Solon's attitude toward tyranny, expressed elsewhere in his poetry, reveals a re-evaluation of some of the traditional standards of praise and blame. In Poem 32, his reply to criticism of his decision not to assume absolute power, Solon maintains:

εἰ δὲ γῆς (φησιν) ἐφεισάμην
πατρίδος, τυραννίδος δὲ καὶ βίης ἀμειλίχου
οὐ καθηψάμην μιάνας καὶ καταισχύνας κλέος,

---

62. Thus, for example, Andromache, grieving over Hektor's corpse, spells out the grim future for the wives and children of Troy (*Iliad* 24.724ff.), and Priam refers to the many children of his whom Achilles has already sold into slavery (*Iliad* 24.751–753).

οὐδὲν αἰδέομαι· πλέον γὰρ ὧδε νικήσειν δοκέω
πάντας ἀνθρώπους.
(Solon 32.1–5)

If I have spared my
fatherland and have not grasped at tyranny [*turannis*] and implacable
violence [*biê ameilikhos*]
staining and shaming my glory [*kleos*],
I am not ashamed [*ouden aideomai*]; rather, in this way I think I will be
victorious [*nikaô*]
over all men.

The poet's insistence that he is not ashamed on this account indicates his unwillingness to accept unquestioningly all popular standards for praise and blame. In his view, becoming tyrant would be a defilement and a disgrace of *kleos*. This suggests a decidedly more restrictive definition of *kleos* than that held by others who evidently would not consider holding tyrannical power to be a violation of *kleos*. Moreover, in the concluding sentence, Solon seems to offer a somewhat idiosyncratic interpretation of what it means to be victorious over people. His victory will not be in terms of *turannis* and *biê ameilikhos*. By suggesting his own specific interpretation of such traditionally potent praise-blame terms as *aideomai, kleos, nikaô,* Solon not only attempts to explain his own actions but also to re-educate, that is, *include* his audience in a departure from traditional standards of praise and blame.

A second reply Solon places in the mouth of a hypothetical critic:

"οὐκ ἔφυ Σόλων βαθύφρων οὐδὲ βουλήεις ἀνήρ·
ἐσθλὰ γὰρ θεοῦ διδόντος αὐτὸς οὐκ ἐδέξατο·
περιβαλὼν δ' ἄγρην ἀγασθεὶς οὐκ ἐπέσπασεν μέγα
δίκτυον, θυμοῦ θ' ἁμαρτῆι καὶ φρενῶν ἀποσφαλείς·
ἤθελον γάρ κεν κρατήσας, πλοῦτον ἄφθονον λαβὼν
καὶ τυραννεύσας Ἀθηνέων μοῦνον ἡμέρην μίαν,
ἀσκὸς ὕστερον δεδάρθαι κἀπιτετρίφθαι γένος."
(Solon 33.1–7)

"Solon is not by nature a deep-thinking nor wise man;
for he himself did not accept good things when the god offered them;
having made a cast about his prey, he was amazed and did not draw up
his great net, having been deprived at the same time of both his
intention and his thoughts;
for if *I* had this power, having seized bounteous wealth [*aphthonos ploutos*]
and ruling Athens for one single day,
I would be willing to be flayed afterward as a wineskin and have my
race [*genos*] after me wiped out."

In this poem, the poet uses traditional concepts to ridicule his opponent. The *persona loquens* is a characteristic device in blame poetry. According to Aristotle (*Rhetoric* 3.1418b 23), if a character's words begin the poem, the procedure is particularly useful for *psogos* 'blame' because it enables the poet to conceal his own identity, and avoid incurring resentment.[63] But Solon is inverting this procedure, implicitly blaming the speaker by revealing the corruptness of his values, and, conversely, implicitly praising the object of the speaker's blame. The speaker is evidently someone who is foolish enough to think that it is possible to take by force *aphthonos ploutos* 'bounteous wealth' (5).[64] Elsewhere, Solon has argued that one can never with impunity take wealth by force (Poem 13). Moreover, this speaker is also willing to sacrifice *kleos* in the process, as indicated by his willingness to forfeit his own *genos* (7). This "critic" appears to be someone whose own standards are so corrupt as to indicate that he has forfeited the right to utter praise or blame—or, at any rate, to be listened to as he does so. In this poem, Solon uses traditional concepts of praise and blame to define and thereby to defuse his opponents.

While other poets, too, cast unfavorable judgements on tyranny, they tend to do so from the perspective of exclusivity, that is, from the perspective of the (potential) tyrant, and conclude that the tyrant's lot is not enviable. Thus, Pindar, for example, maintains:

τῶν γὰρ ἀνὰ πόλιν εὑρίσκων τὰ μέσα μακροτέρωι
{συν} ὄλβωι τεθαλότα, μέμφομ' αἶσαν τυραννίδων·
(*Pythian* 11.52–53)

> for, having searched
> into the city's ways, and having learned
> that moderation blooms
> with a longer happiness,
> I have no fondness for the tyrant's lot.

Similarly, Archilochus presents the carpenter Charon's critique of the wealth and power of Gyges:

οὔ μοι τὰ Γύγεω τοῦ πολυχρύσου μέλει,
οὐδ' εἷλέ πώ με ζῆλος, οὐδ' ἀγαίομαι

---

63. Gentili, *Poetry and its Public in Ancient Greece*, p. 109.

64. For *phthonos* as an important term in the diction of praise-blame poetry, see Nagy, *The Best of the Achaeans*, pp. 224–228.

θεῶν ἔργα, μεγάλης δ' οὐκ ἐρέω τυραννίδος·
ἀπόπροθεν γάρ ἐστιν ὀφθαλμῶν ἐμῶν."
(Archilochus 19)

I do not care for the life of Gyges and his abundance of gold;
jealousy has never seized me; nor do I envy the works of the gods,
and I have no love for great tyranny;
for that is far away from my eyes.

Still, it is not a tremendous leap from favoring the rule of the few to accepting the rule of a single man. Thus, Simonides, for example, suggests that tyranny is acceptable if one can still enjoy life's pleasures (584). These comments consider only the advantages or disadvantages of tyranny for the tyrant himself or for a select and fortunate few under his tyranny.

In contrast, Solon's rejection of tyranny derives not merely from a concern for his own welfare but from a desire to find a balance between conflicting factions in his community. Thus, in Poem 34, he maintains:

οἱ δ' ἐφ' ἁρπαγῆισιν ἦλθον· ἐλπίδ' εἶχον ἀφνεήν,
κἀδόκ[ε]ον ἕκαστος αὐτῶν ὄλβον εὑρήσειν πολύν,
καί με κωτίλλοντα λείως τραχὺν ἐκφανεῖν νόον.
χαῦνα μὲν τότ' ἐφράσαντο, νῦν δέ μοι χολούμενοι
λοξὸν ὀφθαλμοῖς ὁρῶσι πάντες ὥστε δήϊον.
οὐ χρεών· ἃ μὲν γὰρ εἶπα, σὺν θεοῖσιν ἤνυσα,
ἄ[λλ]α δ' οὐ μάτην ἔερδον, οὐδέ μοι τυραννίδος
ἁνδάνει βίηι τι[. .].ε[ι]ν, οὐδὲ πιεί[ρ]ης χθονὸς
πατρίδος κακοῖσιν ἐσθλοὺς ἰσομοιρίην ἔχειν.
(Solon 34.1–9)

But some came for the purpose of robbery; they had rich hope,
and each of them thought that he would find much prosperity,
and that although I was chattering gently I would reveal a harsh mind.
They thought foolish things then, and now, angry at me,
they all look at me aslant, as at an enemy.
It is not necessary, for with the help of the gods, I accomplished what I
      said,
and as to the rest, I acted not without reason, nor was it pleasing to me
[to do] anything by force of tyranny, nor for the base
to have an equal share of the rich fatherland with the noble.

Theognis, like Solon, contemplates the prospect of tyranny from the perspective of the well-being of the community. In two almost parallel passages, he maintains:

Κύρνε, κύει πόλις ἥδε, δέδοικα δὲ μὴ τέκηι ἄνδρα
εὐθυντῆρα κακῆς ὕβριος ἡμετέρης.
ἀστοὶ μὲν γὰρ ἔθ᾽ οἵδε σαόφρονες, ἡγεμόνες δὲ
τετράφαται πολλὴν εἰς κακότητα πεσεῖν.
(Theognis 39–42)

Kyrnos, this city is pregnant, and I fear that it may give birth to a man
 who will be a straightener of our [*hêmeterê*] evil wanton violence
 [*hubris*];
for these citizens are still temperate, but their leaders
 have been turned so that they are going to fall into great evil.

and:

Κύρνε, κύει πόλις ἥδε, δέδοικα δὲ μὴ τέκηι ἄνδρα
ὑβριστήν, χαλεπῆς ἡγεμόνα στάσιος·
ἀστοὶ μὲν γὰρ ἔθ᾽ οἵδε σαόφρονες, ἡγεμόνες δὲ
τετράφαται πολλὴν εἰς κακότητα πεσεῖν.
(Theognis 1081a–1082b)

Kyrnos, this city is pregnant, and I fear that it may give birth to a man
 of wanton violence [*hubristês*], a leader of harsh discord:
for these citizens are still temperate, but their leaders
 have been turned so that they are going to fall into great evil.

The two passages might seem to reflect some ambivalence regarding the emergence of a tyrant. The first seems to view it somewhat favorably, the second without doubt unfavorably,[65] but any contradiction between the two statements may be more apparent than real. The two passages may be evidence of the sort of tact or etiquette required at symposia, the former for use when the would-be tyrant is

65. Nagy sees some contradiction between the two passages, arguing that whereas the latter passage is "one-sidedly negative about the emerging tyrant," the former reveals "a more even-handed—one might say 'Solonian'—stance" ("Theognis and Megara: A Poet's Vision of his City," p. 46). But this use of "Solonian" seems questionable, since Solon is unequivocally opposed to tyranny. The contention is in support of Nagy's argument that the two stretches of the Theognidean corpus—1–1022, containing 39–42 (tyrant as regulator of *hubris*) and 1023–1220, containing 1081a–1082b (tyrant as exponent of *hubris*)—are from different phases of the Theognidean poetic tradition. He suggests that the two passages may represent "the 'same' poem in different phases of Megarian history, the former corresponding to a later 'pan-Hellenic' orientation, the latter to an earlier, more 'provincial' period" (pp. 46–51). In this view, Nagy is in disagreement with M. L. West who argues that the two stretches are superior and inferior excerpts (*Meliora* and *Deteriora*) from a larger corpus (*Studies in Greek Elegy and Iambus* [Berlin and New York, 1974], pp. 40–61).

present in the audience, the latter for use on other occasions. Still, it is hardly inconsistent to acknowledge that a tyrant can be the regulator of *others' hubris* (39–42) (note *hēmeterē* at line 40), and at the same time to recognize the tyrant's inability to regulate his *own hubris* (1081–1082b). Thus, Theognis, too, recognizes that tyranny is no solution to the problem of human acquisitiveness and its regulation. No single individual can create communal unity and harmony, since he is unlikely to be able to control his own greed, to observe distinctions between that which is his and that which is not, between that which is private and that which is public.

Solon concludes his discussion of the problems confronting the city and their results with a striking and unusual metaphor:

> οὕτω δημόσιον κακὸν ἔρχεται οἴκαδ᾽ ἑκάστωι,
> αὔλειοι δ᾽ ἔτ᾽ ἔχειν οὐκ ἐθέλουσι θύραι,
> ὑψηλὸν δ᾽ ὑπὲρ ἕρκος ὑπέρθορεν, εὗρε δὲ πάντως,
> εἰ καί τις φεύγων ἐν μυχῶι ἦι θαλάμου.
> (Solon 4.26–29)

> Thus the public evil comes homeward to each man,
>   the courtyard doors [*auleioi ...thurai*] are no longer still willing [*ouk ethelousi*] to keep it out,
> but it leaps over the high wall [*herkos*], and inevitably finds a man,
>   even if, fleeing, he runs to hide in the corner of a room.

Although it is quite comprehensible, the picture Solon has drawn is odd. What does it mean to say that the courtyard doors are *unwilling* to keep evil out, particuliarly since it is over the fence, not through the doors, that the evil enters? A simple explanation is that Solon is not overly concerned with these details,[66] but perhaps one need not dismiss the puzzle quite so readily, for, alternatively, perhaps Solon intends the oddness of the metaphor to be arresting. And, indeed, although the metaphor is unusual, one Homeric antecedent in particular may help to clarify the implications of this passage.

---

66. Thus, Adkins explains that "one might suppose that the gates do not wish, or are unable, to keep out the woe either because they open to let it through or because the woe jumps over them. (If the woe can jump, presumably the gates can have wishes.) But the woe jumps over the high fence. The wishes of the gates are consequently irrelevant, and it is the fence which is unable to protect its owner." Adkins concludes that "Solon is more concerned to present an emotive image than to offer reasoned exposition" (*Poetic Craft in the Early Greek Elegists*, p. 121).

The *aulê* 'courtyard', *thurê* 'door', and *herkos* 'wall' (or *herkion*) are standard domestic features in the Homeric epics. Solon's image generally recalls Homeric similes in which lions attack domestic animals in the fold such as, for example, *Iliad* 5.136–142.[67] More specifically, however, in *Iliad* 9, Phoenix relates that, having been tempted to murder his father, he managed to flee his home, in spite of being closely guarded by his kinsmen, by leaping out over the courtyard wall. He explains:

> εἰνάνυχες δέ μοι ἀμφ' αὐτῶι παρὰ νύκτας ἴαυον·
> οἱ μὲν ἀμειβόμενοι φυλακὰς ἔχον, οὐδέ ποτ' ἔσβη
> πῦρ, ἕτερον μὲν ὑπ' αἰθούσηι εὐερκέος αὐλῆς,
> ἄλλο δ' ἐνὶ προδόμωι, πρόσθεν θαλάμοιο θυράων.
> ἀλλ' ὅτε δὴ δεκάτη μοι ἐπήλυθε νὺξ ἐρεβεννή,
> καὶ τότ' ἐγὼ θαλάμοιο θύρας πυκινῶς ἀραρυίας
> ῥήξας ἐξῆλθον, καὶ ὑπέρθορον ἑρκίον αὐλῆς
> ῥεῖα, λαθὼν φύλακάς τ' ἄνδρας δμωιάς τε γυναῖκας.
> (*Iliad* 9.470–477)

Nine nights they slept nightlong in their places beside me,
and they kept up an interchange of watches, and the fire was never
put out; one below the gate of the strong-closed courtyard,
and one in the ante-chamber before the doors of the bedroom.
But when the tenth night had come to me in its darkness,
then I broke the close-compacted doors of the chamber
and got away, and overleapt the fence of the courtyard [*huperthoron herkion aulês*]
lightly, unnoticed by the guarding men and the women servants.

The verb *huperthrôskô* (476) occurs elsewhere in epic or lyric poetry only three other times, all in the *Iliad* and all three in reference to horses leaping over the *taphros* 'ditch' of the Greeks (*Iliad* 8.179 and 16.380) or fearing to leap over it (*Iliad* 12.53). Phoenix's use of it in reference to his leap over the courtyard wall is, therefore, unusual, and the phrase *huperthoron herkion aulês* (9.476) is noticeably similar to Solon's *huper herkos huperthoren* (4.28).

As the barrier to the *aulê*, the *herkos* seems to be that which separates the private residence from the rest of the community—in civilized societies. It may be worth noting that the cave of Polyphemos, in *Odyssey* 9, although it has an *aulê* (184, 239, 338, 462), *thurai* (243, 417), and

---

67. Adkins, *Poetic Craft in the Early Greek Elegists*, p. 118.

even a *thureos* 'doorstone' (240, 340), has no *herkos*. By jumping out over his *herkos*, Phoenix, one individual man, reduced the trouble accruing to the community. Solon's metaphor is, in a sense, an inversion of this situation: in his view the communal trouble jumps *in* over the *herkos* to *cause* trouble to an individual man. Solon's *ouk ethelousi* 'they are not willing' might simply be equivalent to *ou dunantai* 'they are not able', but the fact that he does not use this or maintain, for example, that the doors are not high enough suggests that the irrelevance of the doors *is* Solon's point. His image seems to emphasize, intentionally, not inadvertently or carelessly, the multiplicity of ways in which public evil penetrates into the house of different individuals and, therefore, the insignificance or irrelevance not merely of the *thurai* or their wishes, but of the *herkos* as well, that is, of all traditional barriers between public and private, when the survival of the community is at issue. Thus, not only is the community threatened by the fact that necessary distinctions between public and private are difficult to discern or maintain (Solon 4.12–13): it is also not protected by the traditional, readily discernible boundaries between public and private.

Just as tyranny is no solution, in Solon's view, neither is the Homeric conception of harmony and order achieved by means of a coincidence of divine and human actions. The solution he proposes in the concluding lines of Poem 4 is in marked contrast with such a view. Solon claims that

> Εὐνομίη δ' εὔκοσμα καὶ ἄρτια πάντ' ἀποφαίνει
> καὶ θαμὰ τοῖς ἀδίκοις ἀμφιτίθησι πέδας·
> τραχέα λειαίνει, παύει κόρον, ὕβριν ἀμαυροῖ,
> αὐαίνει δ' ἄτης ἄνθεα φυόμενα,
> εὐθύνει δὲ δίκας σκολιάς, ὑπερήφανά τ' ἔργα
> πραΰνει· παύει δ' ἔργα διχοστασίης,
> παύει δ' ἀργαλέης ἔριδος χόλον, ἔστι δ' ὑπ' αὐτῆς
> πάντα κατ' ἀνθρώπους ἄρτια καὶ πινυτά.
> (Solon 4.32–39)

Thus Good Order [*Eunomiē*] makes all things orderly and fitting
    and often places fetters around those who are unjust;
it smoothes the rough, stops *koros*, enfeebles wanton violence [*hubris*],
    withers the blooming flowers of ruinous folly [*atē*],
straightens crooked judgements, and gentles overweening deeds;
    it stops acts of dissension,
and stops the anger of troublesome strife; and by its action
    all things among men are made fitting and wise.

Does Solon understand *Eunomiê* as a divine force? Experts are not in agreement,[68] but the more popular view recognizes that *Eunomiê* for Solon is not a divine force but rather a desired social condition,[69] a goal of Solon's personal policy.[70]

Moreover, the conflict, as Solon has described it, is not amenable to resolution explained in terms of divine intervention. He has stressed that human beings, not gods, are responsible for the city's troubles. Human beings, therefore, must find entirely human solutions. One may contrast the Homeric resolution presented in *Iliad* 24, in which order is restored by means of a coincidence of divine and human actions. In that passage, divine intervention figures prominently,[71] and the strands of human and divine will are tightly intertwined. Achilles agrees *because* Zeus wills it.[72] The importance of human will is not

---

68. Adkins argues that *Eunomiê* is, in fact, a divine agent and that Solon's description functions like multiple determination in which there is both a divine and a human agent. He comments: "Note that many of the good results ascribed to *Eunomiê* suit the actions of a person but not the existence of a condition of 'good order' in which the bad situation would not prevail at all" (*Poetic Craft in the Early Greek Elegists*, p. 124). But it is not at all clear that the continual restoration of order can only result from the actions of a person or that a condition of 'good order' can only be one which precludes trouble from ever arising in the first place.

69. M. Ostwald, *Nomos and the Beginnings of the Athenian Democracy* (Oxford, 1969), p. 64.

70. V. Ehrenberg, *Aspects of the Ancient World* (New York, 1946), pp. 84–85. Solmsen explains it as "sound moral condition" (*Hesiod and Aeschylus*, p. 116).

71. Apollo protects Hektor's body from defilement (*Iliad* 24.18–21), and Zeus determines that Priam should give gifts to Achilles and that Achilles should release Hektor's body (74–76). He sends Hermes to guide Priam (334ff.). Hermes tells Priam that the gods are protecting Hektor's body (411–423), and also helps Priam to leave Achilles' camp safely (679ff.). Zeus' message to Achilles (113–116) is repeated by Thetis (134–137), and his message to Priam (117–119) is repeated three times during the book (145–147, 175–176, 194–196). The repetition not only serves a narrative purpose in helping to advance the plot: it also emphasizes the fact that the resolution is both predetermined and determined by multiple agency.

72. Achilles answers Thetis:

τῆιδ' εἴη· ὃς ἄποινα φέροι καὶ νεκρὸν ἄγοιτο,
εἰ δὴ πρόφρονι θυμῶι Ὀλύμπιος αὐτὸς ἀνώγει.
(*Iliad* 24.139–140)

So be it. He can bring the ransom and take off the body,
if the Olympian himself so urgently bids it.

minimal in the Homeric model; the resolution is based no less on human will than on divine.[73] But Solon's description of *Eunomiê* seems, by contrast, to prescribe an *entirely* human solution—by referring to *that which needs to be done* in order to achieve good order—and suggests that

---

73. Although the ransom has been mandated by Zeus, and in spite of the emphasis throughout the book on the gifts Priam brings to Achilles, these gifts do not actually determine Achilles' decision. Although he will later excuse his action to Patroklos by citing the gifts he has received (*Iliad* 24.592–595), Achilles becomes angry when Priam offers him gifts, insisting

> μηκέτι νῦν μ' ἐρέθιζε γέρον· νοέω δὲ καὶ αὐτὸς
> Ἕκτορά τοι λῦσαι, Διόθεν δέ μοι ἄγγελος ἦλθε
> μήτηρ, ἥ μ' ἔτεκεν, θυγάτηρ ἁλίοιο γέροντος.
> (*Iliad* 24.560–562)

> No longer stir me up, old sir. I myself am minded
> to give Hektor to you. A messenger came to me from Zeus,
> my mother, she who bore me, the daughter of the sea's ancient.

This speech indicates the importance of Achilles' will as well as Zeus', for in spite of the divine message, in spite of the knowledge that Priam could never have entered the camp without divine aid (*Iliad* 24.563–567), Achilles is still dangerous. He still suggests the possibility that he may attack Priam, warning him:

> τῶ νῦν μή μοι μᾶλλον ἐν ἄλγεσι θυμὸν ὀρίνηις,
> μή σε, γέρον, οὐδ' αὐτὸν ἐνὶ κλισίηισιν ἐάσω
> καὶ ἱκέτην περ ἐόντα, Διὸς δ' ἀλίτωμαι ἐφετμάς.
> (*Iliad* 24.568–570)

> Therefore
> you must not further make my spirit move in my sorrows,
> for fear, old sir, I might not let you alone in my shelter,
> suppliant as you are; and be guilty before the god's orders.

Priam's actions also emphasize the importance of human will and action. Hermes may presage the resolution when he tells Priam φίλωι δέ σε πατρὶ ἐΐσκω 'You seem to me like a beloved father' (*Iliad* 24.371). He advises Priam:

> τύνη δ' εἰσελθὼν λαβὲ γούνατα Πηλείωνος,
> καί μιν ὑπὲρ πατρὸς καὶ μητέρος ἠϋκόμοιο
> λίσσεο καὶ τέκεος, ἵνα οἱ σὺν θυμὸν ὀρίνηις.
> (*Iliad* 24.465–467)

> But go you in yourself and clasp the knees of Peleion
> and entreat him in the name of his father, the name of his mother
> of the lovely hair, and his child, and so move the spirit within him.

But, in the event, Priam only entreats Achilles in the name of his father (*Iliad* 24.486–506), and the appeal has the desired effect. It enables Achilles and Priam to grieve together (507ff.) and causes Achilles to feel pity (516ff.)

the harmony he envisions for the *polis* is not a Homeric harmony of conflict utterly resolved but an ongoing, controlled tension.

As such, it encompasses neither tyranny nor the conception of political order embraced by praise-blame poetry: aristocratic rule, the idyllic exclusion of the *kakoi* exemplified by the symposium paradigm.[74] Solon recognizes that, like tyranny, aristocratic political organization has only produced, and *can* only produce, conflict and disorder since, again like tyranny, it does not account for individuals' inability to control their own acquisitiveness.

In sum, thematic similarities betweeen Poem 4 and Poem 13 suggest that there is little to be gained from viewing the former as "political" and the latter as "ethical" or "religious." Both poems emphasize the importance of intellectual understanding, both recognize the difficulty and dangers in achieving human satisfaction, and both attribute to human beings responsibility for the outcome of human actions. Unlike Poem 13, however, which seems merely to hint at a solution, Poem 4 offers a deliberate prescription. And yet, if viewed as political theory, this prescription seems vague at best.

If, however, one examines the emotional impact and imagery of Poem 4 as well as its literal content, one finds a number of archaic passages which provide the context for Solon's reflections. Comparison of Poem 4 with these passages reveals the way in which Solon is able to present an unprecedented analysis of Athens' problems, while drawing upon familiar themes, as well as traditional images and language. Solon's solution to the problem of civic conflict becomes not only more comprehensible than it might otherwise appear, but also all the more strikingly novel in comparison to the solutions presented by other poets.

---

74. The virtue of *Eunomiê* is that:

παύει δ' ἀργαλέης ἔριδος χόλον
(Solon 4.38)

It stops the anger of troublesome strife [*eris*].

If, as Nagy maintains, in the diction of praise poetry *eris* is (like *neikos* 'quarrel'), in fact, a programmatic word which has the specific function of designating the opposite of praise poetry (Nagy, *The Best of the Achaeans*, p. 224), Solon's assertion that *Eunomiê* can put a stop to it may specifically indicate his rejection of the use of invective, and, therefore, of the attempt to achieve social harmony by strengthening the bonds of *philotês* 'friendship' among members of a select portion of society (*The Best of the Achaeans*, p. 241, and see also "Iambos: Typologies of Invective and Praise," *Arethusa* 9 [1976], pp. 191–206). Solon attempts, instead, to strengthen *philotês* not by exclusion but by inclusion.

The difference between Solon and other poets in their prescriptions for the resolution of civic conflict and the restoration of order may provide something of an answer to those who would argue, with Havelock, that "Solon's elegies make no conceptual contribution" beyond that of earlier poets.[75] Sensitivity to differences between an individual's perceptions of himself and his world and others' perceptions of that individual makes the relationship between public and private intensely problematic for Solon. Unlike other poets, he recognizes that, where wealth is concerned, human insatiability can find no analogy in other human desires which have inherent physiological limits. The traditional poetic imagery is, therefore, inadequate because it is inaccurate. Moreover, Solon recognizes the universality of the problem of human acquisitiveness. The *agathoi* are no more immune than the *kakoi.* This understanding of the danger of human insatiability thus dictates the social function of Solon's poetry. In rejecting the exclusivity of the aristocratic solution—which is no solution—Solon attempts to make his poetry equally comprehensible and acceptable to all hearers, not merely a select few.

The implication in Poem 4 is that harmony is possible within the *polis* but it is neither a Homeric harmony in which divine and human will act together and conflict can be resolved utterly nor an aristocratic, utopian vision in which conflict never arises. Solon's solution would neither preclude problems nor ever resolve them completely. Rather, he envisions a community in which *Eunomiê* is a dynamic force perpetually creating balance and order. It is not a divine agent, but a communal commitment to good order.[76] It prevents *hubris* from getting out of hand by dictating the limits of satiety.[77] By advocating the determination of limits not by individuals but by the community, Poem 4 thus progresses from the attribution of individual responsibility to the attribution of communal responsibilities. Solon's vision suggests, unlike other poets', that the potential for human concord, for mutual identification, understanding, and compassion, lies not in the individual but in the community as a whole.

---

75. Havelock, *The Greek Concept of Justice,* p. 262.

76. See note 16 above.

77. Contrast Theognis 39–42. Theognis can only envision the act of setting limits being the work of an individual, that is, a tyrant. See p. 107 above.

Chapter Three

Poem 36: Poet and Polity

Poem 36 is generally considered part of Solon's "political" poetry, and, undeniably, in it Solon defends his political actions. But just as in Poem 4 the lack of specificity limits any attempt to understand the poem as political theory, in Poem 36 Solon's omission of legislative particulars leaves open many questions regarding the specific details of his political reforms. Moreover, emphasis on the political aspect of both poems does not adequately account for the emotional power of either. Poems 36 and 4 both explore many of the same themes, and, like Poem 4, Poem 36 evokes and manipulates the imagery, implications, and emotional resonances of epic and praise-blame poetry. This intensifies its emotional impact and reveals Solon's awareness of the social purposes of his poetry. Although in structure and style this poem appears less Homeric than either Poem 4 or Poem 13, it gains persuasive power through being simultaneously Homeric and un-Homeric. Moreover, in rejecting the exclusivity of praise-blame poetry in this poem, as he did in Poem 4, Solon does not so much reject the terms of evaluation as reverse them. The reversal enables him to use the familiar theme of the scapegoat for his own political and poetic purposes. In the process, he reveals an acute awareness of his own poetic activity, of the relationship between poet and audience, and of the interrelationship between his poetry and his political activity.

While Poem 4 considers the possibilities for conflict and resolution in the relationship between citizens of the *polis*, Poem 36 reveals most clearly Solon's view of himself and his own relationship to his fellow citizens and to his city. Nevertheless, in their concern for communal harmony, both poems emphasize some of the same themes. The threat of slavery, for example, both real and metaphorical, receives particular attention in both poems. In Poem 4 Solon criticizes the unjust actions of the Athenians and the inevitable vengeance of *Dikê* 'Justice', insisting

τοῦτ' ἤδη πάσηι πόλει ἔρχεται ἕλκος ἄφυκτον,
ἐς δὲ κακὴν ταχέως ἤλυθε δουλοσύνην,
ἢ στάσιν ἔμφυλον πόλεμόν θ' εὕδοντ' ἐπεγείρει,
ὃς πολλῶν ἐρατὴν ὤλεσεν ἡλικίην·
(Solon 4.17–20)

This comes immediately upon every city as an inescapable wound;
it swiftly comes to evil slavery,
which wakens intestine discord and sleeping war,
that destroys the lovely youth of many.

The danger derives not only from factional strife and civil war, but also, no doubt, from the threat of resultant tyrannical rule. And slavery is not merely a future possibility: it is a present condition for many Athenians, for

τῶν δὲ πενιχρῶν
ἱκνέονται πολλοὶ γαῖαν ἐς ἀλλοδαπὴν
πραθέντες δεσμοῖσί τ' ἀεικελίοισι δεθέντες
(Solon 4.23–25)

many of the poor
are wandering in a foreign land
having been sold and enslaved in shameful bonds.

In Poem 36, Solon describes the metaphorical enslavement of the earth

τῆς ἐγώ ποτε
ὅρους ἀνεῖλον πολλαχῆι πεπηγότας,
πρόσθεν δὲ δουλεύουσα, νῦν ἐλευθέρη.
(Solon 36.5–7)

whose mortgage stones,
fixed everywhere, I once took away.
Enslaved before, the earth is now free.

He describes, too, the literal enslavement of Athenian citizens whom he himself freed:

πολλοὺς δ' 'Αθήνας πατρίδ' ἐς θεόκτιτον
ἀνήγαγον πραθέντας, ἄλλον ἐκδίκως,
ἄλλον δικαίως, τοὺς δ' ἀναγκαίης ὑπὸ
χρειοῦς φυγόντας, γλῶσσαν οὐκέτ' 'Αττικὴν
ἱέντας, ὡς δὴ πολλαχῆι πλανωμένους·
τοὺς δ' ἐνθάδ' αὐτοῦ δουλίην ἀεικέα
ἔχοντας, ἤθη δεσποτέων τρομεομένους,
ἐλευθέρους ἔθηκα.
(Solon 36.8–15)

And I brought back to their god-founded fatherland
many Athenians who had been sold, one according to law,
another contrary to law; and some who fled under constraint of dire
    necessity
and no longer spoke the Attic tongue,
as might be expected in men who had wandered far and wide;
and some right here who endured shameful slavery
trembling before the moods of their masters,
these I made free.

As well as emphasizing the dire effects of enslavement, both poems stress Solon's view that human, not divine, actions are directly responsible for the consequences that result. In Poem 4 the contrast between divine and human responsibility is unequivocal. The opening lines of the poem contrast divine and human action and place responsibility for the city's troubles on the latter:

ἡμετέρη δὲ πόλις κατὰ μὲν Διὸς οὔποτ' ὀλεῖται
    αἶσαν καὶ μακάρων θεῶν φρένας ἀθανάτων·
τοίη γὰρ μεγάθυμος ἐπίσκοπος ὀβριμοπάτρη
    Παλλὰς Ἀθηναίη χεῖρας ὕπερθεν ἔχει·
αὐτοὶ δὲ φθείρειν μεγάλην πόλιν ἀφραδίηισιν
    ἀστοὶ βούλονται χρήμασι πειθόμενοι
                (Solon 4.1–6)

But our city will never be destroyed by the dispensation of Zeus
    and the intentions of the blessed immortal gods;
for such a great-hearted guardian, daughter of a mighty father,
    is Pallas Athene who holds her hands over it;
but the citizens themselves, persuaded by money, are willing
    to destroy this great city by their folly.

In Poem 36, too, Solon emphasizes human action, not divine, and human responsibility for the outcome of human actions. Aside from insisting that *Gê* 'Earth' would be his witness, in this poem Solon makes no other reference to the gods or their role in the amelioration of the city's troubles. Instead he insists upon his own actions, and his own responsibility for their favorable results. He uses the pronoun *egô* 'I' three times in the poem's twenty-seven lines, and of the sixteen finite verbs in the poem, eleven are in the first person singular in the indicative mood (ten aorists, one imperfect). The remaining five all occur in conditional sentences.

But most striking, perhaps, is the sensitivity in both poems to the relationship between the individual and the community. As discussed in

Chapter 2 above, Solon's use of *koros* 'satiety, surfeit' and his description of *Eunomiê* 'Good Order' in Poem 4 underline the potential differences between the perspective of the individual and that of the community, and Poem 36 concludes with a powerful simile in which the relationship is no longer abstract—for Solon himself is the individual at odds with the community.

Such thematic similarities might suggest the continued presence of epic and praise-blame overtones in Poem 36 as in Poem 4, but literary critics have focused more upon the lack of archaic features in the poem[1] and the scarcity of Homeric references.[2] Admittedly, the poem contains few epic words or phrases (which its meter would tend to exclude) and its structure does not typify archaic structural patterns. And yet, although it may not recall the compositional technique of an epic poet, the poem does recall the self-assertiveness of an epic character. The self-referential quality of the speech, Solon's emphasis on his own actions, his repetition of *egô*, the preponderance of verbs in the first person singular are reminiscent of many speeches in the *Iliad*.

Most striking, however, is that Solon concludes his speech with an arresting, unmistakably Homeric-sounding simile:

τῶν οὕνεκ' ἀλκὴν πάντοθεν ποιεόμενος
ὡς ἐν κυσὶν πολλῇσιν ἐστράφην λύκος.
(Solon 36.26–27)

Therefore, producing defensive valor from every direction,
I turned about like a wolf among many hunting dogs.

Although this simile might seem to be an unHomeric use of a Homeric image, in that its subject is the poet himself, rather than a character in a narrative,[3] the strategy is not entirely unprecedented. One might recall, for example, Achilles' analogy between himself and a mother bird in his heated reply to Odysseus in *Iliad* 9:

---

1. H. Fränkel comments that the poem resounds like a great speech out of classical tragedy, and, noting the lack of ring composition and other characteristics of the archaic course of thought, concludes that there is nothing archaic in the style of this poem (*Dichtung und Philosophie des frühen Griechentums* [New York, 1951], p. 300).

2. A. Masaracchia, *Solone* (Florence, 1958), p. 355.

3. G. Else comments that in this simile Solon uses a Homeric image unHomerically in that instead of the poet's presenting an analogy between the hero and a fierce animal (as in Homer), "now the poet himself is the wolf" (*The Origin and Early Form of Greek Tragedy* [Cambridge, Mass., 1965], pp. 35, 42, and 117, n. 28).

ὡς δ᾽ ὄρνις ἀπτῆσι νεοσσοῖσι προφέρῃσι
μάστακ᾽, ἐπεί κε λάβῃσι, κακῶς δ᾽ ἄρα οἱ πέλει αὐτῆι,
ὣς καὶ ἐγὼ πολλὰς μὲν ἀΰπνους νύκτας ἴαυον,
ἤματα δ᾽ αἱματόεντα διέπρησσον πολεμίζων,
ἀνδράσι μαρνάμενος ὀάρων ἕνεκα σφετεράων.
(*Iliad* 9.323–327)

For as to her unwinged young ones the mother bird brings back
morsels, wherever she can find them, but as for herself it is suffering,
such was I, as I lay through all the many nights unsleeping,
such as I wore through the bloody days of the fighting,
striving with warriors for the sake of these men's women.

Instead of *describing* Achilles with this analogy, the poet has placed the simile in the mouth of Achilles himself to heighten its impact on the audience's emotions.

The emotional impact of Solon's simile is similarly powerful. And yet, Solon's intention is not merely to touch his audience's emotions but to persuade. For that purpose, poetry may have distinct advantages over oratory, largely because listeners are able to retain it more readily.[4] But if poetry is well-suited to the purposes of persuasion, it is perhaps surprising that Solon, nevertheless, uses few epic-sounding similes.

The simile of the wolf, therefore, is particularly notable, first of all, in that it is one of only four similes in Solon's extant poetry.[5] Even though relatively few of Solon's verses have survived, and the extant sample may not be representative, the preponderance of metaphor over simile is overwhelming. Undeniably, in prose, stylistic considerations are likely to limit the use of similes.[6] It may be that the presence of a simile in

---

4. I. Linforth points out that in Solon's time the art of written composition in prose was not yet known, and the remarkable aspect of Solon's approach was not that he used verse instead of written prose, but that he made his appeal through poetry rather than oratory. He argues that poetry has the persuasive advantage of being repeatable, portable, and rhythmical, and, by making a permanent appeal to the feelings, can slowly mold popular opinion (*Solon the Athenian* [Berkeley, 1919], p. 124).

5. The three others: 13.14–16 (ὥστε πυρός...); 13.18–25 (ὥστ᾽ ἄνεμος...); 37.9–10 (ὥσπερ...ὄρος).

6. In discussing Aristotle's theory of simile (*eikōn*) and comparison, M. H. McCall explains that Aristotle distinguishes *eikōn* by the presence of *hōs* (although Aristotle does not adhere rigidly to this distinction in his own selection of examples), and quotes Aristotle's comment that χρήσιμον δὲ εἰκὼν καὶ ἐν λόγωι, ὀλιγάκις δέ· ποιητικὸν γάρ: 'simile is useful also in prose, but seldom, because it is poetic' (*Rhetoric* 3.4.1406b 24–25). McCall explains that "*eikōn* will be used only occasionally in prose because it is poetical,

prose is jarring because it suggests a different genre. As a result, it inter-feres with the audience's ability to grasp intellectually that which the author wishes to convey. By calling attention to itself, by inviting intel-lectual scrutiny (in a way that a metaphor tends not to do), the simile calls attention to the "vehicle" rather than to the "tenor"[7] so that it dis-tracts from the author's argument. This might account for the relative paucity of similes in Solon's poetry, given his intention to persuade.

But, by the very fact of calling attention to itself, the simile can also contribute to the argument. The appeal, unlike that of the typical metaphor (one may contrast mixed metaphors), is as much to the intellect as to the emotions of the audience. Solon's similes demand intellectual scrutiny because they often do not make sense without it. His *lukos* 'wolf' simile, in particular, gains persuasive power by simultaneously evoking and departing from Homeric connotations. It *is*, in fact, both Homeric and un-Homeric, and possibly self-consciously so, not so much because the tenor is the poet himself, as has been suggested,[8] as because of the terms Solon has selected for the vehicle.

Arguably, all of the similes and metaphors in Solon's poetry in which Solon and his actions comprise the tenor are odd in some quite striking way. Of the five such examples (two similes, three metaphors), three, it is true, are not unequivocally Homeric, but they may be worth discussing in this context because their vividness derives from their unexpectedness, and the strategy involved is similar to that of the *lukos* simile. In Poem 37 Solon defends his political actions and, as in Poem 36, concludes with a remarkable simile:

δήμωι μὲν εἰ χρὴ διαφάδην ὀνειδίσαι,
ἃ νῦν ἔχουσιν οὔποτ᾽ ὀφθαλμοῖσιν ἂν
εὕδοντες εἶδον...
ὅσοι δὲ μείζους καὶ βίην ἀμείνονες,
αἰνοῖεν ἄν με καὶ φίλον ποιοίατο.

---

which reduces its power to persuade" (*Ancient Rhetorical Theories of Simile and Comparison* [Cambridge, Mass., 1969], p. 32 and p. 41).

7. I am following M. S. Silk in his understanding of the distinction introduced by I. A. Richards. Silk explains "tenor" as the underlying idea in a poetic image and "vehicle" as "the other idea, the one brought in from outside, the one to which the tenor is, in logical terms, compared" (*Interaction in Poetic Imagery: With Special Reference to Early Greek Poetry* [London, 1974], p. 6).

8. See note 3 above.

If it is necessary to reproach the people openly,
that which they have now they never would have envisioned
in their dreams...
And those men who are greater and stronger
might praise me and consider me their friend.

[According to Aristotle, Solon proceeds to explain that if another man
had held this honor:]

οὐκ ἂν κατέσχε δῆμον, οὐδ' ἐπαύσατο
πρὶν ἀνταράξας πῖαρ ἐξεῖλεν γάλα·
ἐγὼ δὲ τούτων ὥσπερ ἐν μεταιχμίωι
ὅρος κατέστην.
                                                (Solon 37.1–10)

he would not have restrained the people, nor would he have stopped
before having stirred up the cream he destroyed the milk;
but I stood like a boundary stone [*horos*] in the space between
these two armies [*en metaikhmiôi*].

The unexpected juxtaposition of *horos* with *metaikhmiôi* conveys
forcefully the sense that Solon has attempted to restructure political
and economic relations in Athens in a radical new way. The simile
emphasizes that what he has done is as unusual as if one were to set up
a boundary marker between two opposing armies. Solon knows he has
not obviated the reasons for the conflict. He has simply tried to prevent
either side from conquering the other. He has tried to establish a
boundary, to give each side its territory, in effect, so that the two sides
may coexist in harmony.[9] Although not a Homeric phrase, *en*

---

9. The substitution of *doros* 'spear' for *horos* is certainly unnecessary and arguably
obtuse. One may compare the Homeric use of the Ionic form οὖροι in the simile at *Iliad*
12.421–426 in which a peace-time boundary dispute between two farmers figures two
armies fighting at a wall. Solon, by contrast, combines both martial and peace-time
aspects into one image in an effort to transmute real political conflict into peaceful
balance.

For an excellent discussion of this image and of the thought underlying Solon's
recourse to Iliadic language in concluding Poems 5, 36, and 37, see Nicole Loraux,
"Solon au milieu de la lice," *Mélanges H. van Effenterre* (Paris, 1984), pp. 199–214. Loraux
explains that in these three images, Solon treats *stasis* 'political faction' as a type of
polemos 'war' and, unlike Alcaeus, rejects partisan combat, choosing instead to champion
the city itself faced by two hostile factions. Accordingly, Solon's *metaikhmion* refers not to a
pacific *meson* 'middle', a place of regulated exchange, but rather to the martial *meson* of
the *Iliad*, a place of bloody combat where the fate of two armies is decided. By
establishing himself as a *horos* between two factions of the same city, not two armies from

metaikhmiôi is culled from military experience and thus evokes a wealth of associations—which are brought up short by the appearance of *horos*. A similarly unexpected juxtaposition occurs in the metaphors in which Solon and his actions comprise the tenor. In Poem 1 Solon maintains:

αὐτὸς κῆρυξ ἦλθον ἀφ' ἱμερτῆς Σαλαμῖνος,
κόσμον ἐπέων † ὠιδὴν ἀντ' ἀγορῆς θέμενος.
(Solon 1.1–2)

I am come as a herald [*kêrux*] from lovely Salamis,
bringing a song [*ôidê*], an ornament of words, instead of a speech.

The incompatibility of the terms of the vehicle is readily apparent: heralds proclaim messages, they do not compose songs. One must suppose that either Solon did, in fact, deliver a song instead of a speech at a real assembly or that he envisions this in the context of a symposium. The latter possibility seems more likely and suggests that Solon is expanding the symposiastic context—since heralds do not usually address symposia—in envisioning himself as addressing a larger group. Although *ôidê* 'song' is, perhaps, more properly to be considered part of the tenor, its presence after *kêrux* is arresting and vividly emphasizes the idea of the poet as vital messenger.

Solon employs the same strategy of producing emphasis by surprising the audience's expectations when he defends his political actions by insisting:

κέντρον δ' ἄλλος ὡς ἐγὼ λαβών,
κακοφραδής τε καὶ φιλοκτήμων ἀνήρ,
οὐκ ἂν κατέσχε δῆμον·
(Solon 36.20–22)

Had another man than I taken the goad [*kentron*],
a foolish and greedy man,
he would not have restrained [*kateskhe*] the people [*dêmos*].

The juxtaposition of *kentron* with *kateskhe dêmon* is quite startling. Prior to Solon, *kentron* is attested only in the *Iliad* and only in the literal sense

---

two cities, Solon attempts to mark an uninvadable space—something unthinkable in a purely military context but potentially possible in a political context. Loraux concludes that Solon, in effect, makes himself the living incarnation of the *kratos* 'power' of the city, fighting to preserve the possibility of a political life which he knows is at present more or less impossible.

of a goad for horses. Its function, moreover, appears to be the creation of impulsion, not restraint. Hera and Athena, hurrying through the sky in their chariot, have κεντρηνεκέας ἵππους 'goaded horses' (5.752, 8.396). The loss of a *kentron* places Diomedes at a disadvantage in a chariot race (23.387), where increasing, not decreasing, one's speed is the object, and Antilochus uses his *kentron* to urge his horses on (23.430). This would seem to be the logical use of the implement: one does not strike or poke a horse to get it to slow down. Even in Pindar, where the word occurs in both metaphorical and literal contexts, *kentron* seems always to have the function of impelling.[10] Theognis, like Solon, refers to the use of a *kentron* with the *dêmos*, but does not fail to mention the *zeuglê* 'yoke' along with it, the one, presumably, intended for impulsion, the other for restraint:

λὰξ ἐπίβα δήμωι κενεόφρονι, τύπτε δὲ κέντρωι
ὀξέι καὶ ζεύγλην δύσλοφον ἀμφιτίθει·
οὐ γὰρ ἔθ᾽ εὑρήσεις δῆμον φιλοδέσποτον ὧδε
ἀνθρώπων ὁπόσους ἥλιος καθορᾶι.
(Theognis 847–850)

Step with your foot upon the empty-minded people, strike them with
the sharp
goad, and place the painful yoke about their neck;
for you will not find among all the men that the sun looks upon
a people who love servitude so.

Given the Homeric examples, in which no yoke or bridle is implied, that is, no restraint, one suspects that Solon's omission is deliberate. He may, it is true, have simply left out the yoke in his metaphor—or, rather, taken its presence for granted—but the omission gives the juxtaposition of *kentron* 'goad' with *kateskhe* 'restrain' a vivid effect it would not otherwise have. The presentation of himself as a man who, with the implement of a goad, has tried to restrain, not impel, emphasizes the difficulty and unusualness of Solon's efforts. He *has* had to push people, but he is well aware of the danger of pushing them too far—and of the subsequent difficulty of restraining them. He insists, in Poem 37, that if another man had had the same power,

οὐκ ἂν κατέσχε δῆμον, οὐδ᾽ ἐπαύσατο
πρὶν ἀνταράξας πῖαρ ἐξεῖλεν γάλα·
(Solon 37.7–8)

---

10. *Pythian* 2.94, 4.236; Fr. Encom. *124a–b.4; Fr. Incert. 180.3.

he would not have restrained the people, nor would he have stopped
before having stirred up the cream he destroyed the milk.

He observes that

λίην δ᾽ ἐξάραντ᾽ ⟨οὐ⟩ ῥάιδιόν ἐστι κατασχεῖν
ὕστερον

(Solon 9.5–6)

a man who has risen up exceedingly it is not easy to restrain
afterward.

These examples as well as his use of *koros* 'satiety, surfeit' throughout
his poetry reveal his great concern for the problem of restraint. One
suspects that Poem 37 may have clarified the point that he saw himself as using both *kentron* 'goad' and *zeuglê* 'yoke'—if, in fact, in
maintaining that the *dêmos* now has things that they could not have
dreamed of, Solon proceeded to explain how he used the *kentron* to
spur on the *dêmos* to achieve its legitimate demands. In any case, his
metaphor in Poem 36 powerfully depicts his predicament as a
conscientious ruler trying to find a balance between impulsion and
restraint.

A third metaphor presents this predicament in a martial, even epic-
sounding, context. Solon explains:

ἔστην δ᾽ ἀμφιβαλὼν κρατερὸν σάκος ἀμφοτέροισι,
νικᾶν δ᾽ οὐκ εἴασ᾽ οὐδετέρους ἀδίκως.

(Solon 5.5–6)

I stood, casting a strong shield about both sides [*amphoteroisi*],
and would not allow either side to conquer unjustly.

Although this metaphor does conjure up the picture of a heroic warrior
struggling on the battlefield,[11] it is worth noting that a warrior
who holds his shield over two opposing armies, simultaneously
defending each side from the attacks of the other or, following an

---

11. W. Jaeger contends that Solon's use of Homeric language shows that he felt that
he was a heroic champion, a Homeric hero of his own times (*Paideia*, translated by G.
Highet, vol. I [New York, 1939], p. 146). Elsewhere Jaeger argues convincingly that, since
human beings can only be held responsible for their own ruinous acts if they are
forewarned, and since in the sixth century gods do not deal directly with human beings,
Solon transforms the epic motif—the sending of a god to warn men—and assumes for
himself the function of "Divine Warner" ("Solon's Eunomia," in *Five Essays*, translated by
A. M. Fiske [Montreal, 1966], pp. 87–88).

alternative interpretation, defending both sides from an external danger, is a very unusual warrior indeed. There is no example of a warrior of this sort in Homer. Scholars have found the metaphor perplexing, in that it is difficult to understand how Solon could use one shield to protect two parties, unless he means that he protected them from external enemies.[12] But Solon's metaphor is strikingly vivid, not vague, and such a solution seems unnecessarily complicated. Solon is using the traditional image of a protector of his people fulfilling his function for a unified body politic. But in changing it, he manages to suggest both conflict and harmony in the same image. The metaphor seems straightforward until one tries to visualize it too precisely. One would have to envision two shields, but this suggests a division in the state which is not Solon's intention. The unexpectedness of *amphoteroisi* 'for both sides' highlights this difficulty and deliberately under-scores Solon's unique and unHomeric effort to protect both sides, not from an external danger but from each other.

All four examples discussed above emphasize Solon's vision of his own isolation and the unprecedented nature of his efforts, but none so powerfully conveys the sense of heroism—a heroism that is simultaneously Homeric and unHomeric—as the simile which concludes Poem 36:

τῶν οὕνεκ' ἀλκὴν πάντοθεν ποιεόμενος
ὡς ἐν κυσὶν πολλῆισιν ἐστράφην λύκος
(Solon 36.26–27)

Therefore, producing defensive valor [*alkē*] from every direction,
I turned about like a wolf among many hunting dogs.

This simile employs much the same strategy as do the previous examples: the unexpected juxtaposition of terms, in this case terms with powerful overtones from epic and praise-blame poetry, to produce its dramatic and persuasive impact.

---

12. Thus, Linforth observes: "Solon's figure is a little vague. He represents himself as offering to both parties the protection of the same shield. This could only be protection against outsiders. But what Solon evidently intends to express is that his laws are for the common service of both parties and make it impossible for either one to take an unfair advantage of the other. There is no thought of danger from the outside, but true harmony within the state is best displayed by presenting a united front to external aggression" (*Solon the Athenian*, p. 180).

Although Solon does not use the device of animal fables in his poetry,[13] nevertheless he does draw upon the traditional ethical and political connotations of animal imagery for metaphors and similes.[14] As a result, the explicit connotations of wolves and dogs in archaic poetry help to elucidate Solon's simile.

Undeniably, the simile sounds like a typical Homeric simile. It resembles most closely Homer's description of the embattled Hektor, who fights

ὡς δ' ὅτ' ἂν ἔν τε κύνεσσι καὶ ἀνδράσι θηρευτῇσι
κάπριος ἠὲ λέων στρέφεται σθένεϊ βλεμεαίνων·
(*Iliad* 12.41–42)

as when among a pack of hounds and huntsmen assembled
a wild boar or lion turns at bay in the strength of his fury.

Hektor may well be the supreme example of the Homeric hero who fights valiantly in defense of his city, and as such he seems a not unlikely analogue to Solon. But on closer examination Solon's simile also appears strikingly atypical, and, while the poet may be implicitly comparing himself to Hektor, he is at the same time carefully distinguishing himself from that kind of hero.

It seems more than mere coincidence that the Homeric simile which most closely resembles Solon's has as its tenor Hektor and his actions. Solon's decision to present dogs as the attacking animals specifically evokes the role of Hektor in the *Iliad* more than that of any other character in the poem or simply of Homeric heroes in general, for Hektor may be the Homeric character most specifically associated with confrontation with dogs. Many similes in the poem involve the image of

---

13. A reluctance to employ the exclusive, riddling language common in praise-blame poetry may explain the absence of *ainoi* in Solon's poetry. (See Chapter 1, p. 20 and n. 27; Chapter 2, p. 94 and notes 46, 47 and 48.) G. Nagy explains that "*ainos* applies not only to the specific genre of praise poetry but also to the general narrative device of animal fables." There is, thus, a "formal connection between fable and praise poetry" in that *ainos* has the "built-in ideology of exclusiveness" which is also found in epinician praise poetry (*The Best of the Achaeans: Concepts of the Hero in Archaic Greek Poetry* [Baltimore, 1979], pp. 238–240).

14. B. Gentili notes that "in the sociopolitical realm metaphors and similes, drawn for the most part from the world of animals, exemplify moral and political attitudes and modes of behavior" (*Poetry and its Public in Ancient Greece*, translated by A. T. Cole [Baltimore, 1988], pp. 45–46). Similarly, regarding *Pythian* 2.72ff., G. W. Most cites Pindar's "use, familiar from the fable, of animals to denote patterns of human behavior or types of human personality" (*The Measures of Praise* [Göttingen, 1985], p. 122).

hunting or herding dogs pursuing or attacking, or fearing to attack, wild animals, and in addition to *Iliad* 12.41–42 in only two others is Hektor the tenor (5.476;15.271ff.). But dogs figure prominently in the poem in still another significant way. They present a perpetual and hideous threat to human corpses which do not receive proper burial. Nearly half of all of the references in the poem to the possiblity that dogs will rend or consume human flesh refer to this possibility specifically for Hektor, that is, fourteen out of thirty-three instances. In two additional instances, Hektor speaks of the possibility in regard to other persons (13.831 and 15.351), and in one other is reproached by Glaucus for not having the courage to ward off the dogs from Sarpedon's corpse (17.153). For no other individual is the threat mentioned with such frequency. Only Patroklos comes close, and only six of the thirty-three instances refer to the possibility that dogs will consume his corpse. Only twice is the possibliity mentioned for Achilles. This is not, perhaps, a trivial point or one easily forgotten, since the theme of burial in general and of Hektor's burial in particular is of such crucial importance to the *Iliad* as a whole. As a result, the function of dogs as not only hunting or herding animals but also as scavengers reinforces the analogy between Solon and Hektor.

With the exception of two references to actual, rather than metaphorical or hypothetical, dogs—the dogs Apollo's arrows strike (1.50), and the dogs Achilles places on Patroklos' funeral pyre (23.173)—and two instances in which a warrior calls the enemy 'dogs' (8.527 and 13.623), all of the references to dogs in the plural in the *Iliad* are references to hunting or herding dogs in the act of opposing a wild beast or to the possibility that dogs will defile human corpses.[15] In conjunction with the references to the latter possibility, numerous scenes involve warriors fighting to protect the bodies of fallen comrades from being despoiled by the enemy and left unburied for dogs to defile. In such a scene the two types of references to dogs begin to merge. A simile not unlike Solon's depicts Telemonian Aias who, fighting for the corpse of Patroklos,

---

15. The singular (*kuôn*) occurs in reference to single hunting dogs and as an insult or self-reproach, but not in connection with the consumption of human corpses. In the *Odyssey*, dogs have the same functions as in the *Iliad*, but they also have additional domestic functions. They appear not only as hunting or herding dogs but also as watch-dogs, pets, ornamental designs. This is not surprising given the vastly greater number of domestic scenes in the *Odyssey* as compared to the *Iliad*.

ἴθυσεν δὲ διὰ προμάχων συῒ εἴκελος ἀλκὴν
καπρίωι, ὅς τ᾽ ἐν ὄρεσσι κύνας θαλερούς τ᾽ αἰζηοὺς
ῥηϊδίως ἐκέδασσεν, ἐλιξάμενος διὰ βήσσας·
ὣς υἱὸς Τελαμῶνος ἀγαυοῦ φαίδιμος Αἴας
ῥεῖα μετεισάμενος Τρώων ἐκέδασσε φάλαγγας,
οἳ περὶ Πατρόκλωι βέβασαν
                                          (*Iliad* 17.281–286)

He steered through the front fighters in pride of strength [*alkê*] like a
    savage
wild boar, who among the mountains easily scatters
the dogs and strong young men when he turns at bay [*helixamenos*] in
    the valley.
So now the son of haughty Telamon, glorious Aias,
turned to charge and easily scatter the Trojan battalions,
who had taken their stand bestriding Patroklos.

The display of *alkê* and the action of turning around (*helixamenos*)
presents a picture not unlike that in Solon's simile and may begin to
suggest a thematic overlap in the two functions attributed to dogs in the
Iliad. The analogy between Solon and Hektor by itself emphasizes that
Solon, like Hektor, has fought both offensively and defensively to
protect his city. The possibility that Solon is implicitly drawing upon
both types of canine connotations in his choice of simile reinforces this
interpretation and even suggests, perhaps, a religious sanction for
Solon's actions in fighting to protect Athens from defilement by 'dogs'
who would rip her to shreds.

And yet, even as Solon's simile suggests strong parallels between
Solon and Hektor, it also pointedly differentiates the two types, for it is
not, in fact, just like a typical Homeric simile, but the surprise does not
come until the last word: Solon likens himself not to a lion or a boar, as
an audience familiar with Homeric similes would expect, but to a wolf.
This seems a strikingly odd choice, for wolves in Homer have very
different connotations than boars or lions do.[16] Boars and lions

---

16. B. Snell comments that, in Homeric similes "the animal is cited for a generic
behavior. The Homeric lion is always a belligerent beast: above all he is known for his
fierce attacks, but even on the retreat he remains forever warlike. Where the lion is not
extolled as the prototype of noble daring, but is disparaged for his savagery, the criticism
presupposes no change in his nature, but only in the way this nature is judged." Snell
adds that all other animals in Homeric similes have the same constancy of disposition
(*The Discovery of the Mind*, translated by T. G. Rosenmeyer [Cambridge, Mass., 1953], p.
201).

connote heroic strength and valor—often in the face of seemingly insurmountable odds.[17] Again and again in the *Iliad* Homer likens embattled warriors to either or both of these two animals.[18] Not infrequently, the warrior's adversaries are like hunting dogs. Thus, for example, Menelaos is compared to a lion harried by dogs and men (17.657), and Odysseus surrounded by Trojans is compared to a boar surrounded by dogs (11.414).

In contrast, Homer has no such similes comparing an embattled warrior to a wolf. Wolves in Homer have only pejorative connotations and never appear in either of the two contexts associated with dogs. They connote not heroic valour but violence, savagery, the absence of civilized relations. In the *Odyssey* they are mentioned only in the wild domain of Circe (*Odyssey* 10.212, 218, 433). There, wolves fawn on men as dogs do on their master (*Odyssey* 10.218). In the *Iliad*, appearing only in similes, wolves are never hunted or attacked by dogs or hunters, as lions and boars are. In fact, they are never just on the defensive; they are either attacking or simultaneously attacking and defending. They are predatory creatures and prey upon animals distinguished by their lack of *alkê* 'defensive valor'. Poseidon implicitly compares the Achaeans to wolves when he claims that in the past the Trojans have been like fugitive deer who, *analkides* 'without valor [*alkê*] become prey for jackals, leopards, and wolves' (13.99–104). The leaders of the Danaans attack the Trojans just as wolves attack lambs or kids who have *analkida thumon* 'a heart that lacks strength' (16.352–356). Both voracious and persistent, wolves travel in packs. In an extended simile Homer likens the Myrmidons armed for battle to *lukoi ômophagoi* 'wolves who eat raw flesh' who have *aspetos alkê* 'unspeakably great strength' and who travel *agelêdon* 'in packs' (16.156–163). But wolves also seem to be devoid of communal feeling. Twice the Achaeans and the Trojans are compared to wolves fighting among themselves (4.471, 11.72). In *Iliad* 22 Achilles explains that just as there can be no agreement between wolves and lambs, so too can there be none between himself and Hektor (22.262–267). Achilles, of course, is about

---

17. Boars are also mentioned as sacrificial victims (four times in the *Iliad*, twice in the *Odyssey*).

18. Menelaos, Diomedes, Agamemnon, Hektor, Achilles each three times; Patroklos, Aias, Odysseus each twice; Aeneas, Sarpedon and Automedon each once. (In the *Odyssey*, Odysseus is likened to a lion four times.)

to destroy Hektor, the defender of the city. These are the only times wolves are mentioned in Homer. They hardly seem to be distinguished by heroic or civilized behavior.[19] The distinction between the connotations of lions or boars and those of wolves is neatly drawn in *Iliad* 10. In this book, both Agamemnon and Diomedes clothe themselves in lionskins (10.23 and 177).[20] Achilles has just refused the Embassy in *Iliad* 9, and the Achaeans are in dire straits. The donning of a lionskin by Agamemnon and Diomedes may signify the assumption of "lion-ness," simply the heroic valor desperately needed by the Achaeans. The Trojan Dolon, however, preparing to spy on the Achaeans, is in need of something else. *He* clothes himself in the skin of a wolf (10.334).[21] Dolon is leaving the city; he is placing himself beyond its protections. When Odysseus and Diomedes encounter him, Odysseus warns Diomedes to take care

μή πως προτὶ ἄστυ ἀλύξηι.
(*Iliad* 10.348)

nor let him escape to the city.

Dolon's donning of a wolfskin seems to symbolize his need for the savage self-sufficiency of the wolf if he is to survive outside of civilization.

If wolves in Homer connote qualities antithetical to civilized relations, Solon's substitution of wolf for lion or boar in his version of the heroic simile is strikingly unexpected and reveals a new understanding of his own relationship to his community. His simile emphasizes that with his policies he has not attempted to defend his

---

19. Even Autolykos conceivably possesses wolf-like attributes suggestive of uncivilized behavior. Like a wolf he hunts in a pack with his sons, and it is he

ὃς ἀνθρώπους ἐκέκαστο
κλεπτοσύνηι θ' ὅρκωι τε·
(*Odyssey* 19.395–396)

who surpassed all men
in thievery and the art of the oath.

Although these attributes would not have had pejorative connotations in Homeric society, nevertheless they are not emblematic of civilized behavior characterized by law and order and are unlikely characteristics for Solon to wish to claim.

20. Lionskins are mentioned only here. Odysseus wears a helmet with the tusks of a boar set on it which, incidentally, Autolykos stole (10.263–267).

21. A wolfskin is mentioned only here.

society as it is, as Hektor does. Rather, in trying to save the *polis* he has had to redefine it, and, in so doing, he has placed himself outside of it, beyond its protections. The word *lukos* is reserved for the last position in the line for effect; it is not the word Solon's hearers might expect. His use of the singular adds a particular poignancy: in Homer, wolves travel in packs. The only singular use in Homer refers to the wolfskin of Dolon. And Dolon, as it happens, does not fare so well.[22] Solon sees himself as a lone wolf attacked from all sides. Given the explicit Homeric connotations, to say "I am like a wolf..." is not simply to say, "I am heroic in the way that a Homeric hero is heroic." It is to say, "I am heroic in a way that no Homeric hero ever had to be."

And yet, the implications of Solon's simile do not end here. In other ancient authors, the symbol of the wolf consistently retains its Homeric sense of outcast or antithesis of civilized relations.[23] The connotations are more explicit, perhaps, than in Homer and suggest still another dimension to Solon's simile, because, in fact, the outcast has a specific social function in the tradition of praise-blame poetry. Alcaeus speaks of exile, claiming

οἶος ἐοίκησα λυκαιμίαις
(Alcaeus 130.25)

alone, I settled in the wolf-thickets.

Banished from civilization, he must frequent the wild haunts of wolves.[24]

---

22. Although obviously Achilles in 22.262–267 is implicitly only a single wolf, he speaks not of 'wolf' but of 'wolves'. Loraux notes that in the language of epic, wolves are evoked in situations when the battle is dangerously equalized. In holding himself against the opposing sides, Solon's solitary wolf is an inconceivable wolf (Loraux, "Solon au milieu de la lice," p. 207).

23. The derivation of Lukourgos from λύκος and (ϝ)έργω (P. Chantraine, *Dictionnaire étymologique de la langue grecque* [Paris, 1968]) corroborates this conception of the wolf. This name for the legendary law-giver of Sparta, "one who shuts out the wolves" by establishing law and order, is thoroughly consistent with a view of the wolf as antithetical to civilization. G. Nagy, *Greek Mythology and Poetics* (Ithaca, 1990), p. 272, n. 13 offers some good bibliography on this subject.

24. Whether λυκαιμίαις is masculine nominative singular meaning "I, a wolf-thicket man," or accusative plural and the object of ἐοίκησα meaning "I settled in the wolf thickets" (the two possibilities suggested by D. L. Page, *Sappho and Alcaeus* [Oxford, 1955], p. 205), this interpretation remains the same.

In legend, too, the wolf invariably symbolizes qualities antithetical to civilization. The temporary transformation of an individual into a wolf is a frequent theme. Herodotus relates this as an annual occurence for the Neuri, inhabitants of the extreme northern part of Scythia (4.105). Plato refers to the legend of Lycaon, exiled and turned into a wolf for tasting human flesh in sacrifice. Socrates suggests that this is a fitting analogy to the inevitable fate of the tyrant (*Republic* 565d–e). Pausanias gives the details of the Lycaon legend and the ritual to which, he claims, the legend gave rise. He emphasizes that the transformation is temporary if, and only if, the individual during his nine years as a wolf refrains from eating human flesh (8.2.3 and 6). In Apollodorus (3.8.1) and Pliny (*Natural History* 8.81) who records the version that Varro got from Euanthes, the details of the story vary slightly; but in both, as in Pausanias, the cause of the transformation is the consumption of human flesh (in Apollodorus' version, it is the attempt to feed human flesh to Zeus, that is, the treating of human flesh as food). The cause of the re-transformation is invariably the abstention from eating human flesh.[25] It might seem that the transformation into a wolf is a suitable

---

H. Lloyd-Jones and M. R. Lefkowitz, however, agree with M. W. Haslam (*P. Oxy.* 53 [1986], p. 123) that the correct reading is not λυκαιμίαις but λυκαιχμίαις. The word is either nominative, meaning 'wolf-man', or 'wolf-spearman', or, posssibly, dative plural, meaning 'wolf-battles'. Lloyd-Jones and Lefkowitz maintain that the word suggests the deceptive cunning of the wolf that is "the antithesis of open and regulated hoplite warfare," with the implication that Alcaeus is referring not to his exile or solitude but, rather, to his guerrilla fighting tactics (Lloyd-Jones and Lefkowitz, "Λυκαιχμίαις" *Zeitschrift für Papyrologie und Epigraphik* 68 [1987], pp. 9-10). But, in any case, whether the reference is to 'wolf-thicket man', 'wolf-thickets', 'wolf-man', or 'wolf-battles', the 'wolf-' part of the word indicates a departure from civilized or harmonious relations with other men.

25. W. Burkert identifies the ritual as one of initiation, explaining that the transformation into a wolf, as Euanthes describes it, is easy to understand as an initiation ritual: removing clothing and swimming across a lake are undoubtedly 'rites de passage' (*Homo Necans* [Berlin, 1972], p. 105).

punishment for the crime of consuming human flesh, since this is something regularly ascribed to wolves.[26] But perhaps the man who eats human flesh is behaving like a wolf not so much because he eats the proper food of wolves—after all, rabbits probably form a more substantial part of the wolf diet—but because he consumes the flesh of his own kind. This is the extreme antithesis of civilized behavior.

Wolves also appear as figures for lawlessness and hostility. Their behavior toward sheep serves as an analogy for violence against defenseless victims (Herodotus 4.149) and for the misuse of law by *ponêroi* 'knavish men' against innocent people (Xenophon *Memorabilia* 2.9).[27] There appears to have existed a mythic tradition anterior to Homer and more explicit, understanding the wolf as a figure for the outlaw and the exile, a demon to be pursued and expelled.[28] This tradition connects the wolf with the idea of the *pharmakos* 'one sacrificed as a purification for others, scapegoat', with ritual condemnation, exile, execution.[29]

The figure of the wolf thus serves an important social function, a function manifest in praise-blame poetry. Pindar reveals that the traditional function of the poet is to be *philos* 'a friend' to the *philos* (that is, to praise), and to be *ekhthros* 'hateful', to the *ekhthros* (that is, to blame) *lukoio dikan* 'in the manner of the wolf' (*Pythian* 2.83–85). This notion is encapsulated in the name *Luk-ambês* 'having the steps of a

---

26. G. S. Kirk asserts that consuming human flesh "is a thing wolves notoriously do. Therefore the man who tastes human flesh is behaving like a wolf, and it is poetically and mythically appropriate that he should become one" (*The Nature of Greek Myths* [Woodstock, N.Y., 1975], p. 240).

27. The two symbolic ranges, wolf as improper consumer and wolf as antithesis of communal law, seem to be linked in Aesop Fable 348 (B. E. Perry, ed. *Aesopica* [Urbana, Illinois, 1952]. This fable about the Wolf as Lawgiver parallels the story of the tyrant Maiandrios in Herodotus 3.142–143, in that both the wolf and the tyrant pervert the principles of community by reserving for themselves special privileges (Maiandrios) or portions of meat (the wolf) before placing all under communal control. (For a discussion, with further bibliography, see G. Nagy, *Greek Mythology and Poetics* [Ithaca, 1990], p. 272, n. 13).

28. L. Gernet, *Anthropologie de la Grèce antique* (Paris, 1982), pp. 214–216.

29. Gernet suggests that, as a result, the *Doloneia* "pourrait avoir sa lointaine origine bien oubliée d'Homère, dans des rites et notions préhistoriques que l'épopée avait complètement transposés" (*Anthropologie de la Grèce antique*, p. 223).

wolf'.[30] The purpose of both praise and blame is a strengthening of the bonds of *philotês* 'friendship'. The blame poetry of Archilochus, directed against *Luk-ambês*, has as its explicit social function the affirmation of *philotês* within the community.[31]

Solon's simile recognizes the efficacy of a symbolic 'wolf', a kind of *pharmakos*, or scapegoat, for the promotion of social cohesion, and gives the tradition a twist, for the poet takes the role upon himself.[32] He transposes the wolf symbol into the hero necessary for the preservation of his society. His tone is a far cry from the lament of Alcaeus' 'wolf-thicket man' (or, possibly, 'wolf-spearman'). In choosing to depict his opponents as dogs, Solon is employing the traditional diction of praise poetry which represents as dogs those who blame without justification.[33] The simile recalls, to some extent, the image of himself holding a *sakos* 'shield' over contending parties (5.5–6). It has the same Homeric cast, and it is illogical in much the same way. The simile suggests a two-way conflict whereas, in reality, it must have been at least a three-way conflict. Just as Solon depicted as one single act the holding of a shield in defense of warring factions, here, too, he presents his adversaries as if they were a unified group, that is, he presents the conflicting elements within the "dog pack" as if they had a single purpose.[34] Thus, with a simile likening himself to a wolf, the poet creates unity where there is none.

---

30. Nagy, *The Best of the Achaeans*, pp. 241–242 and n. 2. Nagy maintains that "Pindar's words apparently connote the stylized movements of a dance that represents the steps of a wolf. So too with the name *Luk-ambês* the second half of this compound, like that of *i-ambos*, seems to indicate an actual dance step."

31. Nagy, *The Best of the Achaeans*, pp. 243ff.

32. The reversal of terms is a strategy he also employs in Poem 33, in which he uses traditional praise-blame concepts in order to define, and thereby defuse, his "critic." (See Chapter 2, pp. 104–105.)

33. Nagy argues that "the language of praise poetry presents the language of unjustified blame as parallel to the eating of heroes' corpses by dogs." Moreover, quarrels in epic poetry incorporate the language of blame, and in these *kuôn* is a prominent word of insult (Nagy, *The Best of the Achaeans*, p. 226). No doubt, therefore, Solon has not overlooked the element of insult in presenting his opponents as dogs.

34. Hence the ambiguity of *enantioi* 'adversaries' (36.23) and *houteroi* 'the others' (36.24). Linforth understands *enantioi* as aristocrats who opposed Solon's policies and the *houteroi* as the popular party (*Solon the Athenian* [Berkeley, 1919], p. 190), but the converse is equally plausible. (See also Chapter 2, note 57 above.)

One can contrast Solon's approach with Alcaeus' attempt to represent factional conflict. In his celebrated poem describing a ship in a storm (326), Alcaeus depicts himself and his men as hopelessly surrounded by two armed and hostile factions. Defeat seems inevitable.[35] Solon's approach is thus not only more optimistic but far more constructive as political poetry.

Solon's effort to create social unity and his alienation from the community are consistent with the traditional relationship between the generic lawgiver and his community. Legend recognizes that the lawgiver's exclusive power to change the code he himself instituted makes him a potential threat to its stability. The solution to this problem is either the lawgiver's death or self-imposed exile.[36] Solon's simile combines acknowledgement of this political necessity with the application of a poetic strategy, neatly fusing his roles as lawgiver and as poet.

Deliberate reference to both his political activity and his poetic activity may, in fact, be encompassed by the phrase *alkēn...poieomenos* 'producing defensive valor' (Solon 36.26). *Poieō* 'make, produce' in this context is both unexpected and unprecedented. The Homeric verb in such similes is, invariably, *peithō*, and the phrase is *alki pepoithōs* 'confident of his defensive valor' (five times in the *Iliad*, once in the *Odyssey*).[37] Homer never uses *poieō* with *alkē*. Perhaps the more crucial question is why Solon would choose the middle of *poieō* with *alkē* and not simply *amunomenos* 'defending [myself] against'. Perhaps it is no coincidence that later poets, including Solon, use *poieō* of poetic composition. Arguably, *poiein* in Theognis 771 indicates poetic fabrication, and the only other archaic instance in which the verb refers to poetry occurs in the compound *metapoiein* in Solon 20.3.[38] But this list may be one short, for the unexpected combination of *poieō* with *alkē*

---

35. As Gentili notes, "the impossibility of carrying on a battle on two fronts makes the enemy's victory very likely" (*Poetry and its Public in Ancient Greece*, p. 204).

36. A. Szegedy-Maszak, "Legends of the Greek Lawgivers," *Greek, Roman and Byzantine Studies* 19 (1975), p. 207.

37. *Iliad* 5.299, 13.471, 17.61, 17.728, 18.158; *Odyssey* 6.130. Theognis uses it as well: 1.949, 2.1280a.

38. L. Edmunds, "The Genre of Theognidean Poetry," in *Theognis of Megara*, edited by T. J. Figuiera and G. Nagy (Baltimore and London, 1985), pp. 107–109.

suggests that *poieomenos* in Solon's simile indicates poetic as well as political activity.[39]

The metapoetic quality of the simile thus provides an additional frame of reference for Solon's actions. Certainly, reference must be made to his role as a legislator,[40] but over-emphasis on Solon's efforts to *legislate* justice can lead one to overlook the "performative" element in his poetry, that is, the extent to which the poetry is itself an attempt to create communal harmony. As a lawgiver, Solon did create an actual law code. Nevertheless, he is still a poet who seeks to accomplish something socially productive with his poetry. In merging his poetry with his political activity, Solon's simile invites reference to the act of poetic composition itself.

Moreover, the defensive tone in Solon's "explanatory" verses attests to his realization that his policies have not succeeded as he had hoped. In Poem 34 he maintains:

ἃ μὲν γὰρ εἶπα, σὺν θεοῖσιν ἤνυσα
(Solon 34.6)

for with the help of the gods, I accomplished what I said.

But Poem 36 begins with the rhetorical question:

ἐγὼ δὲ τῶν μὲν οὕνεκα ξυνήγαγον
δῆμον, τί τούτων πρὶν τυχεῖν ἐπαυσάμην;
(Solon 36.1–2)

But as for me, for the sake of these things I gathered together
the people. Why [*ti*] did I stop myself before I attained these things?

The question seems to contradict the assertion at 34.6 as well as a later comment in Poem 36 that διῆλθον ὡς ὑπεσχόμην 'I came through as I

---

39. One might dismiss this assessment by arguing that the presence of *pantothen* 'from every side' necessarily precludes the use of *peithô* with *alkê*. No less plausible, however, is the contention that rather it is the substitution of *poieô* for *peithô* that makes possible the use of *pantothen*. D. Campbell notes that in Sophocles *Oedipus at Colonus* 459 *alkên poieisthai* means 'to help' (*Greek Lyric Poetry* [Basingstoke and London, 1967], p. 253, n. 26).

40. Nagy argues that (in contrast to Hesiod or Theognis) "the primary frame of reference for *dikê* 'justice' in the poetry of Solon is not the poetry itself but rather his law code" ("Theognis and Megara: A Poet's Vision of his City," in *Theognis of Megara*, edited by T. J. Figuiera and G. Nagy [Baltimore and London, 1985], p. 70). Nagy contrasts Theognis for whom "the only frame of reference for *dikê* is the actual poetry."

promised' (36.17). It amounts to an admission that he did not, in fact, accomplish what he said he would. If *ti* translates as 'what' instead of 'why', the question remains rhetorical, with the implication that Solon himself carried out his program as intended. If problems still remain, the fault lies with the citizenry, not himself. In either case, the point is that Solon did what he promised, but the *results* were far from what he had anticipated. There is, perhaps, a sad irony that as a great proponent of the necessity of understanding which predictable consequences necessarily result directly from specific actions, Solon himself undertook actions whose consequences he failed to predict accurately. Possibly, it is not a coincidence that Poem 36, which opens with such an admission of his frustrated political efforts, concludes with an affirmation of his poetic efforts, as if the poet began to have more confidence in his ability to create communal harmony by means of poetry than in the possibility of legislating communal harmony. The poet, after all, unlike the lawgiver, can still function effectively even as an 'outcast'.

Perhaps Solon has this in mind even in Poem 1 when he claims:

αὐτὸς κῆρυξ ἦλθον ἀφ' ἱμερτῆς Σαλαμῖνος,
κόσμον ἐπέων †ὠιδὴν ἀντ' ἀγορῆς θέμενος.
(Solon 1.1–2)

I am come as a herald from lovely Salamis,
    bringing a song [*ôidê*], an ornament of words [*kosmos epeôn*],
    instead of a speech.

The phrase *kosmos epeôn ôidê* is certainly puzzling[41]—but not if one recognizes it as a reference to the unique ability of poetry, in contrast to a political speech, or to unilateral legislation, to promote order and unity of purpose among members of the audience.

The concluding dissonance of Solon's *lukos* 'wolf' simile culminates a series of dissonances expressed in the poem: *douleusa...eleutherê* 'slave...free' (7), *allon ekdikôs, allon dikaiôs* 'one contrary to law, one according to law' (9–10), *biên...dikên* 'force...justice' (16), *kakôi te kagathôi* 'for the base man and for the noble man' (18), *kentron...ouk an kateskhe* 'goad...would not have restrained' (20–22). Whereas Poems 13 and 4 discuss more general subject matter, Poem 36, in referring to

---

41. B. A van Groningen, for example, comments that the phrase "reste une expression peu claire, et certainement surprenante pour une élégie" (*La composition littéraire archaïque grecque* [Amsterdam, 1960], p. 131, n. 2).

Solon's own actions, emphasizes this series of antitheses. Iambics, rather than elegiacs, seem the appropriate choice for the expression of dissonance—particularly if Solon recognizes his own position as that of the politically and poetically necessary scapegoat.

Perhaps Poem 36 was Solon's farewell address upon leaving office. Perhaps he delivered it as a speech immediately prior to his self-imposed ten-year exile from Athens. In any case, the simile which concludes the poem suggests that it was far more than simply an attempt at self-justification, far more than an explanation and defense of his political legislation, of his refusal to become tyrant. It contains little reference to specific legislation. To be sure, a contemporary audience would be well-acquainted with the specifics of his political activities. But no doubt Solon's poetry is intended for posterity as well, not in the sense of preserving an historical record for uninformed people, that is, not lest important facts and events be forgotten, as in epic poetry or the work of Herodotus, but, rather, in the sense of providing important information for like-thinking men to use in similar situations—in which case the specifics are not indispensable. Certainly the fact that poetic verse is readily remembered makes it both useful for public dissemination and likely to be passed on for generations. If so, the lack of specificity in Solon's poem may have more to do with the fact that the specific legislation he created did not appear to be achieving the results he desired. His failure to legislate the unity he envisioned for Athens may have lead him to greater reliance upon poetry's ability to create harmony and order.

Just as in Poem 13, discussed in Chapter 1, Solon's address to the Muses attests to his vision of himself as a poet, so, too, in Poem 36 his relationship to his audience is self-consciously that of a poet no less than a lawgiver. The *lukos* simile which concludes the poem, understood as a reference to both his political activity and his poetic activity, demonstrates Solon's awareness of the political and poetic function of the 'scapegoat' in the promotion of communal harmony. This simile, like the other four similes and metaphors in Solon's extant poetry in which the poet himself forms the tenor, emphasizes Solon's isolation and unique heroism. While the simile recalls Homeric heroism in general and Hektor's heroism in particular, the unexpected choice of a wolf rather than a lion or a boar forcefully distinguishes Solon from Hektor and reveals the poet's optimism. The simile invites reference to the Homeric would-be savior of Troy to emphasize that the hero struggling to preserve Athens must be of a different sort. Solon's predicament differs from Hektor's in two important ways: his opponents are not foreign enemies but fellow citizens, and, whereas Hektor ultimately fails to protect his city, Solon intends to succeed.

This optimism derives less, perhaps, from confidence in his political actions than from confidence in the power of his poetry. The total absence in his poetry of specific references to his legislation[42] is consistent with the view that Solon saw his verses not merely as an explanation or defense of his political ideas and actions but as a separate route to the creation of a unified, harmonious polity. This seems to be the case not only in his elegies, which are more overtly didactic, but also in his tetrameters and trimeters, which scholars tend to see as largely self-justifying or defensive. Indeed, Poem 36 seems unmistakably so, but as a poem in defense of Solon's political actions it is baffling in its lack of specificity. And yet, if lack of specificity is a drawback in a political treatise, it is no failing in a poem. Just as in Poem 4, discussed in Chapter 2, lack of specificity assisted Solon in his effort to unify his *polis* by an appeal to all members of his audience not merely a select few, so, too, Poem 36, although sacrificing intellectual clarity, vividly demonstrates the poet's ability to create a poetic vision of the very unity lacking in the polity.

Poem 36, like Poem 13, suggests that Solon recognized the traditional archaic sense of the poet as an arbiter of values.[43] Perhaps the *lukos* simile, and indeed all of the similes and metaphors in which Solon himself and his actions form the tenor, attests to the fact that this is a role the master of words can perform more successfully than the master of deeds.

---

42. No accident of survival, according to W. J. Woodhouse (*Solon the Liberator* [London, 1938], p. 12).

43. Marcel Detienne, *Les maîtres de vérité dans la Grèce archaïque* (Paris, 1981), p. 19. And see Chapter 1, p. 16 above.

Conclusion

If there is a way to appreciate both the content and the form of Solon's message, it is by examining the connection between his political activity and his poetic activity, and, more specifically, the way in which Solon himself understood and expressed that connection. Such an approach derives clarification from archaic parallels and conventions without overlooking either their political function or Solon's aesthetic contribution. A unified, thematic approach to Solon's poetry acknowledges the similarities between poems and reveals the poet's consciousness of his own poetic activity and of his relationship to his audience. Comparison with the themes, imagery, and poetic conventions of other archaic poetry helps to clarify both his reliance on tradition and his departure from it. Drawing upon the associations of traditional language and imagery and adapting them to his own purposes, Solon repeatedly endeavors to express new ideas, the novelty of which can only be appreciated by reference to conventional views and forms of expression. While the social function of much of the poetry during Solon's period and earlier was customarily exclusionary, Solon attempts to use traditional themes, language, and imagery to promote communal harmony—which, he recognizes, must include all members of the *polis*. Examination of his poetry as a unit and in this larger context thus enables one to evaluate the extent of his poetic contribution, to locate him in an understanding of the Greek moral consciousness, and to appreciate his lack of reference to specific political actions or legislation.

In Poem 13, Solon self-consciously allies himself with epic and lyric poetic tradition by commencing with an appeal to the Muses. This opening address may be interpreted as an appeal to that aspect of *Mnêmosunê* 'Memory' which provides knowledge of the logical causal connections between actions and their consequences. This, too is the essential element in the *olbos* 'prosperity' and *doxa* 'reputation' Solon seeks. Far from being unconnected to the remainder of the poem, the opening invocation thus encapsulates all that follows. In this poem, Solon takes issue with the traditional view that human fortunes determine human attitudes. Rather, he recognizes that human attititudes—optimism and acquisitiveness in particular—exist independent of, even in spite of, actual fortunes. These attitudes are responsible for the ceaseless activity of human beings in all its diverse forms and thereby contribute substantially to the form that human fortunes take. This assessment thus acknowledges that human beings, no less than gods, are responsible for human fortunes. The cease-less pursuit of wealth, Solon argues, is dangerous for the individual as well as for the community—not simply because the gods inevitably punish evil-doers, an argument that often seems empirically false, but because indiscriminate and insatiable acquisitiveness necessarily results in unpleasant consequences in and of itself. Accurate identification of the causal relationship between actions and their consequences is, thus, a persuasive contribution to the preservation of communal harmony.

This view is expanded in Poem 4, which reveals that in his efforts to use poetry to create harmony in the *polis* as a whole, Solon must contend with archaic poetic conventions designed to promote social cohesion among small aristocratic groups. Accurate appreciation of the logic of causality is therefore essential, and in this poem Solon emphasizes the responsibility of individuals for the consequences of their own actions, and the interdependence between individual fortunes and the fortunes of the *polis* as a whole. Here, too, Solon recognizes, as do other archaic poets, the dangers of excessive, unrestrained consumption. But Solon perceives the flaws in the traditional assessment of the problem. Identifying the inadequacy of the symposium as a paradigm for communal organization, he implicitly criticizes partisan poetry for its failure to achieve social cohesion. In rejecting the exclusivity of the a istocratic approach, Solon recognizes that his own verses must incljde, that is, be comprehensible and acceptable to, all members of the *polis*. To this end, the ambiguities in his poetry are not intended to veil his meaning to one segment of his audience rather than another. They are equally ambiguous to all and often result simply from the difficulties of his material. The solution Solon proposes in this poem excludes both tyranny and aristocratic utopianism, since neither can achieve true civic harmony. Rather he insists that harmony in the *polis* can only result from the citizens' accurate recognition of their interdependence and their ongoing acceptance of communal limits and responsibiliities.

In Poem 36, Solon personalizes the problematic relationship between the individual and the community in examining his own relationship to his city. As in Poem 13, his relationship to his audience is self-consciously that of a poet no less than a lawgiver. In the simile which concludes the poem, Solon produces emphasis by surprising the audience' expectations, a strategy he also employs in other similes and metaphors. With an unexpected juxtaposition of terms in this simile, he merges his poetic activity with his political activity. Drawing upon the resonances of epic and praise-blame poetry, Solon takes upon himself the role of the 'scapegoat', which he recognizes is both politically and poetically necessary for the creation of harmony within the *polis.*

Solon's originality and creativity as a poet is thus most evident in his reassessment of the social function of the poet and the purpose of his poetry. In confronting both political realities and poetic conventions, Solon seems to appreciate that perhaps his greatest weapon is not so much ambiguity but surprise. Although he does use ambiguity to appeal to disparate factions in his audience, to suggest one thing to one group and at the same time another to another, more often he endeavors to surprise the expectations of his audience as a whole in his selection of imagery and of specific words. This shifting of emphases, the playing with the audience's expectations, is, for him, a potent method of specifying the meanings of words and images. Surprise thus gives Solon's poetry its powerful impact and at the same time its specificity. That specificity is not always easy to ascertain at first sight, but Solon's intentions are equally accessible to all members of his audience. The strategy of surprise is, for him, a way to include people, to unify his audience. It contrasts markedly with the use of riddling language intended to address a select few, that is, with the effort to exclude or to divide, as in the poetry of Theognis or Archilochus, for example. Solon's strategy of surprise seeks to ensure that we all understand the same things when we hear the same words and attempt to visualize the same images. The strategy indicates that Solon does not intend for his verses to be understood on a superficial level, for the poet's task is not, in his view, the promotion of superficial understanding.

The superficial understanding that Solon most vehemently rejects is the mere acceptance of conventional views of causality. True knowledge, for Solon, is the ability to understand the logical connections between actions and their consequences. But the recognition that only such knowledge can lead to communal harmony nowhere envisions the modern notions of moral self-consciousness[1] or a sense of moral duty. Rather, it is possible to analyze Solon's conception as one of a much simpler kind of interdependence analogous to that which exists among *philoi* 'friends, dear ones' in the Homeric world.

Far from espousing a modern conception of moral responsibility, Solon embraces the traditional ethical view inherited from Homer and Hesiod which distinguishes friends from enemies and understands appropriate conduct as seeking to benefit the former and harm the latter. Thus, Solon asks the Muses to grant to him

εἶναι δὲ γλυκὺν ὧδε φίλοις, ἐχθροῖσι δὲ πικρόν,
τοῖσι μὲν αἰδοῖον, τοῖσι δὲ δεῖνον ἰδεῖν
(Solon 13.5-6)

And so to be sweet to friends [*philoi*] and bitter to enemies [*ekhthroi*],
an object of reverence to the former, but to the latter terrible to
look upon.

Homeric heroes use the word *philos* as a means of differentiating from the rest of the environment a person or thing essential to their survival. *Philoi* are entitled to mutual reliance and support as well as to the consumption of available basic necessities. The verb *philein* denotes the act of creating or maintaining this cooperative relationship, not any feeling of friendliness (which is not a necessary part of it).[2] The

---

1. Poem 33 does, however, suggest a movement away from the archaic shame-ethic identified by E. R. Dodds in *The Greeks and the Irrational* (Berkeley, 1951), pp. 18ff. A. W. H. Adkins explains that "the Homeric hero cannot fall back upon his own opinion of himself, for his self only has the value which other people put upon it" (*Merit and Responsibility: A Study in Greek Values* [Oxford, 1960], p. 49). Solon seems to dispute this attitude in giving voice to a critic's opinion of him. In implicitly ridiculing the critic, he implies that the standard for judging Solon correctly is set by Solon himself, not by some other person voicing his own or "public opinion.

2. Thus Adkins interprets the Homeric use of *philos*, in "Friendship and Self-Sufficiency in Homer and Aristotle," *Classical Quarterly* 56 (1963), pp. 34–36. Adkins explains that in the Homeric world, in wartime "success is so imperative that only results have any value; intentions are unimportant. Similarly, and for similar reasons, it is [*aiskhron*] 'shameful' to fail in time of peace to protect one's family and guests, whatever one's intentions." Therefore, "actions must be judged by results; for it is by results that

situation which obtains in the world of Homer's heroes, the concept of interdependent *philoi*, might well be Solon's model for the ideal relationship between citizens in the *polis*, relying on and cooperating with one another, each seeking his own benefit. Such a view seems no more compatible with Kant's categorical imperative than it is with the New Testament injunction to love one's enemies.

It is within this view of appropriate ethical behavior that Solon emphasizes the logical connections between human actions and their consequences. He does not claim, of course, that if one does good, one will prosper. Experience will not support that (Solon 13.67-70). Instead, he recognizes that the actions of individuals inevitably have a direct affect on the well-being of the entire community, the *polis*. The greed and licentiousness of individuals with *adikos noos* 'unjust mind' (Solon 4.7), for example, lead to civil strife, slavery, and bloodshed in the *polis*, and οὕτω δημόσιον κακὸν ἔρχεται οἴκαδ' ἑκάστωι 'thus the public evil comes homeward to each man' (Solon 4.26). Scholars have appreciated this element in Solon's thought, and indeed in that of other poets such as Homer and Aeschylus,[3] but the observation has led some to conclude that Solon understands this connection in a very modern

---

the household continues to exist or fails to do so" (*Merit and Responsibility*, pp. 35–36). Not surprisingly, then, the verb *"philein"* requires of the subject of the verb not primarily emotions or intentions which one might still have when the object of the verb was not present, but actions and results" ("Friendship and Self-Sufficiency in Homer," p. 34). Comparison with Kant's view that nothing is good except a good will (I. Kant, *Foundations of the Metaphysics of Morals*, translated by L. W. Beck [Indianapolis, 1959], p. 9) and that to be truly moral an action must be independent of self-interest (p. 27) suggests how distinct the Homeric attitude is from modern ethical views.

3. For example: C. M. Bowra, *Early Greek Elegists* (Cambridge, Mass., 1938), p. 84; W. Jaeger, *Paideia*, translated by G. Highet, vol. I (New York, 1939), p. 142, and "Solons Eunomie," In *Five Essays*, translated by A. M. Fiske (Montreal, 1966), p. 93; G. Vlastos, "Solonian Justice," *Classical Philology* 41 (1946), p. 71; F. Solmsen, *Hesiod and Aeschylus* (New York, 1949), pp. 91–92, 112–114.

way.[4] Solon does not, however, make any claim for universal truths or immanent laws binding every community. He asserts rather that human actions have logical consequences, and evil actions have, logically, harmful consequences for everyone. He gives this point particular emphasis in Poem 4. Hesiod *Works and Days* 265-266 may contain the germ of this idea, but for Hesiod the wrongdoer suffers through the action of Zeus, not through the logical consequences of the actions themselves.[5] In stressing human responsibility for the consequences of human actions, Solon is not necessarily thinking in moral terms.[6] His insistence that every individual must look to the consequences of his actions is an attempt to appeal not to individuals' sense of moral responsibility but rather to their own self-interest. Indeed, he argued that he was framing his laws so that it would be clear that it was to everybody's advantage to keep them (Plutarch *Solon* 5).

---

4. Jaeger, for example, makes Solon sound rather like Kant when he insists that "recognition of the universal truth that every community is bound by immanent laws implies that every man is a responsible moral agent with a duty to be done" (*Paideia*, vol. I, p. 143).

5. In contrast, Solon argues that, just as natural events have natural causes, human events have human causes:

> ἐκ νεφέλης πέλεται χιόνος μένος ἠδὲ χαλάζης,
> βροντὴ δ' ἐκ λαμπρῆς γίγνεται ἀστεροπῆς·
> ἀνδρῶν δ' ἐκ μεγάλων πόλις ὄλλυται, ἐς δὲ μονάρχου
> δῆμος ἀϊδρίηι δουλοσύνην ἔπεσεν.
>   (Solon 9.1–4).

The force of snow and of hail is from a cloud,
    and thunder comes from shining lightning;
But from great men a city is destroyed,
    and through ignorance the people fall into the slavery of monarchy.

H. Fränkel explains that here again human responsibility for human destiny is established and notes the marked absence of any mention of Zeus as the producer of the bad weather and the lightning (*Dichtung und Philosophie des frühen Griechentums* [New York, 1951], p. 302).

6. "Responsibility" is an ambivalent word. It can have a moral sense or a morally neutral sense. For example, the sentence "Joe is responsible for shutting the door" can mean: Joe is in charge of shutting the door and he is culpable if he fails to do so (or, in the same way: Joe shut the door and it should/should not have been shut; so he is to be punished/rewarded). Alternatively, it can have the morally neutral meaning: Joe's action of placing his hand on the door and pushing caused the door to shut.

Solon's vision of intelligent, far-sighted self-interest on the part of citizens in the *polis* thus seems to derive from an appreciation of the relationships of *philoi* in the Homeric epics. Occasional poetry, too, recognizes the social importance of *philotês* 'friendship', but only within small, exclusive groups of *philoi*. Solon expands the social context to cover civic relationships. This accounts, for example, for his assertion that

ὅσοι δὲ μείζους καὶ βίην ἀμείνονες,
αἰνοῖεν ἄν με καὶ φίλον ποιοίατο.
(Solon 37. 4-5)

And those men who are greater and stronger
might praise me and consider me their friend.

Although *philos* is not a particularly powerful word of praise in Greek,[7] Solon's statement is surprising only if one fails to perceive the social importance of *philotês* in epic and occasional poetry.

If, therefore, Solon's conception of communal relations owes much to the archaic understanding of the relationship between *philoi*, any contradiction perceived between his innovations in the realm of political justice and his traditionalist views of acquisitive or distributive justice[8] is not so much of a contradiction after all. Solon is considered a great innovator in recognizing that the security of individuals is interdependent, that the common security is inevitably imperiled by any unjust action,[9] but if this recognition actually owes a great deal to the archaic conception of relations among *philoi*, then Solon is a traditionalist in terms of political justice as well—albeit an extremely creative one.[10]

---

7. Adkins, *Merit and Responsibility*, p. 31.

8. Vlastos, "Solonian Justice," p. 76.

9. Vlastos, p. 69.

10. Although it may be unscientific to seek corroborative evidence in the legislation attributed to Solon in antiquity, since, as I. Linforth notes, it is impossible to know which laws were really Solon's (*Solon the Athenian* [Berkeley, 1919], p. 70ff.), a consistency of pattern might at least suggest that ancient scholars understood, though perhaps not consciously, the motivation underlying Solon's actions, even if some of the laws attributed to him were not actually his. And there does seem to be remarkable consistency in "Solon's" laws regulating the relationship between members of the same family. All seem

Solon's ethical position may be understood in this way, but his lack of specificity as to the details of his political program must encourage the view that he himself hoped that his verses would be understood and appreciated for their permanent contribution to the political and ethical discussion at Athens. The absence of reference to specific political actions or legislation renders these verses far more persuasive to a factionalized contemporary audience. It also allows them to speak across centuries in making them applicable to modern political realities no less than sixth-century ones. More important, perhaps, it enables Solon to demonstrate poetry's ability to succeed where political programs fail, to create communal harmony within the *polis*—at least in the imagination, which is, after all, where concord must begin.

---

designed to strengthen family ties—but none seem likely to create tensions *between* families. This does support a desire to strengthen existing *philoi* relationships, but not at the expense of civic relationships. In fact, virtually all of "Solon's" laws regulating the relationship between citizens seem consistent with the notion of a return to the *philoi* relationship, the category now broadened to include all citizens. It seems difficult to explain them otherwise. They do not appear to be purely economic reforms, and they cannot be understood in the political context as a remedy for tensions between rich and poor unless something like the Homeric model is the basis. Perhaps the fact that Solon felt such legislation necessary indicates how far removed sixth-century Athens was from Homeric attitudes of family unity. Freeman argues that Solon's extension to all citizens of the right to prosecute on behalf of an injured citizen, a right previously reserved for the relatives of the injured person (Aristotle *Constitution of the Athenians* 9, Plutarch *Life of Solon* 18; cf. Diogenes Laertius 1.59) indicates "the development of the idea of state responsibility for the prevention and punishment of crime" (K. Freeman, *The Life and Work of Solon* [London, 1926], pp. 131ff.). But it is unclear how this is the case, since it seems to show instead the development of the idea of individual responsibility, an extension of the notion of family to include all citizens.

"Solon's" retention of Draco's laws regarding homicide, distinguishing unintentional physical injury from intentional (Freeman, pp. 123ff.) and extending only to relatives the right to prosecution in cases of homicide seems to Freeman a conservative element in Solon's reforms whereby "he preserved the connection with tribal custom in the most serious instance of criminal injury" (Freeman, p. 132).

Editions Cited

Allen, T. W., ed. *Homeri opera*, 2d ed. Vols. 3 and 4, *Odyssey*. Oxford, 1917 and 1919.

Allen, T. W., ed. *Homeri opera*. Vol. 5, *Hymns, Epic Cycle*. Oxford, 1912.

Hude, C., ed. *Herodoti historiae*. 3d ed. Oxford, 1927.

Lobel, E., and Page, D. L., eds. *Poetarum Lesbiorum fragmenta*. Oxford, 1955.

Monro, D. B., and Allen, T. W., eds. *Homeri opera*. 3d ed. Vols. 1 and 2, *Iliad*. Oxford, 1920.

Page, D. L., ed. *Aeschyli septem quae supersunt tragoedias*. Oxford, 1972.

———. *Poetae melici Graeci*. Oxford, 1962.

———. *Supplementum lyricis Graecis*. Oxford, 1974.

Pearson, A. C., ed. *Sophoclis fabulae*. Oxford, 1928.

Snell, B., and Maehler, H., eds. *Bacchylides carmina cum fragmentis*. Leipzig, 1970.

———. *Pindari carmina cum fragmentis*. Leipzig, 1984.

Solmsen, F., ed. *Hesiodi Theogonia, Opera et Dies, Scutum*, with Merkelbach, R., and West, M. L., eds. *Fragmenta selecta*. Oxford, 1970.

Stanford, W. B., ed. *The Odyssey of Homer*. 2d ed. 2 vols. London, 1958.

West, M. L., ed. *Iambi et elegi Graeci ante Alexandrum cantati*. 2 vols. Oxford, 1971–1972.

Bibliography of Works Cited

Adkins, A. W. H. "Friendship and Self-Sufficiency in Homer and Aristotle." *Classical Quarterly* 56 (1963), 30–45.

——. *From the Many to the One.* London, 1970.

——. "Homeric Values and Homeric Society." *Journal of Hellenic Studies* 91 (1971), 1–14.

——. *Merit and Responsibility: A Study in Greek Values.* Oxford, 1960.

——. *Poetic Craft in the Early Greek Elegists.* Chicago and London, 1985.

Allen, A. A. "Solon's Prayer to the Muses." *Transactions of the American Philological Association* 80 (1949), 50–65.

Barrett, W. S., ed. *Euripides Hippolytus.* Oxford, 1964.

Bergk, W. T., ed. *Poetae lyrici Graeci.* 3 vols. Leipzig, 1914.

Bowra, C. M. *Early Greek Elegists.* Cambridge, Mass., 1938.

Burkert, W. *Homo Necans.* Berlin, 1972.

Burnett, A. P. *The Art of Bacchylides.* Cambridge, Mass., 1985.

Campbell, D. A. *The Golden Lyre: The Themes of The Greek Lyric Poets.* London, 1983.

——. *Greek Lyric Poetry.* Basingstoke and London, 1967.

Chantraine, P. *Dictionnaire étymologique de la langue grecque*, Vol. I. Paris, 1968.

Christes, J. "Solons Musenelegie." *Hermes* 114 (1986), 1–19.

Cole, A. T. "Archaic Truth." *Quaderni Urbinati di Cultura Classica* 13 (1983), 7–28.

Croiset, M. "La morale et la cité dans les poésies de Solon." *Comptes Rendus de L'Académie des Inscriptions* (1903), 581–596.

Dawe, R. D., ed. *Sophoclis tragoediae.* Leipzig, 1975–1979.

Detienne, M. *Les maîtres de vérité dans la Grèce archaïque.* Paris, 1981.

Diehl, E., ed. *Anthologia lyrica Graeca.* 2 vols. Leipzig, 1925.

Diels, H., ed. *Die Fragmente der Vorsokrater.* Re-edited by W. Kranz. Berlin, 1903.

Dodds, E. R. *The Greeks and the Irrational.* Berkeley, 1951.

Ehrenberg, V. *Aspects of the Ancient World.* New York, 1946.

—. *From Solon to Socrates.* London, 1968.

Eisenberger, H. "Gedanken zu Solons 'Musenelegie.'" *Philologus* 128 (1984), 9–20.

Else, G. F. *The Origin and Early Form of Greek Tragedy.* Cambridge, Mass., 1965.

Figueira, T. J., and Nagy, G., eds. *Theognis of Megara.* Baltimore and London, 1985.

Fränkel, H. *Dichtung und Philosophie des frühen Griechentums.* New York, 1951.

Freeman, K. *The Life and Work of Solon.* London, 1926.

Gentili, B. *Poetry and its Public in Ancient Greece.* Translated by A. T. Cole. Baltimore, 1988.

Gerber, D. E. "Semonides, Fragment 1 West: A Commentary," in *Greek Poetry and Philosophy.* Edited by D. E. Gerber. Chico, California, 1984, 125–135.

Gernet, L. *Anthropologie de la Grèce antique.* Paris, 1982.

—. "Dolon le Loup." Mélanges Franz Cumont *Annuaire de l'Institut de Philologie et d'Histoire Orientales et Slaves* 4 (1936), 189–208.

Gildersleeve, B. L. *Pindar: The Olympian and Pythian Odes.* New York, 1979.

Groningen, B. A. van. *La composition littéraire archaïque grecque.* Amsterdam, 1960.

Havelock, E. A. *The Greek Concept of Justice From Its Shadow in Homer to Its Substance in Plato.* Cambridge, Mass., 1978.

Jaeger, W. *Paideia.* Translated by G. Highet. 3 vols. New York, 1939.

—. "Solons Eunomie." In *Five Essays,* translated by A. M. Fiske. Montreal, 1966.

Kant, I. *Foundations of the Metaphysics of Morals.* Translated by L. W. Beck. Indianapolis, 1959.

Kirk, G. S. *The Nature of Greek Myths.* Woodstock, N.Y., 1975.

Lattimore, R. "The First Elegy of Solon." *American Journal of Philology* 68 (1947), 161–179.

—. *Greek Lyrics.* Chicago, 1960.

Lefkowitz, M. R., and Lloyd-Jones, H. "Λυκαιχμίαις." *Zeitschrift für Papyrologie und Epigraphik,* 68 (1987), 9–10.

Leinieks, V. "'Ελπίς in Hesiod, *Works and Days* 96." *Philologus* 128 (1984), 1–8.

Linforth, I. *Solon the Athenian.* Berkeley, 1919.

Lloyd-Jones, H. *The Justice of Zeus.* Berkeley, 1971.

Lloyd-Jones, H., and Wilson, N. G., eds. *Sophoclea: Studies in the Text of Sophocles.* Oxford, 1990.

Loraux, N. "Solon au milieu de la lice." *Mélanges H. van Effenterre.* Paris, 1984, 199–214.

Masaracchia, A. *Solone.* Florence, 1958.

McCall, M. H. *Ancient Rhetorical Theories of Simile and Comparison.* Cambridge, Mass., 1969.

Michelini, A. "Ύβρις and plants." *Harvard Studies in Classical Philology* 82 (1978), 35–44.

Most, G. W. *The Measures of Praise.* Göttingen, 1985.

Nagy, G. *The Best of the Achaeans: Concepts of the Hero in Archaic Greek Poetry.* Baltimore, 1979.

——. *Greek Mythology and Poetics.* Ithaca, 1990.

——. "Iambos: Typologies of Invective and Praise." *Arethusa* 9 (1976), 191–206.

——. *Pindar's Homer: The Lyric Possession of an Epic Past.* Baltimore, 1990.

Ostwald, M. *Nomos and the Beginnings of the Athenian Democracy.* Oxford, 1969.

Page, D. L. *Sappho and Alcaeus.* Oxford, 1955.

Perry, B. E., ed. *Aesopica.* Urbana, Illinois, 1952.

Podlecki, A. J. "Three Greek Soldier Poets: Archilochus, Alcaeus, Solon." *Classical World* 63 (1969), 73–81.

Silk, M. S. *Interaction in Poetic Imagery: With Special Reference to Early Greek Poetry.* London, 1974.

Smyth, H. W. *Greek Melic Poets.* Re-issued, New York, 1963.

Snell, B. *The Discovery of the Mind.* Translated by T. G. Rosenmeyer. Cambridge, Mass., 1953.

Solmsen, F. "The Gift of Speech in Homer and Hesiod." *Transactions of the American Philological Association* 85 (1954), 1–14.

——. *Hesiod and Aeschylus.* New York, 1949.

Szegedy-Maszak, A. "Legends of the Greek Lawgivers." *Greek, Roman, and Byzantine Studies* 19 (1975), 199–209.

Vlastos, G. "Solonian Justice." *Classical Philology* 41 (1946), 65–83.

West, M. L. *Studies in Greek Elegy and Iambus.* Berlin and New York, 1974.

Wilamowitz-Moellendorff, U. von. *Aristoteles und Athen.* Vol. II. Berlin, 1893.

——. "Solons Elegie εἰς ἑαυτόν," in *Sappho und Simonides.* Berlin, 1966.

Will, F. "Solon's Consciousness of Himself." *Transactions of the American Philological Association* 89 (1958), 301–311.

Woodhouse, W. J. *Solon the Liberator.* London, 1938.

Index

About the Author

Emily Katz Anhalt holds a B.A. from Dartmouth College and a Ph.D. in Classical Philology from Yale University. Her current research plans include a forthcoming article on the poetics of metaphor in Homer and a book on historiographical traditions in Greece, Egypt and the ancient Near East.

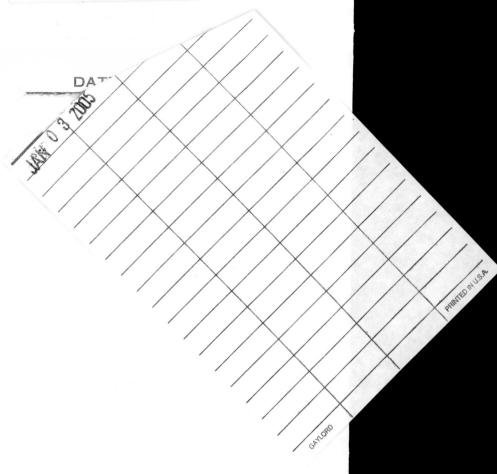

DAT

JAN 0 3 2005

GAYLORD

PRINTED IN U.S.A.